BUFFALO HUNTING IN ALABAMA

BUFFALO HUNTING IN ALABAMA

A NOVEL

DON ERWIN

Bluff Park Press

Copyright © 2020 Donald Louis Erwin

This is a work of fiction. Names, characters, companies, organizations, places, and incidents either are the product of the author's imagination or are used fictitiously. Any references to real people, events, establishments, organizations, or locales are intended only to give the fiction a sense of reality and are used fictitiously. Any resemblance of fictional entities to actual persons, living or dead, events, or locales is entirely coincidental.

All rights reserved.

No part of this book may be reproduced, or stored in a retrieval system, or transmitted in any form or by any means, electronic, mechanical, photocopying, recording, or otherwise, without express written permission except in the case of brief quotations embodied in critical articles and reviews. For permission, contact the author at www.donerwin.net.

ISBN 9798685344755

Front and back cover design and layout by Don Erwin.

Bison silhouette licensed from Pixabay and courtesy of the artist, John Huxtable.

Permission granted to quote from Jim Clifton's *The Coming Jobs War*, 2011, Gallup Press.

Permission granted to quote from Dan Ariely, James B. Duke Professor of Psychology and Behavioral Economics at Duke University.

DEDICATION

To Willis Carrier, the patron saint of
Southern economic developers.

buf·fa·lo hunt·ing

/ˈbəf(ə)ˌlō/ /ˈhən(t)iNG/

noun

1. the activity of hunting a humpbacked shaggy-haired wild ox native to North America and Europe, especially for food or sport.

2. the practice of attracting large firms to locate in a state or community, often with a variety of financial inducements. Sometimes derisively known as "smokestack chasing."

CONTENTS

1	Montgomery, Alabama, Spring 2012	1
2	New York, Almost Two Years Later	5
3	Milltown, Alabama	13
4	New York	15
5	SOHO Walk Around	20
6	Birmingham, Alabama	25
7	Highlands Bar & Grill	30
8	Dinner	36
9	Exploring Birmingham	42
10	Lou's Pub & Package Store	47
11	Dreamland	53
12	Back in New York	56
13	Dinner at Piordo's	59
14	Economic Development	63
15	The Secret Sauce	69
16	Back in Birmingham	73
17	The Quants	80
18	Conditional Job Offer	83
19	Job Loss	87
20	Shrink Exam	89
21	Howland's	97
22	Decision Time	100
23	The Drive South	104
24	Visit to the Black Belt	106
25	The Goethe-Institut	116
26	Journey to Munich	120
27	Dinner with the Governor	126
28	Leading Milltown to Prosperity	135
29	The Art of Persuasion	144
30	A Tech Park	149
31	An Italian Story	151
32	First day on the Job	155

33	Big Data	161
34	Go-Go-Going	168
35	Simon's Charge	170
36	Dinner at Hot and Hot	174
37	Death in the Family	179
38	The Goodie Vault	182
39	Bio, Baseball, & Beer	186
40	Foreign Investment	191
41	Training	194
42	Drinks at the Collins Bar	199
43	Trip to Japan	201
44	Tokyo	209
45	Gotemba	215
46	Family Picnic	220
47	Site Trouble	223
48	Interview with Clara Ogg	225
49	Meeting in Augsburg	229
50	The Project	233
51	Existential Threat	240
52	Ono Island	242
53	The Hypnotist	250
54	Site Visit	255
55	Solving a Puzzle	260
56	Sailing off Mallorca	262
57	Bioprospecting	270
58	The Woodpecker	277
59	South Carolina	281
60	Giving the Farm Away	284
61	In the Ditch Again	292
62	A Unique Incentive	296
63	Making Sausage	301
64	The Announcement	303
	Author's Note	307
	Acknowledgments	311

1

MONTGOMERY, ALABAMA, SPRING 2012

The front door of the antebellum mansion bore a cast-brass plate. A symbol like the number "8" turned sideways stood in bas-relief as if made with flat brass tape and given a half-twist. Below were the words:

Möbius LLC
There is only one side to every issue

Montgomery possessed many fine old houses, including those in the Cottage Hill District, which sat on a low hill overlooking the riverfront. Most of the Cottage Hill houses were Queen Anne Victorian, painted in pastel blues and pinks and whites and decorated with gingerbread trim and occupied by lawyers and lobbyists and trade associations.

The Möbius mansion was arguably the most magnificent of them all, but it was ominous rather than whimsical. Built during an earlier age when antebellum mansions were generally whitewashed, it was constructed of grey stone with dark trim. It had been built in 1860 when Montgomery had the most central and conspicuous slave market in the South.

The original owner, a slaver, could look down from the heights of his mansion and see slaves being herded up from the paddlewheel riverboats and the rail line that ran along the riverfront. Their destinations were the holding pens and slave warehouses along Commerce Street, and ultimately the slave market at Court Square.

Inside, the Möbius mansion featured period-correct furnishings except for an armored steel door off the first-floor hallway. The contents of the basement were the subject of much speculation, from weapons to documents to blackmail videos. Some joked it contained a torture chamber. Montgomery was a city of politics and intrigue, and people naturally thought such things.

Dr. James Carter, the current owner, had earned an undergraduate psychology degree from Princeton and then served ten years as a psychological warfare officer with the U.S. Army Special Forces. Many regarded his doctoral thesis on political campaign communications, earned at the University of Alabama, as a masterpiece.

Carter had black belts in karate and Aikido and was supposedly always armed. Much heard about him was rumor and shadow-talk. He drove a large black SUV, said to be armored, and he once remarked he didn't play golf because there were "too many uncontrolled sightlines."

A lifetime member of the NAACP, Carter had managed far more Democratic campaigns than Republican, but that ratio was changing, as there were few Democratic officeholders or viable candidates left in Alabama.

Dr. Carter had three criteria for accepting a political consulting job: The candidate had to have a chance of winning, they had to listen to him, and they had to have the money to pay him. Sometimes a campaign allocated half its total budget to Möbius and its operations.

The politicians and aspiring politicians from both parties would come calling, wanting Carter and his firm to help them become elected officials or get re-elected.

If he judged a possible client could win, Carter would tell them to come back in two weeks. He would generally begin the second meeting by opening an iPad and showing a video—a sixty-second commercial that painted the prospective client in a very unflattering light. He would then tell the prospective client, whose face by this time was often sheet-white, "This is what your opponent is going to do to you."

If the allegations were too damaging, he would then say, "I can't help you. Sorry." Otherwise, he would lay out a campaign plan, including the message and media buys and opposition research, and what it would cost.

On this warm early-Spring day, Carter sat in his office on the second floor of the mansion. Through the windows to his left, he could see tourists disembarking from a paddlewheel steamboat moored at the riverfront.

BUFFALO HUNTING IN ALABAMA

Two of his best operatives sat on the other side of his desk. Behind them, through the windows, he could see the white dome of the Alabama State Capitol gleaming in the distance.

Both operatives were former newspaper reporters. The media business had been a bloodbath in recent years, and Carter had found that former newspaper reporters made some of the best operatives. They knew politics, knew how to dig, and he took a secret pleasure in seeing formerly self-righteous reporters become skilled political operatives when given the opportunity to make some real money.

Not that they broke the law. Carter repeatedly warned his operatives against that and required them to sign quarterly compliance forms. If they broke the law, Carter said, they were stupid because in Alabama, one can legally do things against the law in other states.

"Gentlemen, we've been retained by our largest client to make sure the voters don't re-elect the Mayor of Milltown. As often happens in Alabama, the voters kicked out a crook and put in a fool. This mayor has essentially stopped all development in Milltown for the last three years. He's pissed off the developers and others who would benefit from a growing economy.

"People want to build a new school in Milltown, and there's no growing tax base to do it. I attended a city council meeting there recently, and they watch the pennies so closely they even took a vote to purchase new tires for a police car. I didn't ask if it was *the* police car."

He continued, "The same time they elected this mayor, they also elected an anti-growth city council, and they've got to go, too. This is not something we've got to move heaven and earth to make happen. Many of the citizens are unhappy with the current regime.

"We're to act as the tipping point to make sure the Mayor and his anti-growth city council friends aren't re-elected. The municipal elections are in August, so that gives us five months. How many other municipal elections are we working?"

"Thirty-six mayoral and city council races, but this one shouldn't be a problem," answered one of the ex-reporters.

"Given the client, I want you personally working on this. Dig into the Mayor's past. We all know that Americans have unreasonable expectations about their politicians. They expect them to be temples of virtue as well as good policymakers. Our polls show we only need a few points. Find that affair, that love child; that DUI or reckless driving conviction. Find the bounced check, the wage garnishment. Everyone has things they don't want known."

"Yes sir," they both answered together.

"As usual, we stay way below the surface. If word of our actions surfaces, that's a failure on your part."

"Yes, sir," they again answered simultaneously. They understood the program.

2

NEW YORK, ALMOST TWO YEARS LATER

The man in the overcoat walked briskly through the New York night, his shoulders hunched, head forward as if deep in thought. The sidewalks had been shoveled clear of snow, but it was starting again, the white flakes swirling in little whirlwinds under the streetlights.

Ezra Drake turned right onto Broadway. It was a couple of miles to his place in SoHo. He walked for the exercise, to walk off the liquor, and to think.

I'm crazy even to consider this. I work for one of the best companies in the world. I live in the best city in the world. I have a beautiful, rich, well-connected girlfriend. People would kill to have what I have. Why would I go back?

As he turned onto Fifth Avenue, Madison Square Park opened to his left. Through the snowy white mist, he could see the twinkling lights and soft silhouettes of tall buildings. *What a city!* He stared for a long moment and then walked south toward SoHo. Ahead, he could see the outline of the Flatiron Building.

The salary would be less, but so would the cost of living—and the taxes! I make a ton of money at Silverman, but I spend a lot, too. In a smaller city, a car would be practical.

How many times have I been to the MOMA or Guggenheim or Frick in the last year? How many times have I walked through Central Park? For a $300 round-trip ticket, I could visit whenever I want. And probably appreciate it more.

He walked around a metal grate, which he knew would be iced-up. He smiled, remembering Jimmy's comment earlier tonight in his distinctive

Southern drawl, "How can any place which gets a foot of snow a year have a great quality of life?"

What about the people? What would I give up in terms of diversity? Would I miss living near eight million other people?

How am I going to miss all the bluntness? he joked to himself. He had never gotten used to it even living in Germany. He remembered telling a German friend one time that people in the American South were so polite because they knew that many of their fellow citizens carried concealed firearms. The German friend wasn't amused.

What about Eleanor? His mind went blank for several moments. *Yeah, what about Eleanor?* She had been all over the world but never south of the Mason-Dixon Line—Florida didn't count—and she wouldn't start now.

Maybe I would get an office and a window, he said to himself ruefully. Here he was, a Vice President at Silverman Bach and no office or window. If they promoted him to Managing Director, he'd get an office but still no damned window. It wasn't the prestige; it was just seeing the world. He remembered that supposedly German law guaranteed every employee a view out a window. *So there you go. What do you want in life?*

His left foot slipped on the snow, and he felt a dagger of pain in his right knee. *And the dojo. That's one of the best things about living here. I do plan to go back,* he chastised himself, *just as soon as the leg feels a little stronger.*

This night had started several weeks ago when Jimmy Adams, who he'd known since the third grade, called him.

"Let's go watch Alabama play in the SEC Championship," Jimmy had said. "We're going to watch it at the Ainsworth."

Jimmy's law firm in Birmingham, Stearns & Markham, had moved him to New York two years ago, and his umbilical cord to Alabama was the New York chapter of the University of Alabama Alumni Association. Stearns & Markham were closely aligned with DG&L, the large Alabama utility, and did securities and lobbying work in New York.

The Ainsworth, on West Twenty-Sixth, was a restaurant and sports bar favored by Southerners who worked in finance and people who loved college football. It featured a large open interior with couches and rows of long tables in the back and round tables in front, and five or six dozen flat-screen TVs scattered throughout. It had a sports-bar/nightclub/cigar lounge feel, with typical sports-bar food—a good fit for Alabama alumni.

BUFFALO HUNTING IN ALABAMA

Last year, Ezra had watched the Alabama-LSU game there, and a middle-aged alumnus had hired girls to be Alabama cheerleaders, complete with uniforms and pom-poms. They looked like the Alabama cheerleaders of his childhood—lush Playboy fantasies—instead of the tiny gymnast cheerleaders of today.

"Doesn't Alabama have to beat Auburn to go to the championship?" Ezra asked, knowing the answer.

"Count on it. That's going to happen. Auburn's been lucky this year, but their luck's run out. I'll be in Auburn next weekend to watch Saban's boys stomp the Tigers."

"OK," Ezra said, "The Ainsworth on December seventh."

Ezra had fled Alabama and the South after high school, and his college football experience had been the crimson and black of Harvard, not the crimson and white of the University of Alabama. Despite Eleanor's attempts to convert him to a New Yorker—with all that implied—he had retained his lifelong love for Alabama football.

Ezra had played tight end in middle school, and the coaches expected great things of him in high school, but he chose debate—of all things. It was an easy choice: The football team played schools thirty miles down the road in rural Alabama while the debate team traveled to Georgetown and Emory and other exotic places for a sixteen-year-old.

At Harvard, Ezra had kept up with Alabama football and even attended a game or two. In the North, pro football was king—especially in towns like New York and Chicago—but in the South, college football dominated.

To Ezra, football was like war—an intricate combination of brute force and sophisticated planning and strategy. Have a ground game but no airpower, and you were a one-dimensional team.

New Yorkers looked down on almost everything about Alabama, but they respected Crimson Tide football and the man who ran it. The Alabama Crimson Tide were the New York Yankees of college football.

Until recent times, Atlanta had been the only Southeast city with a pro football team, and some years people wondered about that. Bear Bryant had supposedly killed Birmingham's chance for a pro team, and by the time the Bear was gone, Birmingham had lost so much ground to other cities that it was no longer a viable prospect. For most Alabamians, Alabama and Auburn football—and high school football—were all that mattered.

It had been a fun evening drinking and talking with Jimmy. The State of Alabama was like an old girlfriend you thought about occasionally but made no effort to contact. Alabama was part of his past, not his future.

***

Ezra had watched the Auburn-Alabama game last Saturday at his flat. They played the game in Auburn, a college town in eastern Alabama, ninety miles from Atlanta. All the drama was there—packed stadium, undefeated Alabama, and one-loss Auburn. Nick Saban, *the Great Satan,* versus Gus Malzahn, Auburn's first-year head coach.

Auburn played tough, but with 4:38 left in the game, they had to kick it away. Alabama was a touchdown ahead with the ball. With 2:38 left, Alabama tried a field goal—which Auburn blocked! *Fuck.*

Now Auburn had the ball. With thirty-two seconds left, the Auburn quarterback threw for a touchdown, tying the game.

Auburn kicked off, and Alabama moved it down the field. One second left, Alabama tried a fifty-seven-yard field goal. It was straight but just short and *caught by an Auburn player,* who then ran 109 yards for a touchdown.

Auburn wins! Ezra had never seen a play like that before, and it looked like Alabama hadn't either.

Auburn fans flooded the field. Cameras cut to the grandstands. Drunk Alabama frat boys stood open-mouthed, wide-eyed, their hands clasped behind their heads. Little kids cried and hugged their mothers. Alabama's elephant mascot was a sad mouse with a droopy nose. The Alabama world was upside down. Two teams, so good, from a state of fewer than five million people, and the whole nation watched.

What now? Ezra had texted Jimmy.

No reply for the rest of the weekend. *He probably tied on a big one.* On Monday afternoon, Jimmy called.

"Let's go watch the SEC Championship game this Saturday."

"You're kidding. You mean Auburn and Missouri?"

"Yeah."

"You hate Auburn."

Jimmy hemmed and hawed around and finally said, "You know, they deserve some credit."

BUFFALO HUNTING IN ALABAMA

This was not Jimmy. Most Alabamians cheered for either Alabama or Auburn and hated the other team. If Alabama played Al Qaeda, Auburn fans would root for the terrorists, and vice-versa.

"Jimmy, you OK? Family OK?"

"They're fine, Ezra. I just thought since we're both stuck up here in New York, and we're both from Alabama, we oughta go and support the state, even if it's…Auburn."

Ezra didn't feel stuck in New York, but what-the-hell; he was as addicted to college football as any Southerner. "OK, Jimmy, we're on. Where do you want to watch the game?"

"Well, the Ainsworth's out. That would be a sacrilege. I'll call you later when I find a good place." *They'll probably be having a wake at the Ainsworth.*

As Jimmy hung up, Ezra reflected on how easy it was to drop into an Alabama accent. He spoke "generic American," but talk to someone from Alabama, and he was like a black executive who spoke flawless English but who dropped into black dialect when hanging with the brothers.

Jimmy called back later and said that Auburn fans were planning to gather at Tavern on Third on the Lower East Side, an Auburn Alumni Association hangout.

***

It was a twenty-minute walk from Ezra's flat. A life-sized blowup of the Auburn Tiger mascot stood outside looking like Tony the Tiger on the cereal box.

The Ainsworth was sleek, Ezra thought, but Tavern on Third was your local neighborhood bar, which fit Auburn's engineering and agricultural roots.

The bar was narrow and deep with a sea of orange and blue. The Auburn fans were mostly white students and older folks. Ezra tried to blend in by wearing loafers, khakis, a white button-down shirt, a dark blue sleeveless vest, and a tie with some orange in it.

Ezra found Jimmy standing at the bar and drinking. He looked miserable.

"I couldn't bring myself to dress in the colors," Jimmy shouted. "That would be like losin' a bet or somethin'."

Fans continued to cram in like rush hour on the subway. Ezra's idea of fun wasn't watching a game standing up, and Jimmy looked miserable, so Ezra said, "Let's find someplace else to watch the game."

Jimmy paid the tab, and they crossed the street to Van Diemen's. They managed to find seats at the bar, directly in front of a flat-screen TV. *The bartender's cute, so what more could we want?* About half the crowd was Auburn overflow, and the other half were lapsed Baptists eager to see Baylor thrash Texas.

They talked football a while, and then Ezra said, "You look miserable. What's up? You hate Auburn."

"No, I don't. Not much, anyway. After all, it's about the state, isn't it? I mean if Auburn beats Missouri, it might be five straight years a team from the State of Alabama has gone to the national championship game. Here we are, this dinky little state, and we're whippin' ass."

Unlike Texans, you rarely heard an Alabamian passionate about his state. "You going to tell me why we're really here?"

Jimmy looked Ezra in the eyes. "Ezra, I've got a job I want you to think about."

Is this what this is all about? "You know I'm not a lawyer. Why would Stearns want me?" *A bit of fucking with him.*

"Not a job with us. We have a client who's interested in you."

"Since when have you been a headhunter?"

"They're a big client. You tired of New York, Ezra? I sure as hell am."

Investment firm in London or maybe Dubai. If it's Frankfurt, I'm not sure I want to live there again. London would probably be fun.

"I might consider moving. Where are we talking about?"

"God's Country for me, and if you'll just listen for a moment, I think you'll agree."

Warning antenna went up. *Uh oh, what's this?* "Where is it? Who is it?"

"The client is DG&L. They want you to come work for them in Birmingham."

Ezra felt as if Jimmy had poured a cold beer down the back of his neck. *Birmingham, Alabama. Police dogs and fire hoses. I spent the first eighteen years of my life trying to escape Alabama, and now they want me to move back? Hell no!*

Be nice. "What's the job?"

"They want you to help them attract new companies to Alabama. They feel your experience in Germany and here in New York can help them attract more industry."

"That sounds interesting, Jimmy, but I have a job—a great job."

"Okay, will you just listen for a second?" said Jimmy defensively.

Ezra turned up the mug of Sam Adams, drained it, and wiped his mouth. "OK, I'm listening." *And drinking heavily. On your dime.*

"Alabama's come a long way. We've got Mercedes and Honda and Hyundai, and we're making almost a million cars a year and kickin' ass. We just landed Airbus, and soon we'll be one of only three or four places in the world making large commercial jets. Huntsville's a tech capital, and downtown Birmingham's comin' alive, and people are moving there and starting bio and tech companies. DG&L is lookin' for people like you who can accelerate the momentum."

"Isn't attracting companies something government does? Why does DG&L want me?"

"DG&L stays low-key, but they're a power behind the scenes, including economic development. When a newly-elected Governor appoints his friends to head the state agencies—and most of them don't know what they're doing—DG&L provides leadership. They've been doing this longer than anybody."

"Jimmy, why would I want to go back to Alabama?"

"Why would you want to stay here?"

"Let's see," Ezra started ticking items off on his fingers. "Good job, greatest city in the world. Did I mention a great-looking girlfriend?" *Eleanor would be like a fish out of water in Alabama*, he thought. *Correction—Eleanor wouldn't go to Alabama.*

"I haven't heard you talk much about her lately."

"All's fine," Ezra said over his shoulder as he adjourned to take a piss. When he returned, a fresh beer sat on the bar.

"Tell you what, Jimmy, I'll think about it—but tonight I want to watch the game." *And maybe get a little drunk.*

Auburn and Missouri turned out to be an offensive battle. By the third quarter, Auburn had the upper hand. *Too bad they lost to LSU, or they might be going to the national championship.* Baylor was beating the crap out of Texas, and Ohio State should handle Michigan State later in the evening, so it looked like FSU and Ohio State would be playing for the national championship. They decided to wander around a bit.

Stopping for a refresher at a bar on West Twenty-Sixth, they watched Ohio State collapse in the fourth quarter against Michigan State and lose 34–24. *By damn*, Auburn was going to the national championship game!

"Oh, God," said Jimmy. "At least I'm here in New York and won't have to listen to the Auburn people talk shit for the next year."

They sat silently for a few moments contemplating the evening's events. Finally, Jimmy asked, "Will you just consider it?"

"Miracles happen," Ezra said. "War Eagle."

"I'll call you tomorrow," said Jimmy as he hailed a cab. Ezra saluted him, "Thanks for the drinks." Jimmy had paid all night. Expense account. He was doing a job. Ezra decided to walk home. It was cold, but he had some antifreeze.

***

As Ezra passed the Flatiron Building, emotion flowed over him like an icy wind down his back. Alabama wasn't even flyover country. It was flyaway *from* country. That's what most people thought. But despite its history and flaws, Ezra had come to realize there was much more to Alabama than the simple stereotype. *And what should they know of England who only England know?* Kipling had said. Ezra had lived away from Alabama long enough to know it had no unique flaws.

Ezra could see his loft in the distance. Several times in the last few months, he had come home to find Eleanor asleep in his bed. Ezra had moved out of her Upper East Side flat almost five months ago, and they had spent a dozen nights together since then. *Will she be sleeping in my bed tonight? Do I want her there?*

As he entered the flat, he saw the security system disarmed. Walking into the bedroom, he sensed Eleanor's presence. Quietly he undressed and slipped under the covers into a place that should have felt warm and secure.

In times past, in this situation, he had felt…excitement, love, longing. Now, he felt only tired and slightly drunk.

3

MILLTOWN, ALABAMA

Billy Jeff Jenkins considered himself blessed. Not that life had always been easy, but the Good Lord never promised that. Billy Jeff had a loving wife, a three-year-old son, a little girl on the way, and a good job. He had much to be thankful for.

It hadn't always been this way. He had been only six years old when his Daddy lost his supervisor's job at the mill. With half the town out-of-work, it had been impossible to find another job in Milltown.

Billy Jeff remembered his Daddy leaving the house in the mornings to drive to Birmingham to look for work. Sometimes his Daddy found a job—for a while—but he was never the same after the mill closed. Most were simple laborer jobs, and it seemed his Daddy had lost his spirit for living. Billy Jeff could still remember the smell of booze on his Daddy's breath when he kissed him at bedtime.

And then one day, his Daddy just left and never came back, and it was just Billy Jeff and his Momma. She did the best she could, running the kitchen of Atkinson's Restaurant, and they were able to keep the small white frame house at the edge of town.

In high school, Billy Jeff had played football and baseball, and though he wasn't big enough or fast enough for Alabama or Auburn, he hoped to get a scholarship to Jacksonville or Troy or the University of West Alabama. That all ended his junior year with the broken leg.

He had been a pretty good student but not scholarship material. In elementary school, math was his favorite subject, but in high school, he had trouble with algebra. Maybe he wasn't smart enough, or maybe the math teacher, who was also the assistant football coach, knew more about Xs and Os than he did about equations.

He graduated and started looking for a job, determined not to end up like his Daddy. He worked in a warehouse for a while, earned his CDL, and then drove a truck for a couple of years. Then he met Emma at church, and the truck-driving job meant too much time away from home. He was still living with his Momma, so he was able to save some money. He kept hearing about the good jobs his friends had gotten who had gone to college, and he knew he needed to step it up.

Then one day, he heard about a company called SangreBio, located on the eastern side of Birmingham. To apply for a job, he had to attend classes at night taught by the state training folks. Billy Jeff went three nights a week for twelve weeks. He never missed a class and was always on time.

SangreBio had been started from research done at the University of Alabama at Birmingham (UAB). They did medical tests on blood that doctors collected from patients. One test could tell a doctor a lot about a patient's health. The training involved learning to operate the testing machines, properly handling the blood samples from doctors' offices across the country, informing the doctors of the test results, and ensuring quality control.

The math was easy the way the trainers taught it. One instructor, who had taught in the Army, told him, "If we can teach high school dropouts and former druggies and gang-bangers to maintain jets and tanks, we can teach you how to operate these machines. It's all in how the material is taught." Billy Jeff had excelled. They told him later he was at the top of the class.

That was five years ago, and Billy Jeff now supervised fifteen people. He and Emma planned to buy a house next year, and when the little girl arrived, Emma would take off work for three months.

Billy Jeff had read somewhere that the middle-class was disappearing in America, but it wasn't disappearing for him. He was becoming one.

4

NEW YORK

Ezra stared at the ceiling. The clock said 3 a.m. Eleanor was out cold. He slid out of bed, stumbled to his study, turned on the computer, and typed "Alabama" into Google.

"Alabama.gov" topped the listing. He clicked on it. *Decent website for government.*

"Alabama-Wikipedia." *Too much information.*

"The University of Alabama." *Pass.*

"Alabama," the country music band. *Pass.*

Alabama's official travel guide. *Pass.*

"Rolltide.com." *Pass.*

ESPN's section on the Crimson Tide. *Pass.*

"Welcome to the Alabama State Legislature." *Pass.*

At the bottom of the search page, Google had a section called *In-Depth Articles,* and the second item on the listing struck his eye—a *Forbes* article about Nick Saban and the University of Alabama written in 2013.

The gist of the article was that the University of Alabama was now a cool place to go to school, and kids all over the country wanted to enroll there. For the past few years, more than half the freshman class had come from out of state.

Alabama a cool place?

He returned to bed and stared at the ceiling awhile.

***

Ezra left at 5:45 a.m. to be at work by 6:15 instead of the usual 6:45. Today was Bonus Day. In past years, this had been the biggest day of the year.

Sunday had been a "nothing day," sleeping late, then lunch with Eleanor, then some reading after she left.

As he neared 400 Warren, he looked up at the forty-five-story, glass-and-steel headquarters. No Silverman Bach sign. The building was like a massive German luxury car turned on end, where the owner paid extra not to display the model and engine size. The intent was to impress but in an understated way. *Lots of horsepower in that building*, thought Ezra.

Shortly after joining the firm, he had asked a colleague why there was no Silverman Bach sign outside. "That's to make it harder for the lynch mobs to find us when the economy crashes," the colleague replied with typical Silverman humor. This was not so long after the Crash of 2008.

The lobby was enormous yet strangely empty. Ezra thought its purpose was to intimidate—to make visitors feel insignificant. The intimidation continued when guests received a keycard at the visitors' desk that controlled where the elevator took them. *No accidentally getting off on the wrong floor and seeing the wizards behind the curtains.*

The building's first nine stories held the football field-sized trading floors. The Partners got glass offices on the outside walls, the Managing Directors got interior offices, and the Vice Presidents got open-space workbenches. His "office" was a big step down from Ezra's Deutsche Bank digs in Frankfurt. About eight thousand of Silverman's thirty-five thousand worldwide employees worked at 400 Warren.

Above the trading floors were Silverman's executive offices, the Research Division, and the Investment Banking Division. Meeting rooms were further up with views to impress the clients.

The eleventh and twelfth floors were the heart of the building: A gigantic food court, with every kind of food known to man, and a massive gym. Ezra found the gym efficient, but bland and soulless, with a sea of cardio machines and company-issued t-shirts and gym shorts.

Like everything else at Silverman, it wasn't free with VPs paying $65 a month. Ezra enjoyed working with most of his fellow employees, but he wasn't interested in spinning or steaming with them.

Until his rehab, Ezra had spent little time in the Silverman gym. Exercise for him was like drinking—a way to remove himself from reality. The Silverman gym reinforced reality. It was the opposite of the dojo.

Ezra enjoyed observing his fellow employees because none of them were normal or average. Whoever said people weren't motivated by money had never met a Silverman employee.

The Bonus Day was a Silverman drama, along with closing deals and firing people. In each case, the passion play occurred in the glass-walled stage of a partner's office, for everyone to see.

On Bonus Day, starting about 7 a.m., the most senior people would get the first calls. A ten-minute meeting in the Partner's office would follow, where the employee would learn their annual total compensation—base salary plus bonus.

Ezra got his call about 9 a.m. He figured he would be OK because even during the 2012 Bonus Day bloodbath, when last quarter profits had been so bad, he had done OK.

"Ezra, the Partners feel you have enormous potential, but compensation is based on performance. You broke your leg in the middle of one of the biggest deals of the year, and we had to bring in others to finish it. If you had closed that deal as the lead, you would be a superstar, but you were in the hospital. Sorry, but actions have consequences. It's all Charlie the Tuna here."

His managing partner, Jason, often referred to a series of Star-Kist Tuna commercials from the 1960s where Charlie the Tuna tried to convince the Star-Kist Company that he had good taste, but what mattered to Star-Kist was that he tasted good. Ezra had watched the commercials on YouTube.

"Competence in karate is not a skill set we value at Silverman," said Jason. "We'd just as soon you take ballet. A few years ago, one of our managing directors went to Pamplona and got his ass stomped by a bull. About killed him. The Partners weren't sympathetic. We have a world-class gym, with every kind of exercise machine known to man, and you chose to take karate down in the Village. You're lucky you didn't break your neck!" he paused. "Ezra, you're a good rainmaker and a good dealmaker, but you don't make us any money lying in a hospital bed."

Ezra knew Jason was right. Silverman was tough, but they were generally fair, and his injury had hurt his ability to generate business. He had only been in the hospital for three days but had been on crutches for two months, and it had been awfully hard to look like a Master of the Universe on crutches, and even harder to hop a flight to visit a client.

"Jason, you know it was a freak accident. Hardly anyone gets hurt taking karate. Hell, you can fall off an exercise machine."

"Yeah, but it happened to you. Tell me you're not going back to karate."

"My leg's not ready for that. I'm using the gym."

"That's not the answer I want," Jason pushed.

"I don't know," Ezra hedged.

Jason was getting visibly pissed. "Look, if you want to be a fucking MMA fighter, that's your business, but don't expect to work at Silverman."

So there it was; the ultimatum. Ezra tried once more.

"Look, Jason, there are people at Silverman who play basketball, who race cars, who ride horses, who ride bicycles—hell, you have to be crazy to ride a bike in New York. Why am I being singled out?"

"You're not. If someone else working for me gets hurt doing something stupid, I'll tell them the same thing."

Ezra left the office, pissed that Jason was forcing him to give up karate, but he was even more pissed at himself because he knew a part of him feared taking karate again and would use Jason's ultimatum as an excuse.

The money wasn't an issue. Ezra's income, even this year, was more than enough; that wasn't the point. There was nothing wrong with taking karate. His fellow students at the dojo were lawyers and doctors and architects and housewives, and what happened was a freak accident. But he also understood Silverman's viewpoint. It was just a shit situation.

He had joined Silverman as a Vice President, coming from Deutsche Bank. The title sounded impressive, but twelve thousand of the thirty-five thousand people at Silverman were Vice Presidents. They were the folks who did the heavy lifting.

He was twenty-nine years old and had been at Silverman for four years. The average employee tenure at Silverman was about five years. If they had the potential, people generally made Managing Director in their mid-to-late thirties. Ezra had hoped to make it by thirty-two. He had to overcome this setback, somehow.

A text whished on his phone. *Drinks? O'Toole's at 6:30?* said the message from Jimmy.

Sure. Why not?

BUFFALO HUNTING IN ALABAMA

***

"How's the Wolf of Wall Street?" Jimmy greeted him.

"Come on, Jimmy, I've had a shit day. Don't *you* give me a hard time." A movie called *The Wolf of Wall Street* was due in theaters later in the month. The advertising blitz was hot and heavy.

"I hear it's a cool movie. Goin' to make guys like you even more famous."

"A lot of people don't like what we do. I might as well be a used-car salesman. Or a lawyer."

"Ouch. Since when have you ever cared what people think? In high school, you pissed off the coaches by debating instead of playing football; you didn't give a shit. Ezra, if you want to serve humanity, go join the Salvation Army. Don't work for Silverman Bach."

Ezra shot back, "Silverman plays an important role in the economy. We may not build bridges or stadiums, but we sure as hell get them financed." Ezra had just finished a bond deal in Florida for a new bridge.

"Ezra, to the average, hard-working person in America, you don't make anything, and you don't help anybody—you just make money."

"Like lawyers," Ezra shot back.

"Maybe like some lawyers," Jimmy half-admitted.

They sat and drank their beers for a couple of minutes, neither saying a word.

"So, why was today shitty?" asked Jimmy, changing the subject.

"Caught shit for breaking the leg."

"I thought that was water over the dam."

"It was, except today was Bonus Day, and I was reminded that actions have consequences."

"Always do," said Jimmy, with what Ezra imagined to be a touch of *Schadenfreude*. Ezra waited.

"You thought any more about the Alabama job?" Jimmy asked.

Ezra looked at him. "Jimmy, I know you love Alabama with all your heart, but have you ever just taken an objective look at the state? The average American thinks Alabama is a shithole."

"That's just another reason why you should consider taking the job. Here, you're just a cog in a wheel. There, you can make a real difference."

It was a twenty-minute walk from the bar to Ezra's flat. He arrived home about 9 p.m. and turned on the TV. The movie channel was showing *Wall Street*, starring Michael Douglas.

5

SOHO WALK AROUND

The following Saturday morning, Ezra wandered around SoHo, Eleanor on his mind. The December weather was brisk, but he stayed warm as long as he kept moving.

He had met her at the Dartmouth winter ice festival almost two years ago. She had looked like a Scandinavian snow queen, her fine-featured face framed by white fur and her pale hair spilling out of the hood. At the time, she was everything he could have imagined.

As they began dating, he found her smart and witty and impossibly bigoted about people she hadn't met and places she hadn't visited. A life of privilege had made it difficult for her to understand how most other people lived.

She did marketing for a New York ad agency, and they fell into a party circuit, two young high-flyers working during the day and partying half the night. To Eleanor, Ezra was an exotic creature from *terra incognita,* and she liked to show off her barbarian.

Her parents had taken to him; her father felt Ezra's upbringing would add vitality to the family stock and prevent some of the inbreeding he said occurred when privilege continuously married privilege. Her mother found him charming.

They had dated hot and heavy that first year, and after six months, he had moved in with her. Last summer, at a party in the Hamptons, her father had pulled him aside and suggested he spend a few more years at Silverman, and then he would bring Ezra into the family firm—a boutique Wall Street investment house.

Eleanor was an only child, so there it was—his future laid out for him like a silver tea service.

Life with Eleanor promised an apartment overlooking Central Park, a home in the Hamptons, recreational use of the corporate jets, children attending the best schools, and Ezra eventually ruling the family firm.

So why wasn't he happy?

For one thing, since leaving Alabama, he had been around enough wealthy people to learn that wealth didn't make people happy. Many of them seemed especially unhappy. Ezra hoped he would be different but wasn't sure.

Eleanor was still as beautiful as always, but the irritations had accumulated. Many of them were petty, so why did they bother him? Was he just not suited for marriage?

Ezra began taking karate because he needed the exercise and hated the Silverman gym. His biggest surprise was the inner peace it gave him. As he stepped-up training, he found it difficult to work all day, take karate in the evening, and then party half the night, so he left the partying to weekends. The parties were part of Eleanor's business marketing, so she kept up the pace, substituting friends for Ezra.

Five months ago, he had moved out of Eleanor's place and sublet the flat in SoHo, and he wondered if they would ever be back together. Maybe he was just unrealistic. What relationship was perfect? Marriage was all about building a family and leaving a legacy.

Ezra stopped at Forbidden Planet on Broadway. More and more, he read books on his iPad, but he still liked reading from a book, especially a used one with some character.

To practice his German, he would sometimes look for a German translation of a book he had already read, so it was easier to understand.

He came across a small thin book, in German, with an English title: *Love Story,* by Erich Segal. Scanning the inside pages, he saw it was a translation. There was no publication date.

It was an easy read even in German. The story was about a rich boy at Harvard and a poor girl at Radcliffe falling in love, and though set in the 1970s or '80s, it brought back memories for Ezra of his time in Boston, though he had been the poor boy among rich people.

DON ERWIN

He sat in Union Square Park on a bench reading the book—with the occasional help of Google Translate—until he finally got cold and moved to a coffee shop where he continued to read. After some time, he came to a chapter where the boy and girl got married and said their vows and recited poetry to each other.

The boy chose a passage from Walt Whitman's *Song of the Road*. The girl recited a sonnet from Elizabeth Barrett Browning. Poetry was sometimes difficult to translate, so Ezra returned to Forbidden Planet and purchased an old copy of Browning's poems in English. He found the passage—*Sonnets from the Portuguese 22*:

> When our two souls stand up erect and strong,
> Face to face, silent, drawing nigh and nigher,
> Until the lengthening wings break into fire
> At either curvèd point,—what bitter wrong
> Can the earth do to us, that we should not long
> Be here contented?

Nice, thought Ezra.

In finding *22*, he came across *14*. He had written a paper about it in high school and gotten a C. His teacher said he hadn't understood it, so he read it again, for the first time in more than a decade:

> IF thou must love me, let it be for nought
> Except for love's sake only. Do not say
> "I love her for her smile—her look—her way
> Of speaking gently,—for a trick of thought
> That falls in well with mine, and certes brought
> A sense of pleasant ease on such a day"—
> For these things in themselves, Belovèd, may
> Be changed, or change for thee,—and love, so wrought,
> May be unwrought so. Neither love me for
> Thine own dear pity's wiping my cheeks dry,—
> A creature might forget to weep, who bore
> Thy comfort long, and lose thy love thereby!
> But love me for love's sake, that evermore

BUFFALO HUNTING IN ALABAMA

Thou mayst love on, through love's eternity.

He read it again. He understood it now, and the words slapped him in the face. Those aspects of Eleanor that attracted him would one day pass away, and while he might have riches, he would have nothing.

He finished the book. It ended with the girl dying.

***

Ezra woke up and stared at the ceiling. He got out of bed, opened Google and Word, and started structuring notes.

Investors created Dixie Light & Electric in the early 1900s to build dams and sell electricity. Later, they acquired a gas company, and the company became Dixie Gas & Light. In the 1980s, it became DG&L, since "Dixie" increasingly had negative connotations. DG&L's rates were lower than the national average and about average for the Southeast. They served about seventy percent of Alabama.

Their rate of return was outstanding and had been for many years. DG&L was the sole provider of natural gas and electricity within its service area, and while the rules allowed "customer choice" for large users, the rules favored the service area provider.

A five-member Public Utilities Commission, elected to four-year terms, regulated DG&L's rate of return. State law prohibited the utility and its PAC from contributing to PUC campaigns, but the prohibition didn't apply to DG&L's suppliers, *including Jimmy's firm*, Ezra thought.

DG&L had spent over $70 million in the last seven years to influence public and political opinion. This was much more than neighboring utilities in Georgia, Mississippi, and Florida. A newspaper article had quoted DG&L as saying the expenses included "civic-related" contributions in addition to lobbying and political spending, and shareholders, not ratepayers, bore these costs.

According to the news stories, DG&L was the dominant political power in the state. Energy sales generated massive amounts of revenue, so even a small percentage spent on political activities was big money.

All in all, thought Ezra, *if I decide to work in Alabama, DG&L seems like a good company to work for.*

***

Ezra flew out of LaGuardia to negotiate an infrastructure deal in Iowa. Locals wanted Silverman to finance a bridge. The traffic numbers looked good, but traffic studies were notoriously unreliable. The tolls would have to be higher than proposed to generate the rate of return Silverman needed to play.

As his plane waited on the runway for the return to New York, Ezra flipped through *The Economist* and came to the employment ads. He always found them fascinating.

Maybe he could be the CEO of "one of the fastest-growing insurance companies in Kenya." He imagined himself wearing a linen suit in a Nairobi office. Middle East and North Africa representative for the Ford Foundation? Sounds mysterious and dangerous, or stiflingly bureaucratic. CEO of the International Diabetes Federation based in Brussels? Probably helps to have diabetes (he didn't). Senior Editor-Dubai for *The Economist*? Sounds interesting. Principal Advisor regarding climate change for the European Commission? He wasn't sure how he felt about the issue. President of the Open Society Foundation, with principal offices in New York, London, and Budapest?

Or he could go work for DG&L in Alabama.

Or he could end this nonsense and continue working for the best company in the world in the best city in the world. Work was a bit of a mess, but it was fixable. Maybe he should take up tennis or handball.

***

As the plane reached flight altitude, the engines throttled down to a muted rush. Ezra began to experience that peaceful state of *plane flight nirvana* that came from sitting in first-class next to an empty seat, savoring the pleasant glow from two Jack-and-Cokes, and watching the surreal puffy-white clouds far below, disconnecting him from Earth.

What to do about Eleanor.

The poem helped him realize what had been bothering him. Don't love someone because they're beautiful or wealthy or have a nice smile because all that can go away. Love them because you're determined to love them no matter what. *Determination* is what sustains a long-term relationship. He didn't know if he would ever meet anyone he felt that way about, but he knew it wasn't Eleanor. It wasn't her fault. They just weren't meant to be.

As he exited the plane at LaGuardia, he turned on his phone to make two phone calls. The first was to Jimmy: "OK, I'm doing this because you're a good friend. Also, I'm hungry for shrimp-and-grits. Make an appointment for me with DG&L."

He dialed the second number. "Eleanor, we have to talk…"

6

BIRMINGHAM, ALABAMA

As a child, Ezra remembered that flying from Alabama to almost anywhere meant transferring in Atlanta, and people joked that when a person died, they had to connect through Atlanta to reach Heaven or Hell. Ezra caught a morning Delta flight from LaGuardia to Atlanta and then a twenty-five-minute hop to Birmingham.

Scott Kling, DG&L's VP of Economic Development, was meeting him at the airport. The visit was a one-day meet-and-greet to see if the chemistry worked. They would talk and have dinner, and then tomorrow, Ezra would wander around on his own to see if he could be happy living in Birmingham. *Happy in Birmingham. That would be incomprehensible to most New Yorkers.*

As a kid, Ezra's aunt and uncle had lived in Birmingham, and he remembered them taking him to the Birmingham Zoo. In high school, he had visited for debate tournaments. It had seemed a big city at the time.

The plane touched down smoothly under calm blue skies. Ezra could see tall buildings in the distance. The airport was near the city center, like LaGuardia, but there was no river in-between.

Stepping into the jet bridge, the air wasn't warm, but it wasn't frigid, either. The airport looked clean and fresh, unlike the rundown pigsties that LaGuardia and Newark had become.

Descending the escalator to the baggage area, Ezra saw a young man holding a sign with his name. Ezra walked up, and the man next to the boy stuck out his hand and said, "Hi, I'm Scott Kling. Welcome to Alabama."

"Ezra Drake. Glad to meet you."

Kling looked about forty, six feet tall, reasonably fit, and wore a dark suit, rep tie, and a white starched shirt. The hair showed touches of gray and looked firmly gelled in place.

"Good flight?"

"Very good. Smooth."

"The weather's a little better here than New York."

No shit. "Much better."

"Sorry you had to connect through Atlanta. We had nonstop service to Newark until recently, but the Great Recession ended that. We hope to get that back soon."

He waved his arm around, "We're in the middle of a $200 million renovation of the airport, so part of it's still closed off. We like our airport because it's conveniently close to the city."

I wonder if we did the financing for this? Ezra thought.

Ezra had a carry-on, so they were ready to go. "We're right outside," said Kling.

A massive dark blue SUV sat at the curb. The young man grabbed Ezra's bag and stowed it in the back.

"I'm driving," said Kling. "You're up front next to me."

As they pulled away, Kling said, "This is Mercedes' luxury, full-size SUV, the GL. It's made about thirty-five miles from here near Tuscaloosa. That's the only place in the world it's made, and Mercedes exports them to 112 countries. Here in the U.S., it outsells the Cadillac Escalade and Lincoln Navigator combined."

The GL featured Mercedes' understated leather-and-wood interior and functional dash, and the vehicle floated down the interstate. *Impressive*, Ezra admitted. It reminded him why he loved cars.

"We're good at making people-movers. About thirty miles in the other direction, toward Atlanta, Honda makes their Odyssey Minivans."

"What cars are made in Alabama now?" Ezra asked.

"Mercedes makes this, the smaller ML, and the R, and they're about to start making the C-Class sedan. Honda makes the Odyssey minivan, the Pilot SUV, the Ridgeline pickup, and the Acura SUV. Hyundai in Montgomery makes the Sonata and Elantra sedans. In all, we make almost nine hundred thousand cars a year in Alabama."

BUFFALO HUNTING IN ALABAMA

Driving toward the city center, they passed an area that reminded Ezra of the worn-out industrial towns of the Northeast and Midwest. A building off to the left belched smoke—hopefully steam. Birmingham looked like any number of second- and third-tier cities he had visited working for Silverman.

Many people thought of Alabama as tropical, but Ezra knew it wasn't. The winters were short, but nights often dipped below freezing. The hardwood trees on each side of the interstate were bare-branched.

"The Birmingham metro area's about 1.1 million people—about a fourth of the state's population. The other major metros—Mobile, Montgomery, and Huntsville—together are smaller than Metro Birmingham.

"Four interstates pass through or connect to the city, and it's a rail hub. Our transportation weaknesses are not having a river, and our airport needs more nonstop flights and an international flight or two. We're working on that."

Much of the interstate was elevated, and Ezra could see that downtown Birmingham sat in a wide flat valley, running east and west, with a low mountain range along its south side. The mountain ridge was crowned with houses, an occasional condo, several radio and television towers, and the famous Vulcan statue, all overlooking downtown.

"What's the mountain called?"

"Red Mountain. That's where they first mined iron ore. Industrialists created Birmingham in the 1870s when they discovered all the ingredients for steel here, and Birmingham became the Pittsburgh of the South."

"You need iron ore …"

"…and coal and limestone. Nowadays, the iron ore and coal are mostly mined-out, but the whole region sits on limestone. Birmingham still makes steel, but with fewer employees and little pollution."

They exited the interstate into the city center. "Downtown's divided by the railroad tracks. The northern half's mostly office buildings, while UAB—the University of Alabama at Birmingham—dominates the southern half of town.

"We call UAB the university that ate Birmingham. It takes up more than eighty square blocks and has an undergraduate college, but it's mostly postgraduate studies, medical care, and research. It's Birmingham's biggest industry today."

Up-close, Ezra could see that Birmingham possessed many late-1800s and early-1900s buildings, both three- and four-story and taller skyscrapers, with decorative brickwork and elaborate stone trim. Birmingham had somehow managed to keep many beautiful old buildings that other cities had torn down.

"People have been moving downtown in the last few years. About five thousand people now live in the city center in buildings that were once offices, warehouses, and retail stores." Ezra had seen this trend nationwide, led by college grads and empty-nesters.

Kling pointed to a warehouse-like building with large windows. "We created the Innovation Depot in 2007 by renovating an old Sears retail store. It now houses about ninety startup companies with more than five hundred employees. In 2011, it won the Incubator of the Year Award, beating out two thousand other incubators from the U.S. and sixty-five other countries."

Kling continued, "Birmingham's always been a railroad town. We've recently opened the Railroad Reservation Park on nineteen acres of land on the south side of the tracks, and it's been a great success. It's Birmingham's Central Park.

"Next to it, we've built a first-class ballfield for the Birmingham Barons. Apartment complexes and hotels are being built around the park and ballfield, creating a critical mass of activity."

"What's the city's population again?" Ezra knew but asked anyway.

"The metro area's over a million. The City of Birmingham is slightly over two hundred thousand. That's down from almost three hundred fifty thousand in 1960, but we think the decline has leveled out and is starting to trend upward. We'll know for sure when the next census comes out."

They were now driving through UAB—block after block of newer eight-to-ten story buildings. "It's one of the leading research universities in the U.S. and the state's largest employer," said Kling. "Ten percent of Birmingham metro jobs and one in thirty-three jobs in Alabama are directly or indirectly related to UAB. The estimated annual impact is almost $5 billion."

They drove northward through a tunnel under the railroad tracks. "See that church? That's the Sixteenth Street Baptist Church where an evil and tragic bombing in 1963 killed four little black girls. And there, across the street, is the Civil Rights Institute—it's a must-see."

Several blocks further north, Kling said, "Here's our office," and pointed to a massive square building, perhaps fifteen stories tall, located near a convention center complex. It appeared to occupy the entire block.

"Impressive," Ezra said.

"It's not the tallest in town. That's not our style."

"I know what you mean," said Ezra. "Where I work, the building doesn't even have our name on it."

"But we do have the largest office by square footage," Kling added.

"How many people work there?"

"About three thousand."

Ezra's leg ached a bit, which reminded him to ask, "Does it have a gym?"

"World-class, with weight machines, exercise bikes, rowing machines—everything you could want."

"That's nice," said Ezra.

Kling parked in the parking deck, and they took an elevator to the fourteenth floor.

The Economic Development Department featured an open central area with offices along the outside and inside walls. The office walls were the easily-moved type, *but they're real walls*, Ezra thought. Through the office windows, Ezra could see downtown and Red Mountain.

"We have ten people total, including admin support."

"If we work out an arrangement, could I have an office with a window?"

Kling smiled slightly. "We could arrange that," he said without hesitation. "We just happen to have one free."

7

HIGHLANDS BAR & GRILL

"Birmingham has a great food culture."
 Ezra and Scott Kling were sitting at the bar of Alabama's holy high church of cuisine—Highlands Bar & Grill. They had thirty minutes to talk before the others arrived.

Highlands was classically simple: Two rooms, the smaller containing a U-shaped bar with the bottom of the U facing the street, and the larger room—the restaurant—with French doors in between and doors from both rooms to the sidewalk. Highlands was dark muted colors, polished and sophisticated.

"Thirty years ago, Birmingham was a meat-and-three and barbeque town. What we thought of as fine dining was mostly done at country clubs," said Kling.

"Now people come from everywhere to eat in our restaurants. Frank Stitt deserves the credit. He created this place. For the last several years, the James Beard Foundation has named Highlands one of America's five most outstanding restaurants. One day, they'll name it the best. Frank's given Birmingham and Alabama a great gift. People here don't mind paying good money for good food."

Ezra had read about Highlands in a recent *Times* article. The New York press was mostly negative about Alabama, but the story about Stitt and Highlands had been positive.

"He's also trained other chefs, hasn't he?"

"Chris Hastings was one of his chefs. My sister's the foodie; she can tell you. She's going to join us tonight."

"Who's going to be here?" Ezra asked.

"A couple of my guys and their wives, my wife, and my sister. That'll make eight for dinner. Before they get here, let's talk business: You wonder why we're interested in you?"

"Yes."

"DG&L mostly promotes from within. That helps build loyalty but makes it harder to acquire some of the rarer skills we need. In Economic Development, we need someone who can not only sell Alabama but who also has a network of national and international business connections and who comes from Alabama.

"Businesses searching for sites know that consultants are hired guns. They want to talk with authentic Alabamians who can really tell them about the state. We put the word out through our network the type person we wanted, and Jimmy Adams gave us your name."

"I know nothing about economic development," said Ezra.

"It's about doing things to improve the economy of a community or state. There are many ways to do it, and no organization can do it all, so each economic development organization has a particular focus."

"What's DG&L's focus?"

Kling's forehead creased. "We want Alabama to have a thriving economy so we can sell more gas and electricity. Economic development is 'big picture' marketing for our company."

"But doesn't government do economic development? Why not let them do it for you?"

"They do," said Kling, "but have you ever seen any truly effective government agency—other than the IRS?" he smiled at his little joke. "We can't turn our company's marketing over to government.

"The Alabama Department of Industry & Trade—ADIT—is our most important partner. The Governor appoints the ADIT Director, who's the gatekeeper for incentives. Just by answering the telephone, ADIT gets more prospects than we get through all our recruiting efforts, because site consultants and companies know it's state government that controls incentives, workforce training, and permitting.

"We work closely with ADIT for two reasons: To make sure as many of their projects as possible locate in our service area, and to help them close on projects.

"Some of the ADIT folks are smart and work hard, and some are...government workers, but our job is to work with all of them. It's like lobbying the state legislature. Some legislators are not, shall we say, totally ethical, but we must work with them, and we must find ways to do it legally." He looked at Ezra for a moment and took a deep swig of his gin and tonic—his second.

"When you say 'projects,' you mean companies interested in moving to Alabama?" asked Ezra.

"It could be that, or it could be a foreign company looking to set up their first U.S. manufacturing location like Mercedes in Alabama. Or it could be a competitive expansion, where a company has several plants across the U.S., and they're trying to decide which one to expand. We, of course, want it to be the Alabama plant.

"Sometimes, a business moves for strategic reasons. Take Porsche. About fifteen years ago, they moved from Reno, Nevada, to Atlanta. God knows why they were in Reno. The air service isn't great, and the time difference with Germany is nine hours, so they had no common office hours. They moved to Atlanta, where the air service is great, and there's only six hours' time difference with Stuttgart."

"So, in addition to helping ADIT, you also generate prospects on your own?"

"We do, and we want to generate more; that's why we're looking for someone like you. We're looking for projects that use large amounts of gas and electricity."

"Like?"

"Chemical plants, steel plants, pharmaceutical operations, data centers. Anything that uses gas or electricity with a high load factor."

"So that's your economic development niche—attracting companies to Alabama?"

"We also try to help communities prepare themselves better to compete for projects. Seventy to eighty percent of the time a company wants to locate in an existing building, rather than take the time and risk to build one, so we have a loan program that helps communities finance a speculative shell building, so they have product to show companies."

Kling was on his third gin and tonic. "We leave export development to ADIT and groups like regional trade centers. We give some money to help with trip arrangements, but most of the big companies are already exporting if they have the appropriate products. Helping a small company develop export markets is time-intensive, and even if it's successful, the electricity and gas component of the goods exported is typically small.

"Business startups are a discussion-in-itself. Most business startups just happen without any involvement by economic developers."

"What's DG&L's core competence?" Ezra asked.

"Transporting and selling gas and making and selling electricity, of course," Kling answered, looking him directly in the eyes.

"And what's the biggest long-term threat to DG&L?"

"Probably alternative energy, but it's an opportunity as well. The Greenies drive around in their Teslas and Leafs, and they're so proud they're *sustainable*, but an electric-powered car is just a coal- or nuclear- or hydro-powered car, depending upon the energy generation mix where it's charged.

"We love electric cars because they're typically charged at night when we have idle power plant capacity. We feel we have enough control of state politics to take advantage of new energy technologies, rather than being threatened by them."

"Speaking of that," said Ezra, "when I did my research, I saw that DG&L spends much more on politics than other utilities. What's the story?"

Kling gave a little smile. "Plato said that one of the penalties for not participating in politics is that you end up being governed by your inferiors. In the late 1960s, we built some expensive nuclear plants, had to raise rates, and became the whipping boy for Alabama politicians. We almost went bankrupt.

"We swore never to be put in that position again, so we became much more politically active. If Plato were alive today, he would probably agree that money is the mother's milk of politics. Whatever long-term threats we face, we deal with them both technically and politically."

"If I come work for you, what will I be doing?"

"First, we want you traveling around the state visiting local economic developers and politicians, getting to know them, and emphasizing to them that DG&L is working to bring companies and jobs to their communities. This will help you build relationships to work with them on projects. You'll also learn about the communities and what they have to offer—their labor force and industrial parks."

"Sounds like a good way to get reacquainted with Alabama," Ezra replied.

"Second, we'll want you to start rubbing shoulders with the ADIT people so they'll include you in their projects. Take them out to dinner, for drinks—that sort of thing.

"Third, we spend a lot of time and effort relationship-building with site consultants because they manage a lot of projects. We try to get site consultants and corporate bigwigs to visit the state by inviting them to golf tournaments, hunting trips, football games, and the like."

Where do the site consultants get projects? Ezra wondered.

"Do you hunt or play golf?" Kling asked.

"Done some of both."

"Good. Important recruiting skills.

"Our CEO also feels it's important for top management to experience what's going on in the world, so we sometimes take our execs to meet with the upper management of international companies who are our customers. The goal is to get these current customers to put their next expansion in Alabama.

"When you're arranging these trips, the execs will tell you to be economical, but you're much better off going nice than cheap. In London, we put them in the Dorchester, the Hyde Park, or the Savoy. In Zurich, it's the Dolder Grand. In Paris, George the Fifth or Crillon are best. Here, these guys are masters of their environment, but overseas they become dependent on you because everything is different."

"How do you quantify what you do?" asked Ezra. "What's the business case for a utility doing economic development?"

"For one thing, it's something we've always done, but we've had consultants evaluate our work, and they tell us we make money for the company. My business development manager will be here tonight; I'll let him explain the calculations."

"Is there much pushback from the public about being a monopoly?" Ezra asked.

Kling sipped his drink. "From time-to-time, we catch crap—mostly from the press. It can be hard to explain that our being a monopoly can be an advantage to the public."

"In what way?" Ezra was interested in hearing this.

"The advantages of competition are overrated. Peter Thiel, the tech guru, recently wrote a *Wall St. Journal* article titled "Competition Is for Losers," where he explains how competition can produce situations where no one has any money to innovate.

"He compares the airlines and Google. In 2012, the airlines together generated $160 billion in revenue but tiny profits. As a result, they're barely surviving. The seats are cramped, the attendants are crabby, and the shareholders aren't happy.

"Google only generated $50 billion that year, but their net operating income was more than a hundred times that of the entire airline industry, so Google is worth three times more than all the U.S. airlines combined.

"Who's doing the innovating? Google—because they have the money to innovate. The airlines have competed themselves to death, but Google doesn't have much competition.

"Granted, DG&L is not an innovator like Google, but we have the financial wherewithal to help the state in many ways, and we can sometimes do things that government is unable or unwilling to do."

8

DINNER

Ezra was about to ask another question when he saw Kling eyeing the front door. Two women were having their coats checked. One was middle-aged—a bleached blonde with her hair in a bun.

The other was younger, taller, and slenderer, wearing a black sleeveless cocktail dress. She faced away from them, but Ezra could see her slim legs and well-defined calves. Her hair was shoulder-length—a dark auburn color. And then she turned around and enchanted Ezra with her oval face, high cheekbones, and large eyes—which caught his.

"Here they come," said Kling, and they both stood without thinking.

"Ezra, I'd like you to meet my wife, Esther, and my sister, Amanda."

"It's a pleasure," Ezra said.

"So, you're the Silverman Bach guy?" asked Amanda.

The eyes were clear grey. "I am, but I'm originally from Alabama."

"Here comes the rest of our group," said Kling, and he introduced his two employees and their wives.

The dining room held perhaps twenty tables. They sat near a window at the front, Esther to Ezra's right and Amanda to his left, and ordered drinks and appetizers.

Ezra chose the Stone Ground Baked Grits, Country Ham, and Mushrooms with Fresh Thyme and Parmesan. He was happy to be in the South. For many Southerners, good grits were like the juiciest steak, the finest wine.

For the main course, he chose the Red Snapper with turnips and a vegetable Ragout. Amanda ordered the Carpaccio for the starter and the Braised beef cheek with butternut squash and buttermilk crushed potatoes.

"I'm going to eat too much," Ezra commented.

"Me, too," said Amanda, "but I'll burn it off working out. Dinner at Highlands is special."

"Amen," said Ezra. He noticed Amanda cut her nails short and finished them with clear polish. No rings, but an old-fashioned wristwatch.

"How do you like Birmingham?" she asked as if the two of them were alone talking.

"I like what I see so far," said Ezra, not looking directly at her because that would be a little too obvious, "but I haven't had a chance to see much." *That would be even more obvious.* "The airport's convenient, and I like the old buildings. And many cities would kill to have UAB. And of course," he swept his hand around, "the people are great." They all chuckled.

"You're not from Birmingham?" she asked.

"I grew up in the Southeast corner of the state more than three hours' drive from here. I left Alabama after high school and haven't been back much since, so I don't know Birmingham well. What about you?"

"Scott and I grew up in Hoover, a suburb on the other side of Red Mountain."

Ezra made polite conversation with Kling's wife and learned they had three children and lived in Vestavia Hills, another Birmingham suburb. The children and their upbringing had filled Esther's life, but now the last one was about to go to college.

The restaurant was full, and Ezra saw happy, prosperous people enjoying good food and conversation. The service was efficient and pleasant, but not flashy. The focus was the customers and the food. As Ezra looked around, there was no clue he was dining in Alabama or even the South.

Scott Kling tapped a spoon against his wine glass, just loud enough for those at the table to hear.

"Ladies and Gentleman, please join me in welcoming Mr. Ezra Drake, a native son, back to Alabama. Mr. Drake is currently with Silverman Bach in New York, but perhaps he will return to help us create a New Alabama—an Alabama that offers more of its citizens good-paying jobs."

They lifted wine glasses and clinked them together, and one of the project managers said, "Hear, hear!"

Amanda caught Ezra's eye. "Hear, hear," she said quietly, so only Ezra could hear. He looked at her and smiled.

The wine flowed freely. In that regard, it felt like a Silverman dinner.

"Do you go to church in New York City," Scott's wife asked? Now Ezra knew he was in the South.

"I'm afraid I've been a bit lax lately, ma'am," he said. *Since middle school, basically, except for some weddings and funerals.*

"We're Southern Baptists," she said. "But we're not fanatic about it. After all, Jesus drank wine," and she finished her glass.

And he apparently liked gin and tonics too, Ezra thought.

"Mandy," Kling said, "I told Ezra you were our resident food guru. Tell him about the restaurant scene in Birmingham."

"Well, Southerners have always appreciated good food, but a lot of traditional Southern food isn't healthy. Frank Stitt changed the restaurant scene when he moved here in 1982 and opened Highlands. He's from Cullman, a little town north of here. Frank went to Boston and Berkley to study philosophy and got interested in food culture, then apprenticed under Alice Waters at Chez Panisse and studied under Richard Olney in Provence, who wrote the best book ever about French cooking.

"The small farms in France reminded Frank of Alabama, so he came back and opened a French restaurant with a Southern accent. Later he opened Bottega not far from here—they have an Italian accent—and Chez Fonfon, which is next door and is the perfect little French bistro.

"A whole generation of chefs have worked for Frank and opened restaurants in Birmingham. My favorite is Chris Hastings' Hot and Hot Fish Club. If Frank is the king, Chris is the prince. Chris won the James Beard Chef of the South award in 2012 and the Iron Chef competition not long ago. Hot and Hot is just a few blocks from here. We're going to have to try it."

We're? Is she part of the recruiting team?

"All these restaurants work together and have created a supply chain of farmers who grow crops and raise pigs and other animals to supply the restaurants. If you decide to move here, you won't starve."

"As you can tell, my sister's enthusiastic about her food," said Scott.

"It'll probably catch up with me, but right now, as long as I work out, I'm OK."

More than OK, thought Ezra.

"Let me tell you about the Iron Chef competition," Amanda said. She was becoming more talkative as the night wore on, and the wine continued to flow.

"Southerners thrive on competition; we're football people, so the idea of two chefs competing against each other is appealing. *Mano a mano* is how we like it. If it's a frying pan instead of a football, then so be it. This is something Alabamians understand and appreciate."

Ezra thought how she said *mano a mano* was both cute and totally absurd.

"They contacted Chris about doing the Iron Chef competition in New York," she glanced at Ezra, "and he told them he would do it but only if they put their best chef against him. So, they put Chris against Bobby Flay, who's competed fifty times and won more than seventy percent of his competitions.

"Have you seen the program? They fix their dishes during a one-hour TV show, and the chefs don't know ahead of time the secret ingredient. For Chris' competition, it was sausage! A natural for a Southern chef.

"Each side provided their own ingredients, trying to guess what the secret ingredient might be and what would best complement it. Chris brought okra, white corn, field peas, tomatoes, and peaches, but also his secret ingredient—peach moonshine—which the celebrity judges loved!

"They held the competition months before they showed it on TV, but Chris couldn't tell anyone whether he won, so a group of us gathered at Hot and Hot to watch the show. Chris won, and it was wonderful! One of my all-time favorite evenings."

Ezra didn't know what he'd expected from this visit, but he hadn't expected to hear about cooking competitions.

Changing the subject, Kling said, "Jim, can you tell Ezra how we measure our effectiveness?" They were well into the alcohol to be talking serious business, but Jim had been drinking water, so he was suited for the task. Whether Ezra could understand it was another matter.

"Sure. If a company locates in our service area, they have a choice of banks or law firms or other providers, but we're almost certainly going to get their electricity and gas business. When we land a company, it will typically generate many years of electricity and gas revenue.

"Each year-end, for those projects where we made a difference, we take the expected future streams of revenue and bring them back to present values and then compare them with our department's operating budget. Every time we've done this, the revenue generated is several times more than the cost."

"As long as you keep bringing home a paycheck, Honey," said Esther to Kling, and they all laughed as people do when the boss or his wife makes a joke. As the evening passed, they emptied more bottles, and the conversation became more and more frank.

Ezra decided to egg things along: "Some say that closing a deal is like seduction. If that's so, then what's your best line?"

Kling eyed Ezra for a moment and then said, "We like to remind people about our great weather. How about 'You can play golf in Alabama eleven months a year. It's sometimes a little too hot in August.' "

"Nice," said Ezra, *though that's not a closing line.*

Jim, the business development guy, said, "How about this? We see these hokey economic development television commercials where states try to attract business by touting their educated workforce and good work ethic. They show a lab worker in a white coat and goggles holding up a test tube or looking into a microscope.

"Instead, how about a beautiful girl in a wife-beater, jeans, and hardhat, with a firm hold on an end wrench, and she says seductively to the camera 'Alabama: A great place to get sweaty.' " Amanda almost choked on her wine, laughing. Kling smiled, but Esther didn't.

Kip, the project manager, was well into his cups and said, "How about 'Is that an economic development project in your pocket, or are you just glad to see me?' " Esther looked shocked. Amanda snickered. Ezra laughed.

Don't believe I'd said that, thought Ezra.

Sometime later, returning from the restroom, Ezra saw Kip approaching. As they passed each other, Ezra said, "Hey, if you guys offer me a job, what do I really need to know about DG&L?"

Kip replied, "The most important thing to understand is that *everything* is always political."

Welcome to the real world, Ezra thought.

Back at the table, Ezra said to Amanda, "You made short work of that food."

"It's a habit," said Amanda. "When Scott and I were kids, our Mother always told us to eat all our food because children in India were starving." She paused.

"Times have changed. Today, I tell Scott's kids to study hard because there are children in India after their jobs."

"What do you do for a living?" Ezra asked.

"Schoolteacher," she said and turned to listen to a joke Kip was telling.

Later, Amanda asked, "You're returning to New York tomorrow?"

"Not until Sunday. I thought I would rent a car tomorrow and just drive around and get a feel for Birmingham."

"If you'd like, I'd be glad to show you around."

"That'd be fun. Thanks." *Should I call you or nudge you in the morning?* Ezra couldn't help but be a smart-ass, if only to himself.

"I'll be at the Westin at 11:30 a.m. Don't keep me waiting," she said.

Ezra smiled. The night ended shortly afterward, Scott's driver dropping Ezra at the Westin.

Not a bad evening, he thought, as he drifted off to sleep.

9

EXPLORING BIRMINGHAM

Ezra opened his eyes and stared at the ceiling. Where was he? Then he remembered: *Birmingham. Amanda. Fun dinner last night.*

Amanda arrived at the Westin at 11:30 a.m. driving a dark blue Z4 convertible with the hardtop folded down. She wore a black baseball cap with a script "B," a windbreaker, and aviator shades.

"Hot car for a schoolteacher. What do you really do?" Ezra asked.

"Mostly give my brother a hard time."

Ezra smiled and slid into the passenger seat. "I had an old MGB in high school. Loved that car. It would be fun to have an old sports car here to drive around town."

"So, you like cars?"

"Love 'em. Used to work on them. You *had* to if you had a British sports car."

"You hungry?" she asked.

"Not so much."

"Then, cover your ears."

"What?"

"Just do it, and don't listen. And turn your head away." She was already dialing her phone.

In about a minute, she shook his shoulder. "OK, let's drive."

"What was that all about?"

BUFFALO HUNTING IN ALABAMA

"You'll see," she said and slipped the car into gear, let the clutch out, and gave it the gas. It wasn't ideal convertible weather, but with the windows up and the heater on, the wind flowed over the windshield and trapped a warm bubble of air in the cockpit. It was perfect. They zipped up the on-ramp of Interstate 20/59 and motored eastward at speed.

"I didn't know these cars still came with manual transmissions," he said over the wind.

"Shows what you know," she teased.

"Special order for schoolteachers?"

She ignored him.

"Where are we going?"

"I called in a favor," she said. "Just for you. You'll owe me."

"I'm sure I will," he said.

They passed the airport and in about ten minutes exited the freeway and turned off a side road. A minute later, an enormous aluminum-and-glass building appeared.

"This is the Barber Motorsports Park, and that's the Barber Vintage Motorsports Museum, the largest motorcycle museum in the world."

"We're here to ride motorcycles?"

"No," she was on her cell. "Doug," she said, "we're here."

They signed in at a security gate and motored down a road that encircled one of the best road racing tracks Ezra had ever seen. Most racetracks were asphalt and concrete, but this one was a beautiful green park with a track flowing through it.

On the opposite side of the track from the museum, Amanda turned into a fenced area, and they drove through a multi-level paddock that sloped down to the track. At each level, Ezra could see dozens of motorhomes, popups, and trailers, with people sitting in lawn chairs, talking, or working on cars.

And what cars! About half of them were Porsches, but he saw Corvettes, Mustangs, BMWs, a couple of Ferraris, several Lotus cars, an old Alfa, and many more. There looked to be a couple of hundred cars in all.

At the bottom level of the paddock, Ezra saw sixty or so red, yellow, blue, and silver Porsches lined up in neat rows. The logo on the side of each said, "Porsche Sport Driving School."

"This track stays busy almost all the time," said Amanda. "There's an Indycar race in the Spring and a vintage motorcycle festival in the Fall, and Barber is the home of the world's largest Porsche school. There's fifteen of these schools around the world, and this is the largest—even larger than Germany's. Porsche uses the track about 160 days a year."

A middle-aged man walked toward them. "When are you going to upgrade to a Porsche?" he asked Amanda.

"When Porsche offers a hardtop convertible," she replied.

"I doubt that will happen," the man said. "Metal hardtops weigh too much."

"Doug Neil," he said to Ezra, shaking his hand. "I'm an instructor with the Porsche Club of America. Ready for a ride?"

"Sure." He led Ezra to a sleek silver Porsche sitting in the paddock hot pit area.

"Just took delivery of this. A 2014 Porsche 911 GT3."

"It's a beauty. I get to drive?" Ezra asked.

"No, but you get to experience a full-blown Porsche race car on one of the best road-racing tracks in the world. Had lunch yet?"

"No."

"That's good because this track is a rollercoaster."

They buckled up and took off with the tires squealing. Neil was right. The track was a series of long sweeping turns, elevation changes, and blind corners. The acceleration was fierce, but the braking was even more violent. They did three laps and pulled into the pits.

"Well, that was fun," said Ezra, taking a deep breath. "How often you do this?"

"My day job is commercial real estate consulting, but I spend a weekend or so a month out here. Different car groups rent the track, and most clubs allow other marques to participate. It's a lot of fun; all you need is a track car. If you just want to drive on the track, take the Porsche school course. They provide the cars and instructors, and they'll make you a better driver."

"I just might," said Ezra. *I know some people in New York who would love this.* Ezra knew that every metro of any size had something special, whether it was the Gateway Arch in St. Louis or the country music scene in Nashville. Barber certainly qualified as "world class" special for Birmingham.

Back in the Z4 with Amanda, Ezra asked, "What's with all the sculptures and statues?" Throughout the park, Ezra had seen art and sculpture, some of them fine art, and some whimsical. There had even been a gigantic metal spider at a turn Neil had called "Charlotte's Web."

"There's different stories about it," said Amanda. "The one I like is that hundreds of thousands of people each year visit Barber, and many of them take pictures of the art and post them on social media, and the park gets much more publicity than it could ever have gotten by spending their art budget on conventional advertising."

"Pretty clever," said Ezra.

***

They were walking in the Railroad Reservation Park, in the middle of the city. The park was perhaps a hundred fifty yards wide and six hundred yards long and ran east and west beside the elevated railroad tracks that divided downtown. It had walking trails, a lake, an amphitheater, and playgrounds for children.

Ezra could tell the park was new because everything was fresh and immaculate, and the trees still had guy lines keeping them upright. Across the street sat a baseball park.

"Five years ago, this area was nothing but overgrown lots and dilapidated buildings, and now it's our own little version of Central Park. It's given the city a green center," said Amanda.

"I saw this photo one time," she said, "of a green plant pushing its way up out of the post-war rubble of Berlin. That's how I think of Birmingham.

"Over there is Regions Field where the Barons play. Apartments are underway over there and there"—she pointed—"and they're planning more."

"You a baseball fan?" he asked.

She tapped her ball cap. "I like the circus atmosphere that's part of minor league games. In high school, the Barons played in Hoover—in the suburbs—and I was a ball girl, and for a year, I wore the mascot costume. It was so much fun!"

"Good things seem to be happening," Ezra said, "but is it enough to turn the city around? The data doesn't look great, but perhaps Birmingham is a caterpillar about to become a butterfly."

"I think we're at an inflection point," she said. "Instead of trending down, we're trending up. You understand?"

Ezra admired her fervor. "I understand, and I wish Birmingham the best."

She continued, "You have no idea how bad it was just seven or eight years ago. Birmingham was on the ropes; the city had lost a third of its population since 1960, and companies were leaving—not just the City, but the entire metro. And then the county bankrupted from corruption and wasteful spending. For several years, almost no new companies located in Birmingham or Jefferson County.

"And then things started happening. Young people and empty-nesters began moving into the city, developers renovated old buildings into condos and apartments, and restaurants and nightclubs and breweries popped up. The people elected a more proactive city government which pushed the city forward. A new generation of businesspeople came to power who weren't tied to the '60s.

"You're never cool when you're trying to be. Birmingham suddenly became cool when it was just trying to survive.

"It's ironic; when we had six Fortune 500 headquarters in the Birmingham area, downtown was a wasteland. Now we only have one, but downtown looks better than it has in forty or fifty years. How does that fit into economic theory?"

Ezra had seen the same downtown trend in many mid-sized cities, but he didn't want to discourage her. "I think you have better leaders than you used to," he said.

"Maybe so. Maybe the old generation of business leaders who lost power during the civil rights years didn't have the vision to build a new Birmingham. It's taken a new generation of leaders to do that."

10

LOU'S PUB & PACKAGE STORE

The Lakeview neighborhood, at the southern edge of downtown Birmingham, was a mix of older houses, apartments, and businesses.

Lou's Pub was tucked into one of three or four connected storefronts from the 1920s or '30s. Lou's had started as a "package" store—a place to buy liquor—and Lou's personality had turned it into a bar and trendy social hangout.

People sat inside at the bar and two or three tables, but there wasn't much room with the liquor shelves, so people spilled outside and drank and talked, standing or sitting at a half-dozen round concrete tables with curved benches.

After a thirty-second tour of the premises, Ezra and Amanda sat outside. The air had a spring warmth, though most of winter was still ahead, and a light wind blew, moving the baby hairs that framed Amanda's face.

What a beautiful woman, Ezra thought. "You look more like Scott's daughter than his sister."

"Thank you. My brothers were half-grown when I came along. I was Mom and Dad's little surprise."

Ezra heard German spoken. Turning around, he saw two men, both in their early thirties, in conversation. The blonde man's dialect was southern German—probably Baden-Württemberg. The taller, darker-haired man spoke *Hochdeutsch* with the clear diction of someone from Hannover.

Without thinking, Ezra leaned back and said, *"Können Sie mir bitte ein gutes lokales Bier empfehlen?"*

"You should try the Good People IPA; it's brewed locally," said the blonde man in English.

"*Vom Fass?*" continued Ezra.

"*Oh ja, das ist das beste,*" replied the German.

"*Ich glaube, das Avondale Saison ist das beste,*" said the dark-haired man.

"*Warum nicht beide?*" asked Ezra. He saw a waiter and inquired, "Do you have a sampler of local draft beers?"

The dark-haired man looked at Ezra for a moment. "*Wohnen Sie hier in Birmingham?*" he asked. He looked at Ezra in a way that made Ezra feel he was being analyzed.

"*Nein, nur zu Besuch.* A job interview." Ezra held out his hand. "I'm Ezra."

"My name's Simon," said the dark-haired one, shaking his hand, and he's Thomas." He pronounced it the German way: Tow-mas'.

"Did you grow up in Alabama," asked Simon? "Maybe Southeast Alabama?"

Damn. "Close," said Ezra, "but I've lived abroad and up north for a while." *I thought I had lost the accent entirely.*

The conversation captivated Amanda, her eyes shining, though she didn't understand much of what they said.

"This is Amanda," said Ezra, introducing her.

"I am pleased to meet you," said Thomas. Simon said nothing.

"Come and sit with us. We have room at our table," said the German, and so they did.

As they talked, Ezra learned that Thomas worked at the Mercedes plant and had lived in Birmingham for two years. He worked in a department that ensured the suppliers met Mercedes' standards. He loved it in the South. With the Mercedes plant located halfway between Birmingham and Tuscaloosa, German nationals could live in either place, whichever best suited them.

"Tuscaloosa is a smaller town. Many students—a big university. Birmingham is a bigger city. All kinds of people. We live where we want, and in the summer we enjoy weekends at the coast. The beaches are incredible!" he said, smiling.

Ezra explained that he was in town to interview for an economic development position with DG&L.

"That's what he does," said Thomas, pointing to Simon.

"You work for DG&L?" asked Ezra.

"No. For the Atmani Foundation," said Simon.

"I'm not familiar with it, but that doesn't mean anything. I was recruited to interview for this job. How do you like doing economic development?"

"I like it a lot. It's about helping create jobs and a better quality of life for people," said Simon. "It's a Great Game, cities and states competing for jobs and investment, and it's rewarding to see good jobs come to a community. These guys are an example of that," he said, nodding his head toward Thomas.

"I make a decent living, and I feel like I'm doing something good. I sleep well at night." Simon paused, "I didn't always feel that way. Now it's your turn. What do you do?"

"I work for Silverman Bach in New York," said Ezra.

"And you're considering doing economic development in Alabama?"

"I know it sounds a bit strange, but I'm originally from Alabama, and hey, it's not such a bad place," he said, looking around. "I mean, right now, people in New York are shivering in their overcoats and walking through slush."

"Where did you learn German?" asked Simon.

"Some as a kid, some in high school and college, and a few years working for Deutsche Bank in Frankfurt."

"Your accent is pretty good," said Simon.

"Not as good as yours," said Ezra truthfully. "Are you German or American?"

"I'm as American as you," replied Simon. "What do you think of the economic development business?"

"I'm not sure," said Ezra quietly. "I need to know more. I've only heard one viewpoint. How is what you do different from what DG&L does? And let me add that her brother is the head of economic development for DG&L."

Simon looked at Amanda and then said, "I think I'm fair in saying that for DG&L, economic development is a tool to help make a profit. They also do it to benefit Alabama, and it has public relations value.

"The Atmani Foundation is a non-profit. We're not selling gas or electricity, or anything for that matter. One of our goals is to bring better jobs to Alabama—to raise the standard of living of the people here.

"Our being a non-profit doesn't mean we're better than DG&L; just different. Making a profit is the cornerstone of American capitalism, and our foundation wouldn't exist without Mr. Atmani having made lots of profits. We're not interested in any public relations value to what we do. We don't have a website; we try to stay anonymous."

He continued, "As to what we do, most economic development organizations try to do so many things they have little time to focus. We spend all our efforts targeting good companies and persuading them to locate in Alabama. We don't fundraise, we don't develop industrial parks, and we don't spend much time networking with other economic development organizations. We don't have a board of directors to please. We don't have investors to please. All we must do is satisfy Mr. Atmani."

The beers arrived, and they paused to drink.

"How do you find the companies and convince them to locate in Alabama?" Ezra asked.

"That's the secret sauce. Most economic developers wait for the phone to ring. Instead, we're proactive—to the extreme."

"You said that economic development was a Great Game. What did you mean?" Amanda asked.

"Rudyard Kipling used the term to describe the behind-the-scenes fight between Great Britain and Russia for influence in Asia in the nineteenth century. Today, we have a Great Game where more than eighteen thousand municipalities, 3,100 counties, and ninety thousand taxing jurisdictions compete with each other to attract companies who will create good jobs and generate new tax revenue."

"It looks as if Alabama has been pretty successful. Everything I've seen so far looks nice," Ezra said, trying to be complimentary.

"Alabama's median household income, adjusted for inflation, is down twenty percent from its peak year of 1998, and within three miles of every place you've visited in Birmingham, I can show you crippling poverty and Third World conditions," Simon said. "They've been treating you like an economic development prospect, showing you the pretty stuff." Simon looked at Amanda. "Show him Southtown; it's just a few blocks from here, near where you work.

"Local economic developers always paint a positive picture because they're cheerleaders for their communities. And it's the same story at the state level because the governor is the chief recruiter, and governors are always running for reelection or polishing their legacies. If you're thinking about economic development as a job, you should understand the real situation," Simon said.

None of them knew what to say, so they sat there looking thoughtful and drank their beer.

BUFFALO HUNTING IN ALABAMA

"Speaking of work," Simon said, looking at his watch, "I have a flight to catch. After years of optimizing their supply chains, Japanese companies again seem interested in the U.S." He looked at Ezra again with that intent stare. "Where are you in this job search?"

"I'm not searching as much as being recruited," Ezra said. "This trip was the first meeting."

"With all due respect to DG&L," he looked at Amanda, "you owe it to yourself to explore all possibilities. Here's my card. Email me if you're planning to come back."

Ezra took the card with both hands, holding the card carefully at the bottom edges. "And this is your email address?" he asked, slightly nodding his head.

"That's quite good," Simon said. He stood up and went inside to pay his tab; they later discovered he had paid theirs as well. Thomas stayed, and they talked about his impressions of Alabama. "The American interstates were more frightening at first than the autobahn. A little like the old Mad Max movies."

Simon emerged from Lou's talking on his phone. As he passed them, he stopped talking and covered the phone with the palm of his hand. "Hey Doc," he said as he stepped onto the sidewalk, "my shoulder's much better. Thanks!"

Ezra turned and looked at Amanda, who looked pissed. "Was he talking to you?"

"Smartass," she hissed.

"I knew you weren't a schoolteacher. What are you—a physical therapist?"

"I'm an orthopod and a sports medicine doctor. I work at St. Vincent's Hospital, not far from here."

"And you've treated him before?"

"I can't discuss patient information."

Later, as they walked to the car, Ezra asked, "Why didn't you tell me you're a doctor?"

"What difference does it make?"

"None, really. It's just something else that's interesting about you."

"While we're being honest here," she said, "tell me about the limp. Most people wouldn't notice it, but that's my business."

"I broke it. Compound fracture. It's fine now."

"How'd it happen?"

"Karate promotion."

"Oh God, another one."

"You see that often?"

"Your friend there. His collarbone."

Interesting, thought Ezra.

Later, in the car, Amanda asked, "I wonder why you're doing this. Working for Silverman Bach in New York is a dream job. It sounds like you're running away from something. Are you married?" She thought for a moment. "Do you have a girlfriend?"

"No," he paused, "and no." *Not anymore.*

"OK," and she paused to change the subject. "So, what haven't you done that you wanted to do on this trip?"

He thought for a moment. "I haven't had ribs. It's hard to get good ribs in New York."

"I know just the place," she said, "and it's less than ten minutes away."

As they drove, Ezra reflected on what he had experienced. This Simon guy was intriguing. In addition to everything he had said, as he left, talking on his phone, it sounded as if he was speaking Japanese.

11

DREAMLAND

"Bib him up," said Amanda. The waitress tied the disposable plastic bib around Ezra's neck. "Serious rib-eating is messy."

They had driven to Dreamland, a rib joint on Birmingham's Southside, near the University. The décor was basic barbeque—tables with red-checkered cloths and a bar with neon beer signs.

"I think I've gained five pounds on this trip," said Ezra. He had heard of Dreamland in Tuscaloosa because the TV announcers bragged about it during Alabama football games. He didn't know they had one in Birmingham.

"The original Dreamland specialized in ribs, white bread, and sweet tea," said Amanda, "but when it expanded to Birmingham, they added corn-on-the-cob, baked beans, mashed potatoes, and the like."

"For a sports medicine doctor, you know an awful lot about food."

"Know thy enemy," she said.

"As they were eating, Ezra asked, "What do you think about all this? About me doing economic development. I mean, your brother does economic development. Does he like it?"

Ezra liked looking at Amanda, even with barbeque sauce smeared around her lips. She had great lips. He had never thought of barbeque sauce as sexy until now.

"Move closer," he said, and she leaned forward.

He reached out with his napkin and gently wiped each side of her lips.

"That's an intimate thing to do," she said. He could sense her increased breathing.

"Do you mind?" he asked.

"No," she said and took his hand and lightly kissed the end of his finger. Now he was the one breathing harder. They looked into each other's eyes for a long moment.

"What were you asking?" she said, breaking the silence. "Oh, about Scott. He's only been doing economic development for six months or so. It's not a passion. As he puts it, it's another machine to be tuned-up. He's just punching his ticket as he climbs the DG&L ladder. The way to get ahead at DG&L is to work in as many departments as possible."

"He did a good selling job on me yesterday."

"He's my brother; he's competent," she said.

"What do *you* think of all this? What advice would you give me?" asked Ezra.

She was quiet for a moment. "I have lots of thoughts. First, I know now why Scott invited me to dinner. He worries about me being single, and from time-to-time, he tries to fix me up with someone. If you started working for him, and you and I started dating, he would have control of both you and me—and he always likes control!" A pause. "I also still wonder why you want to leave New York."

"I'm not sure I do. I'm just exploring possibilities," Ezra paused. "Maybe I like wiping barbeque sauce off pretty girls' faces."

"Have you thought about where to live if you moved here?" Amanda asked.

"No idea. What do you think?" Ezra said.

"Most people our age want to live downtown. That's where I live."

"I'd love to see your place," he said.

"Maybe I'll show you one day."

***

Once the sun set, it had quickly turned colder, and Amanda had raised the Z4's metal hardtop. Ezra had a flight the next morning, and Amanda had hospital rounds, so she drove them to the Westin and parallel-parked on the street near the entrance.

Seated, Ezra turned to Amanda. "I've had a great day. Thank you for showing me around."

"I had fun doing it," she said and looked into his eyes.

Ezra leaned toward her.

"Looking for more barbeque sauce?" she said with a twinkle in her eye. That stopped him. She leaned over and kissed him gently on the cheek. "Please come back again."

"I will," he said. "One way or another."

12

BACK IN NEW YORK

As the Delta jet made its final approach, Ezra looked down at the incredible density of New York. *Life in Birmingham would be very different.*

Paying bills on Sunday evening, he thought about the visit. Alabama had been fun, but as Simon had said, DG&L had given him a very selective tour.

Ezra used Google to build a basic profile of Alabama: In 2010, Alabama's median income was the fifth-lowest in the U.S. Nineteen percent of the population lived below the poverty line. Alabama was among the twenty worst states for every category measured in the 2012 *Gallup-Healthways Well-Being Index* and among the ten worst states for physical health, healthy behavior, and work environment.

Alabama had the third-highest rate of obesity, the seventh-highest rate of cancer, the highest rate of heart disease, and the third-lowest life expectancy.

And yet, when Gallup asked people if they would move to another state if they had the opportunity, some states with the highest incomes had the highest percentage of people wanting to move, while some states with lower incomes had the fewest who wanted to leave.

Fifty percent of people in Illinois wanted to leave the state, forty-nine percent in Connecticut, forty-seven in Maryland, and forty-one percent in New Jersey, New York, and Massachusetts. In Mississippi, the poorest state in the U.S., thirty-nine percent would leave. Thirty-eight percent wanted to leave Georgia, and thirty-six percent leave North Carolina.

BUFFALO HUNTING IN ALABAMA

Only thirty-two percent of the people in Florida, Kentucky, Tennessee, and Arkansas wanted to leave. Only thirty percent of Vermonters wanted to leave. West Virginia was near the bottom of state income rankings, but only twenty-eight percent of West Virginians wanted to move.

Only twenty-four percent of Texans wanted to move—that made sense. Only twenty-three percent of Hawaii and Montana residents wanted to move. That was understandable, too. Hawaii is a paradise, and Montana is actually what people think Texas is.

And only thirty-one percent of Alabamians wanted to move. *Not the most satisfied state, but pretty damn happy.* Life is about more than money or climate—look at Vermont. Maybe the type of high-achieving people who live in places like New York and Connecticut are never happy with life.

Does the happiness of people in some of the poorer states reflect a lack of ambition, or do they know something that people in some of the wealthier states don't?

Alabama didn't have much wealth, but it was a beautiful state with wonderful rivers and huge forests and mountains in the northeast and beaches in the south. Ezra had heard or read somewhere that Alabama was one of the most biodiverse places in the entire world. *Where did I hear that?* He thought.

Ezra liked Birmingham. It was different from the "firehoses and police dogs" image that haunted it. Birmingham was a mid-sized city large enough to have lots to do but not so big that getting around was a hassle. It had been fun to zip around with Amanda in her little sports car with the top down in mid-winter. The food scene was great, the people seemed nice, and he liked what he saw.

Growing up, Ezra had often wondered if he was a true Southerner because his parents had come from the Midwest. He could speak Southern when he wanted yet mostly spoke generic American because of his parents, his debate training, and his belief that parts of America discriminated against people with Southern accents.

Am I crazy? He had spent most of his early life trying to escape Alabama. Was he now seriously thinking about returning there?

Find the next cool place or thing before everyone else, and there are good margins to be made. Savvy money people had told him that. Birmingham was an overlooked place. Was it one of the next cool places?

DG&L was a quality company with a firm control of their market and Alabama politics, but could they control technology? In recent years, the giant

German utilities had suffered mightily from the progress made in renewables. New technology was disruptive. Digital cameras had destroyed the film camera industry; smartphones had devastated digital cameras. Would solar cells and batteries destroy the electric and gas industry?

Is lusting after your potential boss's sister a sign you're not taking a job possibility seriously?

He liked Birmingham, but ultimately it was the job. If the job-fit wasn't good, then everything else was irrelevant. He wasn't convinced he wanted to work for DG&L. He couldn't see it as a step forward. Doing economic development intrigued him, but lots of things intrigued him.

Next the Atmani Foundation: He looked up their 990 Form, which didn't reveal much. He read and took notes, and one website led to another.

Samir Atmani was born in Alexandria, Egypt in 1936 to a Coptic Christian family. He worked for Citibank in Egypt, then got crossed with Gamal Abdel Nasser and fled, supposedly in the baggage compartment of an Ethiopian Airlines plane. One rumor said he'd spied for the U.S.

He became friends with Haile Selassie, the Emperor of Ethiopia, and ended up the head of the National Bank of Ethiopia at age twenty-five.

In 1962, he immigrated to the United States and moved to Birmingham, working as a currency trader for Stein Stewart & Taft, a regional, privately-owned brokerage house based in Birmingham. He was now the chairman and sole owner of Stein Stewart, as well as other companies. People thought him to be worth many hundreds of millions, at least. He was a widower with no children.

Ezra was about to start researching Amanda Kling when an email popped up. Scott Kling wanted him to return to Birmingham to discuss a formal offer.

Five minutes later, a text message whished on his phone:

I'm in town tomorrow evening. Are you free for dinner? Simon.

13

DINNER AT PIORDO'S

It's not the cold; it's how long it takes till spring arrives, thought Ezra as he walked to work on a gray and chilly New York Monday.

They met for dinner that evening at Piordo's on Greenwich Street in the West Village a dozen blocks north of Silverman. The dining room was wood beams and dark leather and a large window overlooking an interior garden. A white-jacketed waiter made cocktails. The menu was Italian, with Korean accents. As waiters came and went, Simon conversed with them in Italian and, presumably, Korean.

"The pastas are good," said Simon. "They suggest the purple red-wine rigatoni with duck sausage and charred figs." Simon ordered for them.

"I've never seen anyone order food in both Italian and Korean," Ezra admitted.

"The owner is Korean, and the chef is Italian," said Simon. "I'm not fluent in Korean; just enough to get around." Ezra said nothing.

"At the Atmani Foundation, we value foreign language fluency," Simon continued. "International companies have invested in Alabama when domestic companies have passed us over. Speaking a prospect's language gives us an advantage."

"How many languages do you speak?"

"Five or six, and I'm passable in another half-dozen. I pick them up easily. How did you like Alabama?" he asked.

"I enjoyed it. Birmingham seems on the rise."

"Has DG&L made you an offer?"

"Not yet, but they've invited me back."

"Are you going?"

Ezra hesitated, "I liked Alabama and the people I met. I'm not totally happy at Silverman, but I can't see moving to Alabama as a good career move. And I'm not sure I'm a good fit for DG&L."

"We guessed that," said Simon. "If you were seriously considering DG&L, we'd stay away. We're not interested in getting crossed with them."

"But you're here," said Ezra, "so what's your interest?"

"We're interested in you possibly being part of the Atmani Foundation's economic development team."

"How would that be different than DG&L?" Ezra replied. "Economic development seems to be mostly done by governments and public utilities."

"Fair question," said Simon. "As a young man, Mr. Atmani came to Alabama, essentially a refugee. Over the years, he built an enormous fortune. In recent years, he's worried about the state's lack of progress, so he decided to try to make a difference."

"What do you mean by 'the state's lack of progress?' " asked Ezra.

"The good news is that between 1929 and 2001, Alabama's per capita income rose from forty-six to eighty-one percent of the U.S. average. The passage of social security, the economic impact of World War II, and the widespread use of air conditioning benefitted Alabama and all the Southern states. Today, the South has a larger population and more Fortune 500 headquarters than any U.S. region. There's still poverty, but there's *huge* areas of prosperity."

"To most New Yorkers, the South is shoeless flyover country," said Ezra.

"And they're wrong," said Simon. "But we do have some challenges.

"In 1998, Alabama's median annual household income reached a peak, and we ranked in the mid-thirties among the states in median household income. We were doing OK.

"Since then, however, our median income, in constant dollars, has dropped ten to twenty percent, and we're now ranked forty-fifth or forty-sixth in median household income. We're only a rank or two better than we were twenty-five or thirty years ago."

"What happened?" asked Ezra.

"In the '90s, Alabama had many good home-grown companies who had matured into large, significant enterprises. Then in 1993, Alabama won

Mercedes and its suppliers, and many companies decided if Alabama was good enough for Mercedes, it was good enough for them.

"But the first decade of the twenty-first century was a disaster. Alabama lost almost thirty percent of its manufacturing jobs, five of its six Fortune 500 headquarters, and two-thirds of its publicly-traded companies. Some went private, but others relocated, went bankrupt, or were acquired.

"Did we become too complacent after winning Mercedes? Maybe, but since 2000, most of the South's taken a beating compared to the rest of the country. North Carolina dropped five places in median income; Alabama, Kentucky, Mississippi, and South Carolina all lost six places; Florida lost nine places, and despite Atlanta's growth, Georgia lost thirteen places. The big winners in the South were Texas, who moved up seven places, and Arkansas, who rose five spots."

"So what happened?" asked Ezra. He thought he knew but wanted to hear what Simon would say.

"NAFTA came into effect in 1994, and China joined the World Trade Organization in late 2001. The South's economy was heavily dependent on manufacturing, and much of it migrated offshore, forcing the remaining domestic manufacturers to become more efficient and lay off workers. In addition, mergers and acquisitions slashed white-collar jobs. Companies were acquired and moved elsewhere.

"Some states benefitted from one-off situations like North Dakota's shale oil boom, and DC and its neighbors benefitted from the growth of the federal bureaucracy. Texas became an alternative for California and Northeast companies fleeing onerous business climates."

"Texas has amazing energy," said Ezra.

"And then we had the Great Recession of 2008 from which we still haven't fully recovered. We don't publicly discuss our downward slide much in Alabama, because economic development is all about keeping a smiley-face.

"Announcing new jobs is one of the few ways politicians can show voters they're doing a good job, and politicians are not interested in talking about job losses. The state announces that Airbus is coming to Mobile or Mercedes is planning another $100 million expansion, and the public thinks all is well. We celebrate our wins and ignore our losses, and that creates a warped perception among the public about our progress.

"Add to this our slow population growth: Between 2000 and 2010, Alabama's population grew 7.5% compared to fifteen percent for South Carolina, eighteen percent for Georgia, and more than twenty percent for Texas. Thirty-one of Alabama's sixty-seven counties lost population between 2000 and 2010."

"So, what's the answer?" asked Ezra.

"That's what Mr. Atmani asked. He wanted to examine how Alabama does economic development, but he got push-back from his friends. Most advised him to focus on improving the state's education system.

" 'Helping educate our children is where you can make a difference,' they said. 'In the global economy, capital is mobile, and companies go where the talent is. Alabama's ability to successfully educate its children will determine its future success.'

" 'You don't want to mess with economic development,' said another, 'There's already enough players, and you *really* don't want to get crossed with DG&L.'

"They eventually persuaded Mr. Atmani to focus on improving education. So he assigned teams to research issues and make recommendations, solicited advice from friends and business leaders, and brought in experts and consultants. After a year of study, we met with the Governor and legislative leaders and presented our recommendations."

"What happened?" asked Ezra.

"Absolutely nothing," said Simon. "We were naïve and thought we could make a difference with education."

"I'd like to hear about it."

"It would take too long. I'll just say this: If someone ever tells you 'It's all about the children,' it rarely is."

14

ECONOMIC DEVELOPMENT

Simon refreshed their glasses and continued the discussion.

"So, we decided to do a deep-dive into economic development. We quickly realized how territorial it was, so we looked for ways to help without competing with what's already being done." He paused for a moment. "Before we continue, tell me what you know about economic development."

"Very little," said Ezra. "I've helped finance some bridges and toll roads, and Scott Kling told me what DG&L does, but that's about it."

"Economic development is about creating or attracting enough good-paying jobs for people," said Simon. "Some parts of Alabama are doing OK, and some aren't.

"Huntsville's the shining star. With NASA and Redstone Arsenal and all the tech companies there, it compares favorably with anywhere in the country. The Auburn-Opelika area and the Alabama Gulf Coast—Fairhope, Orange Beach, Gulf Shores, and Foley—are fast-growing. Tuscaloosa is doing OK. But Birmingham, Montgomery, and Mobile—three of the four largest metros—have slow or stagnant population growth, and almost half of Alabama's counties are losing population. How do you persuade people or companies to move to an area that's losing population?

"We're all about having enough good-paying jobs for Alabamians, so it's essential you understand how jobs happen. Every day new companies start up. Most are small and stay small. Half of them fail within five years. A tiny fraction of a percent grow into big companies. The fate of these companies depends on the economy, the business climate, their management—and luck.

"Economic developers help startups by funding business incubators and making sure the business climate stays good so companies will grow and expand. Overall, Alabama's doing OK in this area.

"Sometimes, existing businesses want to expand their operations to new locations, and occasionally they want to relocate altogether, and that's when economic development typically makes the news.

"The public hears about company X wanting to relocate their headquarters or company Y planning to construct a new billion-dollar manufacturing plant that will employ thousands. This gets the attention of the public—and politicians. A 100-employee, $20 million project can provide a boost to a community. A 5,000-employee, billion-dollar project can boost an entire state.

"Each year, there are typically three to five thousand economic development projects with flexibility where they locate. Two-thirds of them create less than fifty jobs. Ninety percent create less than 250 jobs. About one percent offer a thousand or more jobs.

"Attracting projects is known in economic development circles as *buffalo hunting* or *smokestack chasing*. Some argue that instead of buffalo hunting, economic developers should spend most of their time doing *economic gardening*—helping companies start-up and grow.

"If those terms sound politically loaded, you're right. Buffalo hunting sounds like killing and violence, while economic gardening sounds peaceful and green. Letting such labels influence your strategy would be a mistake.

"Almost every community needs both strategies. Communities become successful by attracting both talent and companies. Few communities have the native intellectual and entrepreneurial talent to be successful in isolation.

"New York is a great city because smart people like you move here from all over the world. Fifty percent of the employed, core working-age population of Silicon Valley are foreign-born, and nearly three-quarters of all Silicon Valley computer workers are foreign-born. Nick Saban is a great football coach, but if he were limited to recruiting players only from the State of Alabama, he wouldn't win any national championships."

Interesting how everything ultimately relates to football in Alabama, Ezra thought.

"Most communities have an economic developer, and some have a whole staff. They prepare sites, train people, help companies startup, and try to prepare the community to grow and attract companies and jobs.

"They generally don't have the time or expertise to go prospecting for companies. Some *do* take recruiting trips because they're expected to, but the trips are typically to team-build with state officials or as a job perk. Local economic developers mostly depend on others to bring them projects.

"ADIT—The Alabama Department of Industry and Trade—is the state agency responsible for economic development. Companies and site consultants interested in Alabama typically contact ADIT because they're the gatekeeper for incentives.

"ADIT has some good people, but it's understaffed, and some of their people are mediocre. ADIT has its hands full simply responding to inquiries. Their marketing is largely ineffective.

"Almost everywhere, the big utilities are involved in economic development. They try to help the state development agency close projects while also steering projects to their service area.

"Alabama's biggest economic development challenge is its reputation: Many company executives and site consultants view Alabama as a low-skill state with narrow-minded people. Even if we have the skills, they worry whether their board or client will approve of having a presence in Alabama.

"According to one survey, the American public has a lower opinion of Alabama than any state except New Jersey. It's like what Jay Leno said not long ago: 'Alabama won a national championship again. They're number one in college football and forty-ninth in everything else.'"

"I run into that all the time," said Ezra. "Sometimes, I just say I'm from flyover country."

"Because of our reputation, fewer companies are interested in locating in Alabama. Even when they consider us, companies and site consultants more often consider us for low-skill, low-wage jobs, and that makes it difficult for us to raise our median household income. There have been times when Alabama was at full employment, and we still ranked forty-fifth among the states in median household income.

"One limit on a state's household income is the education level of its people, and we've got some work to do there, but Alabama has a significant *underemployment* problem, where workers aren't able to make full use of their skills and abilities. A recent study concluded that the underemployment rate in Alabama is about 24%. That's 480,000 workers.

"Communities fit into one of three categories: Those who can't attract or grow enough jobs, those who have enough jobs but they don't pay enough, and those communities who have enough good-paying jobs. We want as much of Alabama as possible to be in the third category."

Simon continued, "There's probably not enough marketing money in the world to change the national public's perception of Alabama in the short- and medium-term, and even if we made progress, a politician would do something stupid and set us back again.

"Instead, we must reach out to growing companies with higher-skill, higher-paying jobs and convince their decision-makers that we're a viable location. That's our primary mission at the Atmani Foundation.

"Alabama's second-biggest economic development challenge is that no Alabama economic development group has, as its first priority, finding and persuading companies to locate in Alabama."

Ezra looked at him blankly, "I thought that's what it's all about, isn't it?"

"It is, and ADIT, DG&L, and the localities all do *some* prospecting, but it's no one's first priority.

"ADIT's first priority is to work the projects brought it by companies and site consultants. DG&L's first priority is to steer ADIT projects to their service area, and the local economic developers' first priority is to prepare their communities for projects.

"Since finding projects is about the hardest thing to do in economic development, it's easy to put off. And for most organizations, when the budgets get tight, it's the first thing that's cut.

"Typical recruiting tactics are to visit site consultants, attend trade shows, and invite prospects to the state for an event like an Alabama football game. Too often, while the event prep is top-notch, the prospect quality and quantity is lacking because the necessary business intelligence work wasn't done on the front-end.

"Good prospecting *always* begins with good intelligence about which companies are growing, have good-paying jobs, and are likely to have projects."

"Which is what you do?"

Simon continued, "A third challenge is that Alabama typically gets cut by data before we ever hear about a project. The internet and Big Data have fundamentally changed site selection. Companies and site consultants now use databases to systematically eliminate thousands of communities without a visit. They use Google Earth and Streetview to check out sites without physically visiting them. Local online news exposes every community's dirty linen.

"Most locations are cut without knowing they were considered. Local officials never meet the prospect and have an opportunity to pitch their community. These days, when a community's contacted, they've usually already made the semifinals for a project. Only then can they try to persuade the prospect that their community is the best location.

"This process hurts us, because Alabama's metrics are weak, especially if statewide numbers are used. Alabama is like a girl with average looks but a great personality. Alabama doesn't show her best until she personally engages with a prospective company.

"If Alabama's going to progress, we can't be cut from most projects by perception or data. We *must* reach out to these companies and persuade them to give Alabama a chance."

"So, that's what you guys do?" Ezra asked.

Simon continued, "A top-notch proactive prospecting effort requires a sophisticated business intelligence operation and superior people to execute it.

"Unfortunately, the economic development business is mostly a cottage industry. The typical local economic development effort is one or two people with a budget of less than a million. They have a website and use Powerpoint and Publisher, and they text and email, but they're not power-users of data.

"ADIT doesn't have the manpower, resources, or vision to develop a consistent, proactive prospecting effort. ADIT's General Manager, Atlas Ogg, is a master bureaucrat who manipulates the ADIT Directors who pass through. The ADIT directors—all political appointees—typically have no idea of how to set up or manage an effective business intelligence effort."

"What about DG&L? This sounds exactly like what they want me to do."

"Which is?"

"Spend time with site consultants, for one thing."

"Building relationships with site consultants is important," said Simon, "but it isn't nearly enough. Only about half of companies with projects outsource any part of the site selection process, and when they do, dedicated site consultant firms are used about a quarter of the time, so do the math: Dedicated site consultants only work ten to fifteen percent of total projects. How do you reach the rest?"

"So, how *do* you?" asked Ezra.

"For one thing, we avoid site consultants. We don't want to compete with DG&L and ADIT."

"How else?"

"We try to make contact with company decision-makers *before* they contact site consultants or brokers and before they start an active site search."

"How?"

"That's the secret sauce. Our techniques are highly proprietary. Would you mind signing a non-disclosure agreement?"

"Not at all," said Ezra. "As long as it doesn't impact my Silverman job."

15

THE SECRET SAUCE

Alabama's economic developers do a good job of winning projects when prospects are interested in the state. Our challenge is to get more companies with higher-paying jobs interested. We do this by proactively reaching out and influencing corporate decision-makers' opinions about Alabama."

"How?" asked Ezra.

"First, we use big data techniques to target companies likely to have projects in the near future. Second, we profile the target company decision-makers and devise strategies for building relationships with them. Third, we employ superior people to represent and personify Alabama to these decision-makers, to engage and build relationships with them.

"Our goal is to have the decision-makers include Alabama on their shortlists or instruct their site consultants to include Alabama in their site searches."

"That's easy to say, but how do you do it?"

"Identifying the target companies and decision-makers is relatively easy. The challenge is influencing them. They're difficult to contact and difficult to influence. Cold-calling rarely works."

Ezra said, "DG&L told me they target chemical and steel plants, data centers, and anything that uses large amounts of gas or electricity. What types of companies do you target?"

"We target growing, traded companies which could increase the state's median income. We generally don't target specific industries for two reasons:

"First, only a few percent of the companies in each industry segment are fast-growing and good candidates for a project. Too often, economic developers waste time recruiting marginal companies simply because they belong to an industry segment they're targeting.

"Second, many labor skills are transferable to other industries. When Mercedes-Benz picked Alabama, the state didn't make a single car. When Airbus chose Alabama, we didn't manufacture airplanes. When Alabama people think 'medical,' they think of Birmingham and UAB, but the Auburn-Opelika area manufactures many more medical devices than Birmingham.

"Our approach also addresses two problems with modern site selection: First, when companies do their own site selection, they often use wrong data. With few exceptions, using statewide data for site selection is totally bogus. All that matters is data relevant to the areas around the sites they're considering.

"Aren't state tax rates important?" asked Ezra.

"They are, but comparing state corporate tax rates is highly misleading. Forty-four states have rates from four to twelve percent, and six states have no corporate income tax. Alabama's rate is effectively five percent, so we're higher than states with no corporate income tax, but Alabama abates its corporate income tax for twenty years for many projects, and four of the six states with no corporate income tax have a gross receipts tax, which can tax a company even when it makes no profit.

"Another example: If a company wants to avoid having a union, comparing unionization rates by state is irrelevant. What matters is the union activity in the area they're considering. Huntsville, Alabama, is closer to Louisville, Kentucky, than to Mobile, Alabama. Statewide data that combines union activity for Huntsville and Mobile is worse than useless.

"Alabama has communities and sites that are competitive with anywhere, but Alabama will often lose site searches based on statewide data because Alabama, *on average*, is a poor, slow-growing state.

"So, we contact company decision-makers before they have projects, build relationships with them, and persuade them not to use irrelevant data sets.

"The second challenge we address is that most site decisions are ultimately emotional 'gut' decisions. Corporate executives like to think they use data and analytics to make decisions, but psychologists tell us it's often their "gut feel," not data, which counts.

BUFFALO HUNTING IN ALABAMA

"Currently, most Alabama sites are cut by data before the decision-makers can get a gut-feel about Alabama and its people.

"We circumvent this by meeting with the decision-makers before they have a project. If you work for us, your primary job will be to create emotional connections with decision-makers so they can rationalize including Alabama on their shortlist. We use data to win the decision-makers' heads, but it's more important to win their hearts.

"That's why we use exceptional people to bypass the traditional site selection process and reach the decision-makers. Our people must personify Alabama and persuade the decision-maker to put Alabama on the shortlist because of his or her gut feeling about them.

"Decision-makers make intuitive judgments based on peoples' looks, their clothes, where they went to school, who they've worked for, and how they communicate. That's why we pick people with impeccable academic and work backgrounds.

"There's also an intangible aspect to persuading people. If you're interested in working for us, we'll put you through a thorough evaluation by psychologists. We may think you're perfect for our team, but if the psychologists give you the thumbs-down, we won't make you an offer.

"Decision-makers also have biases, and one secret to winning projects is to identify their biases quickly and play to them. We try to know many of those biases before we ever meet them.

"Perhaps the most impactful 'gut' decision in recent times was described by Professor Enrico Moretti in his must-read book, *The New Geography of Jobs*. He tells how Seattle in the late 1970s had a struggling economy, high crime and unemployment, and thousands of people leaving the city.

"In 1975, Bill Gates and Paul Allen founded Microsoft in Albuquerque, New Mexico. Four years later, they made a non-business decision to move it to Seattle, their hometown.

"Seattle then became a hot place for high-tech companies. Amazon, T-Mobile, and many other tech companies located there. This concentration of money and brains created more companies. Microsoft alumni have started four thousand new businesses, most of them in the Seattle area.

"Microsoft transformed Seattle. Today it's a cool, high-tech city where software workers there earn more than one-fourth of all salaries paid to software workers in North America, and people at every socioeconomic level have benefited. Microsoft has created 80,000 jobs for workers with college or advanced degrees, but 120,000 jobs for service workers with limited education, like cleaners, taxi drivers, carpenters, and small-business owners.

"The gut decision to move Microsoft to Seattle fundamentally changed the city forever. We want to swing some gut decisions for Alabama."

"I've never heard that story," said Ezra.

"So, now you have some idea of what we do. Interested in working for us?"

"Is that an offer?"

"Not yet," said Simon.

"I might," said Ezra. "Who would I work for, and what would I do?"

"You'd work for the Atmani Foundation and me," said Simon. "I suspect you've already researched the Atmani Foundation."

"And you," Ezra said, "But I didn't find much."

"Our economic development effort has two groups: The Analytics Team—we call them the Quants—builds and crunches databases, recommends target companies, and builds the decision-maker profiles. The GO Team uses the Quant data to go after companies.

"If you work for us, you'll spend half your time analyzing and refining the Quants' decision-maker profiles and developing strategies for building relationships with the decision-makers. The other half of the time, you'll be traveling and executing the strategy."

"Traveling where?"

"To wherever the prospects are, and your skill set allows you to be successful. Certainly Germany and parts of Europe. Certainly New York. We'll do an in-depth evaluation."

Ezra smiled, "It sounds interesting." He paused. "Why do you call it the GO Team?"

"That's a long story. Why don't you go ahead and accept DG&L's invitation to visit again but also come meet with us?"

Ezra realized they had been talking for several hours, and it was late. "I appreciate the invitation. It's been interesting and informative."

They shook hands outside the restaurant. As Ezra walked away, he turned around and said, "I want to hear about Amanda Kling sometime."

Simon nodded and smiled and kept on walking.

16

BACK IN BIRMINGHAM

Ezra took a cab from the airport to the hotel. He liked talking with cabbies—they were a city's ambassadors. This one was upbeat and said good things about Birmingham but was adamant about not letting that "damn Uber" operate in the city.

They also talked about the Auburn–FSU national championship game. "Auburn had them on the ropes and let them come back," lamented the cabbie. "That Jameis Winston was just too good. Course you know he's from Birmingham, don't you? Right out there in Hueytown."

Scott Kling had offered to meet him at the airport, but Ezra had declined, saying he wanted to rent a car and wander around. They had reserved a room for him at the Aloft Hotel in Homewood just over the mountain from downtown Birmingham.

January was Alabama's coldest month, but Ezra knew in six weeks or so that yellow-and-orange jonquils would bloom, and the pine trees would spread their pollen everywhere, coating cars in yellow dust.

Ezra had flown into Birmingham late Thursday afternoon. The meeting with DG&L was Friday morning, and he would meet with the Atmani Foundation on Friday afternoon.

***

They offered him an Assistant VP position and an office with a window. The salary was higher than he expected, though still lower than his Silverman salary.

"Ezra, we think you'll be a strong addition to our economic development team," Scott Kling had said. "Of course, we can't pay you as much as Silverman Bach, but we're offering you an outstanding salary with great opportunities for advancement."

"I appreciate the offer. Let me have a few days to think about it," Ezra said.

They're decent folks, Ezra thought, *but I'm not moving to Alabama to work for DG&L.*

***

Simon met Ezra at the Aloft Hotel. They drove south and in ten minutes or so turned left off the main highway onto a heavily wooded two-lane road. Three hundred yards later, they came to a black metal gate that opened for them. Shortly afterward, the road terminated in a gravel roundabout with parking spaces. On the far side sat a natural wood-beam and glass building, like a large modern house.

Two crepe myrtle trees framed the walkway to the front door. To the left of the entrance sat a pocket garden with orange and yellow koi swimming in a shaded pool. The front doors were glass, and Ezra could see entirely through the building to a lake on the other side.

Nice, he thought. They were not far from a busy main thoroughfare, yet the impression was a modern house overlooking a secluded wooded lake.

A receptionist sat behind the front desk, and a waiting area lay to the right. Four Knoll Barcelona chairs framed a coffee table, and on the wall behind were enclosed glass shelves with an extensive collection of Egyptian *shabtis*, small exquisitely-carved and painted statues found in ancient Egyptian tombs.

The floor plan was open, with partial walls concealing different areas and artwork everywhere. The art was mostly modern, except for several Egyptian pieces, including a fine statue of Bastet, the Egyptian cat god.

"I expected your offices to be downtown," said Ezra.

"The view's nicer here," said Simon.

"Mr. Atmani is ready for you," said the receptionist.

The reception and waiting area sat several feet higher than the rest of the office. As Simon led him down a short flight of steps, Ezra asked, "Is this the Atmani Foundation's headquarters?"

"This office serves several purposes," said Simon. "It's the headquarters for Mr. Atmani's holding company as well as the Atmani Foundation's offices."

BUFFALO HUNTING IN ALABAMA

In the middle of the building, light poured in from skylights and glass walls, giving an outdoor feeling.

"The office is 35,000 square feet on two floors," said Simon. "This floor holds the Atmani Enterprises' and Foundation's offices. The lower floor has accounting, administrative, the data center, and a nice little gym."

***

The back wall of Mr. Atmani's office was entirely glass and overlooked the lake. A pair of white swans glided gracefully in the distance.

At the opposite side of the room, Mr. Atmani sat behind a large desk, facing the lake. *He could be fifty-five or seventy-five*, Ezra thought. Atmani had a round face, grey mustache, and short grey fringe framing a bald head. His skin shone like dark, fine leather.

Ezra noticed only two items on his desk—a *Wall Street Journal* and a *New York Times*. Mr. Atmani stood up, walked around his desk, and shook hands with Ezra. He was perhaps five-and-a-half feet tall. In another world, Ezra could imagine him as a shopkeeper in a *souk*.

Mr. Atmani saw Ezra eyeing the newspapers. He smiled and swept his hand across the desk. "Mr. Drake, you live in New York. Which newspaper do you prefer?"

"A safe answer would be the *Wall Street Journal* for work and the *New York Times* for leisure, but I find much wit and humor in the *Wall Street Journal*."

"My choice too," Mr. Atmani said, again smiling. He spoke with a strong accent, and Ezra somehow knew, even if he lived to be a hundred, Mr. Atmani would always speak that way.

"I hope we have shown you our famous Southern hospitality?"

"Very nice," said Ezra.

"And you have some interest in working with us?"

"Yes."

"And we have interest in you, too," Mr. Atmani said with a smile in his eye. "I'm sure my people have filled your mind with *many* reasons why you should work for us, but to me, it is simple: What does all the world want?"

"Sir?"

"What do people in the world want more than anything else?"

"World peace?"

"An obvious answer, but not the right one. Do you know the Gallup Poll people? They have been studying this issue for several years. This is not so easy to determine because it is difficult to create opinion surveys independent of language and culture, but they did it. What they found, all over the world, is that more than anything, people want a good job.

"A good job is more important than love or religion. Most of the trouble in the Arab world is not about religion; it's about not having good jobs. If you have a good job, you're too busy to cause trouble. If you don't have a good job, and your life is miserable, you start thinking about *jihad* and those seventy-two virgins, though why anyone would want seventy-two *virgins*, I don't know." He said.

"It's possible to have little and be happy; Mahatma Gandhi showed us that, but prosperity is about materialism. It's not about intellectual or spiritual enlightenment. You do that on your own time. Alabama must win its share of good jobs to be prosperous.

"I will tell you a story. I was born in Alexandria to a Christian family. You know there are Christians in Egypt? I worked for Citibank as a currency trader but left Egypt because of Nasser. I ended up in Ethiopia. Then I immigrated to the United States. I settled in Birmingham because I like warm weather.

"I also liked Birmingham because it was different. The English and Scots-Irish settled most of the South, but many ethnic groups settled Birmingham—Blacks, Lebanese, Russians, Italians. They came to work in the coal mines and the steel mills. Birmingham wasn't just the British Empire transplanted to America.

"Still, when I first came here during the early 1960s, it wasn't easy being dark-skinned." He smiled. "A lot has changed.

"I made many friends; I worked hard. I helped grow Stein Stewart & Taft and eventually gained majority control and ownership. I started or bought a few other companies. My wife and I could not have children, but we eventually accepted that and were happy. Then she died three years ago." He was silent for a moment. "I have no children; no grandchildren."

He raised his hands, open-palmed. "So, what do I do with my life? Alabama has been good to me; I decided to give back. I have always given to my church and charity because I am a Christian, but I decided to do more.

"I tried to help fix the school system in Alabama, but there was too much resistance. I decided to improve education indirectly by attracting companies that would demand world-class skills. It's easier for the education system to train people when companies tell them what they need.

BUFFALO HUNTING IN ALABAMA

"There's a lot of money in Birmingham," said Mr. Atmani. "In the old days, you made money from farming or digging wealth out of the ground. Birmingham had coal and iron ore, and many people got rich. Some of their children even held on to some of it. Some have used their money to buy yachts and vacation houses all over the world, but some have used their money to do good. I decided that's what I wanted to do.

"You have heard the saying: 'Give a man a fish, and he eats for a day, but *teach* a man to fish, and he eats for a lifetime?' I could give more money to charity, but if I help find good jobs for people, that helps them the rest of their lives. By doing economic development, I teach men to fish.

"We have created an organization that requires very particular skills. We think you may be useful to us. Simon will tell you more. I hope to see you in the future."

Simon had said nothing during the entire conversation. Ezra thanked Mr. Atmani for his time. In the hallway, Ezra said, "An interesting man."

"Our President & CEO, Hakim Abdelkarim, and all the GO Team people are out of the office now—and that's not unusual—but I want you to meet two other people."

At the front of the building were more offices. Simon lightly knocked on a door. It opened, and the man inside welcomed them.

He was medium height, probably close to sixty, with well-trimmed grey hair. He had a full face with a big smile. His nicely-cut suit failed to disguise a substantial belly.

"Now come in, come in. I'm Jack Brannon. Really glad to meetcha." Jack vigorously shook Ezra's hand, and he spoke with a soft southern drawl. "Simon says you may be joinin' us, and he wants me to tell you what I do. That's easy. As far as I'm concerned, I have the greatest job in the world, and that's no bullshit.

"Economic development is one of the three most important jobs in the world. Doctors keep you from getting sick, lawyers keep you out of jail, and economic developers help you get a job. And of the three, economic developers may be the *most* important because, without a job, you're much more likely to get sick and go to jail!"

Ezra didn't know what to say, so he just stood there and smiled.

"All my life, except for a little tour in Vietnam, I've worked in economic development, and I loved it. But I also knew it was done mostly half-assed.

Economic developers are some of the finest people in the world, but the business is very competitive, and no one can guarantee results. So, economic developers often substitute activity for results.

"I had known Mr. Atmani a long time, and then one day he asked me to join his organization, and finally—finally, toward the end of my career, I see a new approach being taken. I can tell you it's damned gratifying!

"Economic development's basically been done in the South the same way since Southerners realized it was easier to pick Yankee companies than to pick cotton—that's a joke, son!

"You have the state economic development organization and lots of local economic development organizations. Most projects come to the state, and it often decides which localities to submit as site candidates.

"The state and the localities know their place. Anything new that enters the picture is threatening. The utilities do economic development, and they're accepted because they've always done economic development and have more money than God, so they can't be ignored."

He stopped to take a swig of Diet Coca-Cola. "Would you like a Co-Cola? Coffee?"

"I'm fine," said Ezra.

"So, Mr. Atmani comes along and does something different. It's all based on computers, and I can barely use email, so get Simon and Sean to give you the details.

"What I do is handle the politics. That includes dealin' with the Governor, the legislature, with ADIT, with local and state politicians, and of course with the local economic developers—who are just a variety of politician. Real politicians have job security between elections, but many economic developers can be fired at-will, so they can be skittish to work with. I know because I was one of 'em for most of my life.

"This group that Mr. Atmani's put together, they're smart as hell, but they've never done economic development, so I help 'em keep from steppin' in it, mostly by helpin' 'em keep a low profile.

"Most of the economic developers in the state don't have a clue what we're doing, but those who do are suspicious: Are we site consultants? Are we working in the prospect's interest? The state's interest? What's our motive? Are we going to threaten their jobs somehow?

"Economic developers run in packs. When it's necessary, they're some of the greatest team players ever born. I've seen 'em do great things, but I've also seen 'em stop some good ideas because they felt threatened. We don't want that to happen here. Are you lookin' to work with the Quants or the GO Team?"

"The GO Team, if it works out."

"The Quants are the big brains, but the GO Team people are smart and quick learners since they constantly deal with people. If I can help you, let me know. Any questions?"

"I'm not sure I know enough at this point to ask any questions," Ezra said, and smiled and thanked him.

"One last thing: You'll hear all this talk about median household income and big data and algorithms, but just remember our whole purpose is to help people have better lives. If you work for us, that's what you'll be doing with *your* life."

Ezra looked at Jack. "Thanks, I'll remember that."

17

THE QUANTS

"Everyone uses the gym—even the Quants," said Simon.

They were downstairs in a large room with floor-to-ceiling glass windows open to the lake. A half-dozen desks, each packed with computer screens, faced the lake. Analysts occupied four of the desks.

One wall featured a large poster of Abraham Lincoln as a young man, tall and rangy before he grew a beard. He had an ax in his hands, and a caption read, "Give me six hours to chop down a tree, and I will spend the first four sharpening the ax."

A worker approached them dressed in jeans and a black *St. Paul and the Broken Bones* t-shirt.

"This is Sean Howard," Simon said. "He's the Team Leader for the Analytics Group."

"Everybody calls us the Quants," said Sean. "We like that better," he smiled mischievously.

Ezra grinned.

"Ezra may be joining the GO Team," said Simon. "Can you give him the five-minute tour?"

"Sure," said Sean. "They asked us if we wanted offices, but we prefer one big room. If we want privacy, we use headphones or the conference room or go outside.

"The GO Team deals with people; we collect and analyze data. First, we work with the GO Team to define the companies to target. Occasionally we get help from the Stein Stewart analysts. That's Mr. Atmani's stock brokerage firm. You'd be surprised what companies will tell you during earnings calls.

"Then, we determine the decision-makers within those companies and find out everything we can about them, so the GO Team can figure out how to build relationships with them.

"Defining the target companies and their decision-makers is easy; most of the data is well-structured in databases easy to acquire and manipulate.

"More difficult is collecting data about the decision-makers. Dun & Bradstreet provides short bios, but we need more in-depth information, so we dig for it.

"For instance, we have an algorithm that takes every single person in our decision-maker database and searches for them on Wikipedia. When it gets a positive result, it fetches and passes the Wiki entry to an algorithm that looks for keywords and phrases to insert automatically into a searchable in-depth profile of the decision-maker.

"Maybe only five percent of the decision-makers have a Wiki bio, but that's OK because we search hundreds of different online databases containing bios of people. And of course, we use Facebook. Even if a decision-maker doesn't use it, their spouse and children often do.

"We collect information about decision-makers to find hooks to engage them. Sorting through ten million pieces of data for maybe a few hundred pieces of useful information sounds inefficient, but not for computers. Everyone talks Big Data, but what matters is Good Algorithms.

"The GO Team folks are the James Bonds, but we're the people behind the scenes directing them. Without us, they're just wandering around at cocktail parties."

The last stop downstairs was the gym. It was large, considering the size of the building, with Nautilus machines, free weights, stair-steppers, and stationary bikes, but what impressed Ezra was an open area about twenty-five-feet square with a wall rack filled with traditional martial arts weapons. *They have a dojo.*

"Our people travel a lot, and we want them to be safe, so we encourage them to learn martial arts. Also, our jobs are stressful, and the exercise helps them cope.

"There's space inside for sparring and *kata* work, but there's also outside. Simon pointed to a large grassed area overlooking the lake. Our people practice multiple styles of martial arts, and there's a healthy competition among them."

"Do you worry about people getting injured?" asked Ezra.

"That sometimes happens. They deal with it."

As they walked back up the stairs, Ezra asked, "You have the GO Team and the Quants. What do you call the Foundation's overall economic development effort?"

"We don't call it anything," Simon said. "That way it's easier to keep quiet about it. Let's go grab some coffee and talk."

As they exited the front door, they met a tall blonde with a slim waist and swimmer's shoulders.

"Ella! I want you to meet Ezra Drake. Ella went to Auburn and then to Wharton," Simon said. "One of her focus areas is the aerospace industry. She came to us from McKinsey almost a year ago."

"It's certainly not been boring," she said.

18

CONDITIONAL JOB OFFER

They sat outside at a Starbuck's a quarter-mile from the office.

"Still interested in the job?" asked Simon.

"Yes," said Ezra.

"I've gotten feedback. You've made a good impression."

"Thanks, what's next?" asked Ezra.

"Shrink exam. Many companies require it to weed out the crazies and non-team players, but for us, it's much more critical. Psychologists have helped us determine the traits useful in persuading decision-makers. They're partially trainable, but many are innate—you either have them, or you don't.

"This is a make-or-break part of the process. If you pass, we'll make you an offer. If you don't, we won't.

"The evaluation helps you, too. It gives you an idea of what it's like working for us. You may decide we're not for you.

"It sounds like overkill, but it's not. We try to maximize our chances of success. Some decision-makers are impressed with people who've attended good schools, or who have worked for prestigious companies. Others judge people by their looks. It's not by accident that GO Team members have outstanding academic credentials, have worked for excellent companies, and are reasonably attractive.

"But personality is also important. I think you might agree there are smart people at Silverman who are a bit irritating and abrasive; we don't want that type of person. At the same time, we don't want a suck-up because CEO types typically despise them. Our ideal candidate can read and adapt to the traits of each decision-maker.

"When a GO Team member meets with a decision-maker, they *are* Alabama to that decision-maker. The decision-maker can't help but attribute to Alabama some of the traits they see in the person, and that makes a difference. ADIT has some competent people, but many are just good ol' boys and girls, and that mediocrity influences how decision-makers view Alabama.

"We also want people who grew up in Alabama because decision-makers wish to speak with someone who can speak from personal experience—not a hired gun. Your growing up in Alabama makes you more *authentic* to the decision-maker.

"Finally, there's an indefinable quality about a person that makes them intriguing to CEOs and decision-makers, and you either have it, or you don't. We want people who have it.

"Most economic development organizations make compromises regarding personnel. They have salary caps; they have people who've been there ten or fifteen years who are maybe not ideal, but they're good people and can't just be tossed out on the street.

"We don't make these compromises. We have no legacy employees. We started with a clean sheet of paper, and we only employ the people we want.

"One issue complicating your possible employment is how badly we're going to piss off DG&L. We've worked hard not to antagonize the major players in economic development, and the fact they recruited you first won't help. Also, the fact you've struck up a friendship with Scott Kling's sister won't make it any easier.

"We've already decided, though, if you pass the shrinks, we'll make you an offer and deal with the situation. Still want to go through with this?"

"Let's do it," Ezra said.

"The shrinks are based in New York, so that's convenient for you. Give me some dates you're available, and I'll check with them. The process starts about 6 p.m. one evening and runs through the entire next day until midnight.

"Don't stress out over the shrink exam," Simon advised. "Just be yourself."

Simon dropped him off at the Aloft in Homewood. Ezra felt a burden lifted from his shoulders. For the first time, he envisioned a scenario where he might be happy and successful in Alabama. He called Amanda.

"Do you have time for me this weekend?" he asked.

"I might. Scott told me you were coming. Why didn't you call?"

He paused. "How happy would we be together if I hated my job?"

She gave him the address of her apartment.

***

"Don't you want to see more of Alabama?" Amanda asked teasingly.

Ezra's eyes were closed, his arms wrapped around her. "I'm experiencing the best part of Alabama right now." They were half-sitting, half-lying on her couch after a Sunday brunch at Café Dupont. Saturday had been a drive through the countryside with stops for hiking and then clubbing around town in the evening.

"I've dated people for months and not had them to my apartment, and then you come along...and here we are," she said.

"So, what do you conclude?" Ezra murmured.

"I don't know, but I like it."

"Me, too," said Ezra. "That's why I recommend we do much more of this."

After a moment, Amanda said, "What are you going to do? Work for my brother?"

Ezra didn't say anything.

"Don't worry; I won't tell him. There are lots of things I don't tell him."

"No," Ezra paused. "But I'm planning to move to Birmingham anyway."

"Has Simon hooked you?" She twisted around and looked at him, face-to-face, with those clear grey eyes.

"They're interesting, don't you think?"

Amanda sat up as if to discuss business, and Ezra's head ended up in her lap. "Mr. Atmani is certainly an icon in this town. Simon's group—they stay low-key. Nobody knows what they do, except beat up each other. I've treated a couple of them."

"I'm going to work for them if I can pass their shrink exam."

Amanda was silent for a moment. "Scott won't be happy."

"I know. I feel bad how it's turned out, but if we hadn't met Simon, I still wouldn't be taking the DG&L job—I'd stay in New York and continue working for Silverman—because I wouldn't be much fun in a job I didn't really like."

"I understand," said Amanda, "but Scott and DG&L don't like to lose; they're used to getting their way."

"We'll make it work. Come down here," Ezra said. She slid down, and Ezra put his arms around her, and they lay face-to-face.

"When I graduated high school, I couldn't wait to leave the South," said Ezra. "I was ashamed of its prejudices and problems. As the years passed, I started to realize that people are basically the same everywhere.

"Each area has its version of the Southern redneck, there are racial or ethnic issues everywhere, most places have some type of historical baggage, and every place has crooked politicians that do stupid things. Once you look beyond that, you start to see the uniqueness of the South."

"That's a difference between you and me," she said, kissing his nose. "I went to Chicago to do my residency, but I've never wanted to live anywhere but Alabama."

19

JOB LOSS

It had begun as just another Monday morning. Emma and the kids were still asleep when Billy Jeff left for work at SangreBio. He met with the night-shift supervisor for the daily handover.

About 9:30 a.m., they called everyone into the auditorium, and the CEO told them the company was bankrupt and shutting down. No Chapter 11 reorganization. Chapter Seven—liquidation of assets. No two weeks' notice or severance pay. Everyone should just clean out their workstations and go home.

"We've got less than $50,000 in the bank. We tried everything we could to stay in business. I'm out of a job, just like you," the CEO said, white-faced.

Everyone was orderly—no yelling. Billy Jeff guessed everyone was so stunned that no one knew what to say.

As they shuffled out of the auditorium, Billy Jeff saw Meg Wallace, the VP of Human Resources, sitting in a chair crying. It was clear this was a surprise to her, too. She wasn't the only one crying.

"Isn't there a law against just shutting down without notice?" asked one employee.

"It's called WARN," said another. "Supposed to give you sixty days' notice of a shutdown, but it's got loopholes. You have to sue the company to get any money, and it doesn't sound like they have any."

Billy Jeff's vice president sat down with him: "We got caught in a perfect storm. You remember a few years ago when that New York private equity firm bought us? They loaded us up with debt, but we handled it because our revenue growth and profits were strong.

"Then the FDA caught one of our competitors, HPR, paying 'draw fees' to physicians to win their blood work. That should have benefitted us, but instead, the FDA clamped down on the entire industry and saddled us with millions in legal and regulatory compliance costs. They've never found fraud at any company besides HPR, but the feds are driving the smaller players out of the market.

"Then, the insurance companies argued that doctors were ordering our tests too often, and they began lowering the reimbursements. We reached a point where the banks wouldn't loan us any more money, and that was it: A perfect storm," he repeated.

Billy Jeff didn't understand it. He just knew that he and three hundred people were out of a job. He kept thinking about Emma and the kids, probably having breakfast together at this moment.

Billy Jeff had often wished he'd gone to college, and maybe life would have been easier. *But college-educated people lost their jobs here today, too,* he reflected. *Much of America is just like me, barely hanging on to a decent life by our fingernails.*

***

"Here I am with a new baby, a son, a wife, bills to pay, and no job." Billy Jeff was meeting with his former boss at the trucking company. He had left on good terms, and his boss had said he would always have a job there if he needed it.

"I can put you on a limited schedule, and maybe we can work you in full-time in a few months," the trucking boss said. "You better take advantage of that CDL while you can. In a few years, we'll probably have trucks that drive themselves."

20

SHRINK EXAM

The snow began shortly after he returned to New York, and it came down heavily. By morning, more than a foot blanketed the ground. Ezra needed to visit clients, but the airports were closed, so he waded through paperwork. On Wednesday, he flew to St. Louis and returned Thursday afternoon.

At 6 p.m. a courier delivered an envelope to his flat. Inside was a letter which said:

Dear Mr. Drake:
Please be at 725 Fifth Avenue, Suite 2000 tomorrow morning promptly at 8 a.m. dressed in business attire. The Atmani Foundation assessment will take the entire day and possibly into the evening.
You will experience several scenarios. The following will require homework on your part: First, you will meet with Senator Morris Smyth, with whom the Atmani Foundation has a good relationship. Many corporate decision-makers have contributed to Senator Smyth's campaigns. The objective of your meeting is to interview Senator Smyth and solicit his help in building relationships with some of his contributors. Pick seven of his contributors and conduct the interview. Senator Smyth will give you twenty minutes.
Second, sometime during the day, you will encounter Mr. Jim Hawkins, the CEO of Travert Industries. Your goal is to secure a follow-up appointment with him. For purposes of this scenario, assume the gentleman in the attached photograph is Mr. Hawkins.

We will reimburse you for reasonable expenses incurred. We look forward to meeting you tomorrow.
Sincerely,
Martha Baringer, Ph. D.

Ezra fired up his laptop and started learning about campaign financing. He quickly focused on the Federal Election Commission website and a watchdog site called *Open Secrets*.

He learned there were several ways individuals or corporations could contribute to federal election campaigns. The massive amount of data deserved hours of analysis. He needed to cross-reference the corporations with their officers and board members, but he didn't have the time. He knew, at some point, additional research effort tonight would lead to decreased performance tomorrow.

After spending two hours reviewing Smyth's donor listings, he focused on business executives with faster-growing companies, rather than old-line firms.

Ezra then researched Jim Hawkins and Travert Industries. He didn't know what to look for, but he was searching for a hook to get a second meeting.

There must be some reason why they chose this person. I've just got to find what it is. By 11:30 that evening, Ezra thought he knew.

He fell asleep, wondering how they would test him the next day.

***

They called him Spot—not to his face, of course, and not out of disrespect—but his name was hard to pronounce, and he had a circular discoloration around one eye. He was one of the Uchi-deshi, the apprentices from Japan who lived and cooked together in a small apartment upstairs from the dojo. They typically stayed a year or two and never seemed to learn much English. They showed how more than they told. They were not bulked up, but lean and hard like slabs of stone. When they weren't teaching class, they were training.

Once a quarter, the dojo had promotion tests. The most important part was the kumite, or sparring. For promotion to Brown Belt, Ezra would have to fight three or four opponents, one after the other.

Ezra's dojo sparred without gloves or pads during promotions. One could punch, but not to the face. One could kick, but not to the knee joints. Roundhouse head kicks were allowed, but not straight head kicks. Typically, the chest and ribs took most of the punishment, and repeated low kicks to the thighs made supple legs stiff. An unblocked roundhouse kick to the head or a hard straight-back kick to the body generally put someone down.

BUFFALO HUNTING IN ALABAMA

He had fought well against the first opponent, and now he was facing Spot.

They traded several punches and kicks. Ezra knew Spot could put him down. Spot trained all day every day, and Ezra spent a lot of time sitting in a chair. But he knew the goal was to test him, not break him.

It was a freak thing. A dojo couldn't stay open by regularly putting its customers in the hospital. Ezra moved side-to-side, looking for an opening. He had a fast front-snap kick, the leg shooting forward in a blur, hitting the opponent with the ball of the foot, the toes pulled back. Ezra had caught Spot once in the ribs already.

Ezra saw the opening, leaped forward, faked a right jab, and his left leg snapped forward, but Spot was aiming a knee kick to Ezra's abdomen, and Ezra's shin snapped forward and slammed into Spot's folded kneecap. Ezra's fibula and tibia cracked like a baseball bat, and he went down and lay there stunned. He felt the warm blood before he saw it.

***

"Mr. Drake, I'm Martha Baringer. We're evaluating you for a job position with the Atmani Foundation. A psychological assessment is standard for many executive positions, but your testing today may be a bit…different. The Atmani Foundation is searching for a person with specific traits and characteristics. They employed us to develop tests to measure whether job candidates have these traits.

"We're not testing your intelligence; we know you're smart. We're looking for specific traits, some of which are innate and others which are learned. The traits are neither desirable nor undesirable; they're just specific to this job. If you lack these traits, it's no reflection on you.

"We'll begin by having you take a battery of written tests. Afterward, we'll test your foreign language fluency. Then you'll experience several scenarios that simulate situations you may face if you work for the Atmani Foundation.

"Also, working for the Atmani Foundation will consist of long hours, high stress, and extensive travel, which will require physical stamina, so we've scheduled an appointment this afternoon for you with a sports medicine doctor. Is this acceptable?"

"Yes." *They want to know if I'm crippled. No sense buying a racehorse with a lame leg.*

"Before we begin, do you have any questions?" she asked.

"Let's get on with it," said Ezra.

The written tests took two hours. Ezra could discern no recognizable pattern to the questions and problems, so he gave up trying and just answered them as best he could. He finished before the time limit.

Dr. Baringer then gave him two letter-sized sheets of paper. On each were fifteen photos of people with their names listed underneath. Most were headshots of varying quality—driver's license photos to corporate portraits.

"Please study these. You have five minutes." She looked at her watch. In five minutes, she took the sheets from him.

"Take a ten-minute break, and then you have a meeting with Dr. Heinrich in the coffee room, straight ahead."

***

"*Guten Morgan, Herr Drake. Möchten Sie eine Tasse Kaffee, bevor wir anfangen?*"

"*Ja, mit etwas Milch bitte,*" said Ezra.

The conversation lasted about forty-five minutes. It ranged from simple pleasantries to discussions about Goethe and the German auto industry. Dr. Heinrich would change accents from time-to-time, first talking in the clear accent of someone from Hannover, then with the distinct accent of Berlin and then the dialects of Baden-Württemburg and Bavaria.

Ezra was comfortable most of the time but occasionally didn't know a word or phrase, which he worked around. Heinrich sometimes saw what he was doing and asked a question differently, which exposed Ezra's limits. Dr. Heinrich then shifted into *Schweizerdeutsch*, of which Ezra could understand very little.

Dr. Heinrich then spoke Spanish and then French. Those conversations were shorter, and Dr. Heinrich quickly found Ezra's limits.

"You have a good command of the German language and a reasonably good command of conversational French and Spanish," Heinrich said, smiling. It was now 11:10 a.m. "Take a break, and Dr. Baringer will see you at 11:30 in the break room."

***

"How's it been so far?" asked Dr. Baringer.

"Just an average morning at Silverman," said Ezra with a smile.

"Yes, well," She took him into a conference room. A large screen hung on one wall. They sat down, and she handed him a remote control.

"I want you to watch this video. It's about ten minutes long. When you recognize someone, pause the video and use the remote's laser pointer to tell me who they are. Go ahead and start the video when you're ready."

Ezra started the video. There were a couple of hundred people milling around and talking over drinks at a cocktail reception. The camera viewpoint was that of a person strolling through the crowd.

Ezra paused the video. "These are the people you showed me earlier, correct?"

"Do you recognize someone?"

"Ezra pointed out several people, and then stopped the video several more times, pointing out others. By the time the video ended, he had identified fifteen people.

"Did I get them all?" Ezra asked.

"You can't be good at everything," she said.

"How many did I miss?" he asked quickly.

"Less than one percent of the population are what we call 'super-recognizers.' They can quickly memorize a series of headshots face-on and then recognize those people when their heads are at different angles—sideways, three-quarters, and so on."

"How many did I miss?"

She just smiled. "The rest of the day will be a series of scenarios, for *some* of which you have prepared. After each scenario, you must dictate a concise contact report into a Notes document on your iPhone and email it to Simon. The report should summarize the meeting and any recommendations you have. If you join the Atmani Foundation, they will expect you to do this after every contact meeting."

She looked at her watch. "Time for you to leave for your meeting with Senator Smyth. Here's the address. Your appointment is at 1 p.m."

Ezra looked at his phone. He didn't have a lot of time to waste. "What happens after that meeting?"

"You'll be given instructions."

Ezra stood and shook Dr. Baringer's hand. "If we don't talk again, it's been a pleasure," he said sincerely and exited the office.

Ezra reviewed his notes for the Smyth interview as he waited for the elevator.

Ding! The elevator door opened, and standing there was Jim Hawkins, the CEO of Travert Industries—or the person impersonating him. Behind him stood two other people.

Shit! I've got maybe 30 seconds, Ezra thought. He couldn't help but smile. *The classic elevator pitch!*

The elevator door shut. "Sir, my name is Ezra Drake, and I know who you are. I've studied your company's financials and its capital budgeting plans. I've read everything I can about your company, and I think that sometime in the next year you plan to build another production plant. I would like fifteen minutes with you to explain why Alabama is a good location for your production plant. Will you give me an appointment?"

16...15...

Hawkins looked somewhat taken aback by Ezra's directness. "I don't think Alabama has the labor force I need for my plant."

11...10

"Sir, when you look at labor quantity and quality, state rankings are irrelevant. What matters is the labor situation near your site. Huntsville, Alabama, is closer to Louisville, Kentucky, than it is to Mobile, Alabama. Much of the Kia auto plant's workforce in Georgia comes from Alabama because the plant is near the border. Let me prove to you that there are sites in Alabama with the workforce you need. I will come prepared to prove that."

4...3...

The executive hesitated.

Ezra urged, "C'mon, give a fellow Yalie a chance to show you why Alabama is a great location for you."

2...1...

The executive hesitated just an instant, then said, "OK, here's my card. Set it up with my assistant."

As the elevator door opened, Ezra stepped out, and the executive said, "But you're no Yalie."

"And you're not Jim Hawkins," said Ezra. The two people behind Hawkins looked at each other. Ezra exited the building, whipped out his iPhone, and started dictating a contact report on the run.

***

Ezra was scheduled to meet Senator Smyth *or the person who will play him* at the offices of a prominent law firm that specialized in investment banking. Ezra had been there before on business.

Ezra spoke to the receptionist, who whispered into her headset. In a moment, she said, "Senator Smyth is waiting for you. Please step through those doors," and she pointed to the left.

As Ezra walked into the office, he saw an older man sitting behind a desk. *Holy shit*, Ezra thought, *it's the real Senator Smyth.*

Ezra was astonished. Sam Atmani had a lot of pull. It also said something about how seriously they took this job search.

"Senator Smyth, it's an honor to meet you."

"Sit down, my boy, sit down," and he motioned to a seat. "You're thinking of working for Sam?"

"I'm considering it, yes sir, if they make me an offer."

"You work for a fine company now, my boy. I know because I'm on the Senate Banking Committee and have occasion to work with them. Why are you interested in leaving?"

They had a good conversation, and Ezra was able to ask him about the donors he had targeted. Senator Smyth offered to make several intros for him. When they finished, Smyth handed him an envelope. "Good luck, son."

"Thank you, sir."

***

Ezra's goal was to make the doctor's visit as brief as possible. He hated doctors and hospitals.

"Your vitals look great. Tell me about this scar."

"I had a compound leg fracture last year."

"How did it happen?"

"I hit a kneecap."

"A kneecap?"

"A hard kneecap—with my shin."

The doctor thought for a moment. "Maybe you need a bone density test."

"My bones are plenty dense enough," said Ezra.

The doctor looked at him for a long moment. "Well, you look fit enough," he said.

"I'm almost a hundred percent. The tibia and fibula both broke cleanly. Only the upper edge of the tibia broke through the skin. I've done rehab religiously. My leg is not an issue." He *had* been religious in doing rehab in the hated Silverman gym. Nine weeks after the break, he had been exercising vigorously and had even done a twenty-mile hike.

He had healed his body but admitted his mind still needed some work.

***

The Jacob Javits Convention Center sat between West Thirty-Fourth and West Thirty-Ninth Streets, near the Lincoln Tunnel to New Jersey. It hosted events virtually nonstop, including toy fairs, fashion shows, restaurant and food shows, and international car shows. Ezra walked through aisles between hundreds of medical device-related companies exhibiting catheters, medical instrumentation, and every kind of medical equipment.

Leaving the doctor's office, the receptionist had given Ezra a manila packet. Inside was the following message:

> *The Medical Design & Manufacturing Show is currently underway at the Jacob Javits Center. Included in this packet are credentials for you to "work" the show. Look for companies who might be prospects to locate in Alabama. Work the show until it closes at 5 p.m. and then email Simon the names of companies you think might be prospects, and why. We will then give you further instructions.*

Ezra knew nothing about medical devices; the vastness of the trade show was bewildering. *Whatever I'm supposed to be doing, I'm screwing it up*, he thought.

As he walked the aisles, he decided to focus on European exhibitors. The larger exhibitors often had color-coded maps showing the company's headquarters, sales offices, and manufacturing plants. Ezra focused on those companies with a U.S. sales presence but no U.S. manufacturing, especially if they manufactured bulky items that might be costly to ship to the U.S.

Ezra asked them about any plans to set up U.S. manufacturing. Generally, the people at the exhibits were salespeople with no idea about the company's plans, but occasionally he was able to talk with a decision-maker. By the time the show closed at 5 p.m., he had identified three companies worth further study. He emailed them to Simon and received the following reply:

> *Proceed immediately to Howland's Bar at West Thirty-Ninth Street. Inside, you will see a middle-aged man with a beard (see attached photo). Your objective is to find out from this gentleman the color of his daughter's eyes. However, you cannot ask him that question. You must elicit that answer from him without asking him the question directly. Good luck.*

Ezra's leg hurt from walking the concrete trade show floors. *This works for me*, Ezra thought. *I need a drink after this.*

21

HOWLAND'S

He had never been to Howland's Bar on West Thirty-Ninth. It looked like a typical New York neighborhood bar—deep and narrow. As he entered the front door, Ezra saw half-a-dozen people seated at the bar to the right. He immediately spotted his subject, but people were sitting on barstools on both sides of him.

Ezra reflected for a minute and then decided on the smaller of the two. *Here goes...*

Ezra slid into the space between the subject and the man sitting to the right of him. Standing at the bar, he ordered a large draft Blue Moon. The head of the beer overflowed the rim of the glass as the bartender placed it on the bar. Ezra picked it up and brought the beer to his lips, and then, *suddenly,* the beer slipped in his hands, and the entire contents dumped into the man's lap to his right.

"I am *so* sorry!" said Ezra, raising his hands. Seeing the man wasn't throwing a punch, Ezra reached into his back pocket. "The least I can do is pick up your bar tab—and here's fifty bucks to get your clothes dry-cleaned. Again, I am so very sorry!"

The man looked at Ezra as if he wanted to punch him. He then grabbed the money and headed to the bathroom.

Ezra took napkins from the bar and began to clean the bar top and the stool where the man had sat. The bartender brought a towel to help.

As they were finishing the cleanup, the man walked out of the restroom and continued out the front door, ignoring Ezra. Meanwhile, the subject watched all this with a slightly amused look.

Ezra sat down at the newly-free barstool. "I *do* need a beer now." He turned to the subject. "Would you like one?"

The man looked at him and said, *"Ich spreche kein Englisch."*

***

Ezra worked three hours to build a rapport with the subject. The man's name was Rainer Siepmann, and he was in town for the Medical Design & Manufacturing show at the Javits Center. It was all bullshit, of course, but the man did a convincing job in the role. He drank like a fish, and Ezra matched him, beer for beer. Ezra still felt no closer to his objective.

Over an hour ago, he had tried spinning a long story about a girlfriend he had loved who had beautiful blue eyes, but the guy hadn't bit, so he couldn't immediately bring up "blue eyes" again, or the subject would get suspicious.

Ezra found this game of deception to be fascinating. He was often so engrossed in the conversation, effortlessly spinning little lies and falsehoods, and trying to come up with subtle ways to—what was the term—*elicit* the information he wanted, that Ezra briefly forgot it was just a scenario. It was also a bit disturbing. As a rule, he had always tried to tell the truth—not just because he believed it the right thing to do—but also because he didn't have to worry about keeping his story straight.

The man playing Rainer Siepmann was very good at this, and Ezra felt Siepmann was often toying with him. It had been over an hour since the last try, so he started again.

"I met this Australian girl one time at a bar in Cancun. What a looker! Sometimes we Americans are not the most popular people in the world, so I told her I was German, and I spoke English with a German accent. It was going good. I was making progress—*more progress than I'm making here*, he thought—and then she told me she didn't believe I was really German.

"At the time, I lived in Frankfurt, and so I showed her my German driver's license, but she was still skeptical. 'Most Germans have blue eyes, but you don't,' she said.

" 'Have you ever been to Germany?' I asked her. She admitted she hadn't.

" 'Most Germans don't have blue eyes,' I said. 'Many German *girls* have blue eyes, but not so many men,' " and Ezra looked at the subject. "What do you think?"

"About blue eyes?" he asked.

"Yes."

He appeared to be thinking for a moment: "Well, my eyes are brown, but my wife and both my daughters have blue eyes."

Bingo! Ezra thought.

For the first time that evening, the subject spoke to Ezra in English: "That will be it for this evening, Mr. Drake. Why don't you catch a taxi and head home? You'll probably have a nasty hangover in the morning. A bit of advice: When you're in a situation like this, try to arrange with the bartender in advance for him to pour you a *Radler* while your subject drinks beer. That way, you can outlast him."

Ezra looked at the bartender, who bowed his head and did a little hand flourish.

Son of a bitch, thought Ezra. A *Radler,* or *Alsterwasser,* as they called it in North Germany, was half-beer and half sparkling lemonade. Visually, it looked like a Pils beer.

"It's been a pleasure," said Ezra as he shook the man's hand.

"I've got the tab," said the man.

Ezra smiled as he exited the bar. The subject spoke English with a distinct Brooklyn accent. Luckily for Ezra, the next morning was Saturday, so he could sleep late because he knew he would feel like shit.

***

Ezra heard his phone buzzing, announcing a text message:

> *Even though you forgot your last contact report, you pass. Congratulations. We will make you an offer at lunch. Artie's Deli at noon. — Simon*
>
> *P.S. — Please submit your contact report before then.*

As Ezra showered, he thought about all that had happened. He had worked hard to get this job offer. He was confident the job would be challenging, but there was still a nagging worry whether he could be successful in Alabama.

22

DECISION TIME

"What did you think about yesterday?" asked Simon. They were having lunch at Artie's Deli on Broadway. Ezra was fighting a hangover.

He thought for a moment, "I've certainly never had a job interview like it."

"That's no answer," said Simon in a neutral tone. He expected Ezra to say more.

"I found it challenging and frustrating," said Ezra. "I feel I bombed the medical show thing; I didn't know what the hell I was doing."

"The purpose of the Javits exercise was to show you the challenges of trying to do this job without being adequately prepared."

Simon looked at Ezra. "You want the job? If you want a job where you help people—a job that's interesting and challenging—we have a job for you."

"What would I do, specifically?"

"We mainly want you to focus on attracting European companies to Alabama. They're desirable to us for many reasons.

"Such as?"

"First, their decision-makers generally don't have hardcore biases against Alabama and the South. They tend to evaluate us with open eyes. Second, foreign companies setting up operations in the U.S. tend to set up traded operations. Third, foreign companies tend to pay higher wages. Finally, Alabama needs the diversity of people from elsewhere. How does that sound?"

"Sounds good. I'm comfortable working in Europe."

"We don't expect to keep you forever. If we can get five years out of you, that would be great."

"What would my job title be?" asked Ezra.

"What do you want it to be? One purpose of a job title is for people to know who reports to who. You'll report to me. If Hakim or Jack asks you to do something, do it. The other reason for a job title is to impress other people. At your age, Senior Vice President is probably not credible, so let's call you a Vice President. OK?"

"That works."

Simon gave him an envelope. The offer from the Atmani Foundation was generous, almost as much as he was making at Silverman. More, given the difference in cost-of-living and taxes. The offer also included an invitation to join Stein Stewart & Taft if he ever wanted to leave the GO Team.

Ezra knew if this job didn't work out, he could probably return to Wall Street, but he would have lost momentum. If he failed in Alabama, he might end up as a middle-aged back-bencher in some Wall Street firm, just trying to hold on till retirement.

Come on, Drake, said Ezra to himself. *Where is the old risk-taker? Where is the guy who decided not to go to law school when everyone told you to go? Where is the guy who went to school up North, when everybody told you to stay in Alabama?* He had plenty of time to recover if this didn't work out. It's not as if he had a wife and kids who would go hungry.

"What's it going to be?" asked Simon.

"A month ago, moving to Alabama and working there was the last thing on my mind. It's interesting how a whole string of unlikely incidents led to where I am now," said Ezra.

"That's how Alabama wins economic development projects—when a whole string of unlikely events come together. So, what's it going to be?"

Ezra remembered as a little kid standing at the end of a high-diving board, looking at the blue water far below, mustering up the courage to jump.

"I want the job," said Ezra. "When do I start?"

"Dr. Heinrich has suggested you do an advanced course at the Goethe-Institut in Frankfurt, to brush up on your German. Let me check when the next one starts."

***

"Scott Kling here."

"Scott, this is Ezra Drake in New York."

"Ezra!" Scott swung his legs off his desk and sat erect, grabbing a legal pad and pen with his free hand. "I hope you're calling to give me some good news."

A pause. "Scott, I am very grateful for the job offer. DG&L is a great company, and you opened my eyes to how cool Birmingham is becoming."

"But you're not taking the offer?" Scott interrupted.

"Again, I appreciate your and DG&L's hospitality—and the great offer—but I just feel it doesn't match up exactly with my skills and interests, so I'm going to have to decline it," said Ezra. "I'm sorry."

"If it's money, I can try to see if we can sweeten the pot a little more."

"No, it's not that," said Ezra.

Scott was silent for a moment. "Well, if I have to lose to somebody, I guess losing to Silverman Bach isn't so bad," he said, starting to digest his disappointment. "But Amanda's not going to be happy. You know she's taken a liking to you."

"Scott, there's something else I need to tell you. It happened purely by accident. While Amanda and I were touring Birmingham, I happened to meet someone from the Atmani Foundation, and we talked, and we've talked several more times, and I feel what they're doing in economic development more closely aligns with my particular skills."

"You're taking a job with them?" Scott almost yelled into the phone.

"Yes," said Ezra quietly.

"They're nothing! We've been doing this a hundred years. They probably won't be around two years from now. Atmani's already had to back off on his education initiative—did you know that?"

"They told me."

"Ezra, you're making one of the greatest mistakes of your life."

***

Ezra's first boss had taught him it was far more important how you left a job than how you started it. When he told the Silverman people he was leaving, they couldn't believe it. Moving to Alabama? Most tried to be nice about it, as nice as New Yorkers could be.

"Is your mother sick?" asked one.

"You know I had this friend of mine who dropped out of Harvard Law and signed up with the Marines to fight in Afghanistan," said the VP who sat next to him. "Got his arm blown off."

"Alabama has such a bad reputation," said another sympathetically.

"At least buy some good clothes before you go," said yet another. "And shoes, too." She paused. "Will you need shoes down there?"

23

THE DRIVE SOUTH

As a kid, during the summer, Ezra would sometimes visit his Aunt and Uncle in Louisville, Kentucky. One year he took the train, another year he flew, and one year he rode with Mr. Morrow, the long-haul trucker who lived next door. It had been a big adventure for a little kid, riding in an 18-wheeler truck, sleeping in the bed behind the seats, and eating at truck stops.

Ezra remembered that now as he drove south from New York in a U-Haul truck with all his worldly possessions. *Long-haul trucker*, he smiled. As he drove, he could see the countryside beginning to wake up from the long winter. Springtime in the South appeared to be two weeks or so ahead of the North.

The Atmani Foundation had offered to move him, but Ezra had declined. He had surprisingly few possessions—no car, not much furniture. Mostly clothes, books, and electronics. As a wanderer, he hadn't accumulated much. All his possessions fit in the smallest U-Haul truck. He drove southward, a road-gypsy, soaking in the countryside and stopping to eat at truck-stops.

Ezra knew that each year there were tens of thousands of people like him who moved from flyover country to New York or DC or LA and later decided to return home. Some hadn't found the success they desired. Others had prospered, but the bright lights and big city hadn't turned out to be the dream they envisioned. Still others had left home because of a lack of opportunity, and after achieving in the big leagues, they were now in demand back home. He smiled. And then there were those like Jimmy who regarded it as an assignment in hell and couldn't wait to return home.

BUFFALO HUNTING IN ALABAMA

He arrived in Birmingham shortly before noon on Saturday. The Atmani Foundation had someone meet him at the storage warehouse to help him store his belongings. He would look for an apartment and unpack after returning from Germany. His cell phone rang as he locked the mini-warehouse.

"You make it to Birmingham OK?" It was Simon.

"I did. Just finishing up storing my stuff."

"Good. We have a challenge for you before you travel to Germany on Wednesday. You haven't met Mrs. Avery, but she works for us. Please call her immediately, and she will fill you in. I'm texting you her number."

Not wasting any time putting me to work, Ezra said to himself. "Will do. See you at the office on Monday?"

"I'll be there, but I think Mrs. Avery has other plans for you."

"Sounds good," said Simon.

He called the number. "Hi, Ezra," said Mrs. Avery. "I work with communities on development issues. We have a situation in Forrest County in the Black Belt. You may be able to help them when you're in Germany. Can you drive down there Monday morning? You'll be back the same day."

"Sure."

"Meet me at the office at 7:30 a.m. Monday morning. We'll do your employee paperwork, and you can get on the road. I'll email you some background."

Ezra rented a car he could drop off at the airport on Wednesday, and he checked-in at the Aloft Hotel. Homewood was the most walkable community in the Birmingham metro, with shops and restaurants of all kinds near the hotel. Ezra planned to chill for the remainder of the weekend, sitting at cafes, drinking coffee, and soaking in the feel of his new home. Amanda was out-of-town at a conference.

Weary from the drive, Ezra lay on the hotel room bed and read emails. Mrs. Avery had sent a hundred-page document about the Black Belt region of Alabama. Ezra took a two-hour nap and then started reading.

24

VISIT TO THE BLACK BELT

On Monday morning, Ezra met with Mrs. Avery, a middle-aged woman with a pleasant smile. *She could be my high-school English teacher*, he thought.

"I head our Community Outreach and Education Program, but I also handle our HR work," she said. Ezra signed the employee paperwork, including a detailed and complex nondisclosure agreement. Mrs. Avery gave him Amex Platinum and VISA Black cards and a box of business cards.

"Now you're official. You have a meeting with Prudence Baker and friends at Judy's Restaurant in downtown Perigee, in Forrest County, at noon. They will tell you about their situation. You should leave here by 9:30 a.m."

"Tell me about the Community Outreach and Education Program," said Ezra.

"We help prepare local communities for economic development projects. Have they told you about Microsoft and Seattle?" Ezra nodded. "We want to know about past graduates of Alabama high schools—where they work and what they do. If they're decision-makers in companies we're targeting, that may give us an advantage. If they're like Bill Gates and started companies elsewhere, we want to encourage them to bring their companies back to Alabama, or at least establish a presence here.

"We've created software to assist locals in putting together high school reunions. It helps them with the entire process, from establishing a budget to printing name tags for attendees. It also helps them locate and communicate with graduates, regardless of where they live.

"We provide the software free to the organizing committees, and also modest organizing grants. If they can't find a particular alumnus, we help locate the person. In return, they agree to let the software automatically upload to us the databases they build. Our goal is to have useful information about every Alabama high school graduate for the last sixty years—where they live and what they do.

"We currently have data for fifty-seven percent of all Alabama high school graduates since 1950. We should hit eighty percent in three years. The data helps with business prospecting. It also helps us understand why some communities are more successful than others."

"That's pretty slick," said Ezra.

"For international prospects, I can offer you our intern program. European colleges expect students to serve an internship as part of their education. It's competitive lining up these internships, and even smart, motivated European kids can have trouble securing good positions. Some European kids try for U.S. internships, but American corporations generally aren't set up to accept European students.

"We've established a program to place European students as interns in Alabama corporations. For the international companies we target, we build profiles of the decision-makers' children. If they're attending university, we send them an invitation to apply for the Atmani Foundation's intern program.

"Currently, we have thirty-four children of targeted international decision-makers doing internships in Alabama. Twice a year, we hold a social event for these young people. You will want to attend those. We find the children's parents often visit Alabama sometime during their internship."

"Have you been with the Atmani Foundation long?" Ezra asked.

"About two years."

"What did you do before that?"

"I was a high school principal."

Simon had arrived as Mrs. Avery was talking. "We didn't intend to give you an assignment your first day, but since you're heading to Germany—where the possible solution lies—we thought we'd give you a challenge."

Ezra smiled. He liked challenges.

As he left Mrs. Avery's office, Ezra ran into Jack, who welcomed him on-board and invited him for a cup of coffee. Jack kept an old-fashioned electric percolator and coffee service on a sideboard in his office, and Ezra could smell the fresh coffee.

On hearing Ezra's mission for the day, Jack commented. "Have you ever visited a famous place that was supposed to be cool or cutting-edge, and when you got there, you were a bit disappointed because it didn't look that different from many other places?"

Jack remembered the first time he visited Cupertino in Silicon Valley and how unremarkable it was. The same for Hollywood and the Sunset Strip. He nodded.

"That's because there are cool places everywhere," said Jack. "Name me someplace more lovely than Fairhope, Alabama. I'd put it head-to-head with anywhere on the Monterrey Peninsula. Name me a finer small town than Oxford, Mississippi or Auburn.

"We're conditioned to believe because the South's median income is lower than some other places that *everything* about the South is not as nice, and that's not so. The only difference between richer states and poorer states is the relative number of nice places they have, and the relative number of not-so-nice places. You're about to visit one of Alabama's not-so-nice places. While it has a certain charm and potential, it's the Alabama the *New York Times* writes about."

***

Following Google Maps, Ezra drove southwest on Interstate 20 toward Tuscaloosa and Mississippi. Just outside Birmingham, the last vestiges of the Appalachian Mountains sunk into the landscape.

Starting over, thought Ezra. *I need to hit the ground running. Start things off with a bang.* Simon had emphasized that results wouldn't come at once—that he would have to be patient and plant lots of seeds, and some of them would hopefully grow into projects.

To hell with that, thought Ezra. He needed to find the first project quickly. All his life, if he weren't getting the results he wanted, he would simply work harder until the results came. That was his plan now.

In about forty minutes, he spied the Mercedes Drive exit sign, and an industrial city of white gleaming buildings appeared on the left—the Mercedes-Benz auto assembly plant. He had read that four thousand people worked there, not counting the suppliers in nearby industrial parks. The entire complex spanned almost two miles along the interstate.

BUFFALO HUNTING IN ALABAMA

Twenty minutes after passing Mercedes, the interstate wound through the southern edge of the City of Tuscaloosa. Crimson Tide land. He had almost gone to school there.

Ten minutes later, he was driving through empty countryside. *It's beautiful land,* Ezra thought, *flat grassland, some agriculture, stands of trees. Great hunting land. Great land for riding horseback or just doing nothing.*

Ezra recalled the briefing paper: The Alabama Black Belt stretched across the middle of Alabama, with Montgomery as the belt buckle. It included eighteen of Alabama's sixty-seven counties and about a quarter of its land area, but only twelve percent of the population.

Fewer people lived in the entire Black Belt than in Jefferson County, where Birmingham was located. Fourteen of the eighteen Black Belt counties had lost population between 2000 and 2010. Five of the counties had lost more than ten percent of their population during that period.

Each Black Belt county had its own story, from the Carolina settlers who moved to Choctaw County to Napoleon's soldiers who tried to establish a wine and olive colony in Marengo County. Some Black Belt counties epitomized the antebellum stereotype with cotton crops and slave plantations, while other counties were mostly white settlers with few slaves.

The Black Belt had been one of the wealthiest areas in the U.S. before the Civil War, but a tiny percent of the population owned the wealth, and it had been accumulated from the sweat of slaves.

The Black Belt name had been coined in the 1820s to describe the rich dark soil of the region, but after the Civil War, it took on a political meaning to designate the swath of counties from Texas to Virginia where more than half the population was black.

Forrest County lay at the northwestern edge of the Alabama Black Belt. Its land area was 650 square miles, with barely nine thousand people. *Fourteen people per square mile. Less, really, when you consider the density of the few small towns. What can one do with that kind of density?*

The median household income was just over $24,000, and the population was eighty percent black. Only six-tenths of one percent of the population was mixed race. Only two-tenths of one percent of the population was foreign-born. *I guess that means*—Ezra did the math—*eighteen Hispanics are living and working somewhere in the county.*

Poor, black, and isolated.

Forrest County had a labor force of fewer than three thousand people, and the unemployment rate was twice the state average. With only three hundred people listed as unemployed, a hundred-person company could slash unemployment by a third.

He couldn't recall the disability rate, but Ezra knew it wasn't as high as nearby Hale County, where almost one-fourth of the working-age population was on disability.

Forrest County wasn't the poorest of the Black Belt counties and not the richest. In most respects, it was about average. Seventy-six percent of the population had a high school degree, and almost thirteen percent of the adult population had a bachelor's degree or higher.

The county issued four building permits in the last year. No manufacturing output, except for a catfish processing plant.

Ezra's destination, the town of Perigee, was located about halfway between Tuscaloosa and Meridian, Mississippi. Economic developers regarded a community with an interstate exit as being born with a silver spoon in its mouth, but Ezra doubted that applied to Perigee.

Forty-five minutes later, Ezra took the Perigee exit. There were no gas stations or restaurants at the end of the off-ramp; just a sign with two arrows— Perigee to the left and Aliceville to the right.

The town center was several miles from the interstate. Driving past the "Welcome to Perigee" sign, Ezra saw two enormous old plantation houses within a thousand feet of each other, the first one in good condition.

Downtown Perigee was a faded, dried-up little town with a main street and several cross streets. The buildings were mostly late-nineteenth- and early-twentieth-century one- and two-story brick buildings, some painted in faded colors. About half seemed empty. Several churches were scattered about. There was a quiet, listless feel to the town.

Ezra parked at Judy's Restaurant and entered the small-town meat-and-three. At a table next to a front window sat two men and a woman. One of the men was white. They noticed Ezra immediately and waved him over.

The woman introduced herself as Prudence Baker, the local economic developer. The black man was Commissioner Wilton Raspberry, and the white man was George Collins, the District Manager for the local electric co-op and Chairman of the Forrest County Industrial Development Board. They went through the buffet line, and Collins picked up the tab.

As they began eating, Commissioner Raspberry said, "Mr. Drake, we hope you can help us get our land back."

"I'll help, however I can," said Ezra. He wanted to be encouraging yet noncommittal. "Can you give me some background?"

"We have this industrial park out near the interstate," said Collins. "Big Sky Industrial Park. About twenty-five years ago, a German company purchased five hundred acres there to build a paper plant. Made a lot of sense. Not much cotton grown here anymore, but we've got lots of trees, and our industrial park sits right on the Tenn-Tom Waterway, which goes all the way to the Gulf, and all the way up the Mississippi River to Chicago or wherever.

"The German company bought the land, and everyone was excited. *Hundreds* of jobs. It would transform our poor little county. I wasn't here then, but this is what I've been told."

"I was here," said Commissioner Raspberry, "and it was the biggest news our town ever had."

Collins continued, "The county waited and waited. Everyone thought the company was working on its plans. And then one day, we learned they had decided to buy a paper plant up in the northwest—Oregon or somewhere.

"Everybody, of course, was deeply disappointed. The local leaders didn't want to give back the money—I think they had spent some of it—and the German company didn't ask for it. Some of the county leaders figured the German company would build the plant in a few years.

"Well, they didn't, and years and years passed. Back in those days, the county hardly ever got looks from industrial prospects. County leaders eventually realized if we didn't do something, our little county was going to dry up and blow away, so we upped our game and got busy trying to attract industry.

"I moved here as District Manager six years ago, and we hired Ms. Baker shortly afterward. We *did* start getting some prospects, but there's been a problem: Every time a prospect looks at our property, they want proof we control it, and telling them we are *sure* we can buy back the land from the German paper company isn't good enough. Either they don't have time for that, or they don't believe us, or whatever."

Site selection is a process of elimination, Ezra remembered hearing. Not owning or controlling a site is a good reason to eliminate it.

"We decided we *must* buy back the property from the German company," said Collins. "The first problem was money—the county is technically in bankruptcy."

"That's when Mr. Collins came up with the idea of selling the other part of the property," said Ms. Baker. As they explained it, the industrial park was initially about a thousand acres. They had sold the best five hundred acres to the German company. The remaining five hundred acres sat next to the Tenn-Tom Waterway and was mostly within the floodplain.

"No one's going to build a plant in a floodplain," said Ms. Baker, "so that land's no good to us. Mr. Collins came up with a good idea. Tell him," she said, nodding her head at Collins.

"The biggest industry in the Black Belt is hunting. People come from all over to hunt here and stay in our hunting lodges. We have some nice ones. They're essentially small hotels and provide jobs for our people.

"There's a guy in Birmingham who owns a big metal-fab company who's interested in buying the land down near the river for a hunting lodge. He'll pay us $2,100 an acre for it."

Hunting lodges are traded industries, Ezra thought. *They bring in wealth from elsewhere. The jobs probably don't pay much—service jobs like guides and cooks and maids—but at least they're jobs.*

"Sounds good," Ezra said.

"We should go ahead and sell that land *now*," said Commissioner Raspberry. It sounded to Ezra as if there was some history there.

Collins ignored the Commissioner, "We want to sell the five hundred acres to the Birmingham man and use that money to buy back the good five hundred acres.

"We've tried to contact the German company. We called their office in Oregon but haven't gotten anywhere. They said they'd talk to Germany, but we never hear anything back. That's happened two or three times, and then we tried to call the company directly in Germany, but we had trouble understanding them, and they couldn't understand us, so that went nowhere.

"We tried to get the state to help us, but they said it's *our* job to put together property for companies—they just bring us the prospects."

"Wasn't there a reversionary clause in the sales contract that required the land to be resold to the county if it wasn't used?" asked Ezra.

"We checked, and it's not there," said Ms. Baker.

"You want me to try and contact the German company?" Ezra asked.

"We would be most grateful if you would help us get back our property," said Ms. Baker.

"If they're willing to sell, how much are you willing to pay for it?" asked Ezra.

"$2,100 an acre—or less—if possible."

"How much did they buy it for?" asked Ezra.

"$2,000 an acre," said Ms. Baker.

"And that was twenty-five years ago?"

"Things don't appreciate much here. Most of the time, we're happy if things don't *lose* value."

"What if they want more?" asked Ezra.

"That's all we have," she said. "And we don't have that yet."

***

After lunch, they stood outside the restaurant on the sidewalk.

"I'm headed to Germany on Wednesday," Ezra said. "I'll be there a month and will try to meet with the company. Can you email me a copy of the old sales contract and the contact information for the people you've tried to contact? Also, do you have a draft sales contract for the land you plan to sell to the Birmingham guy? It's not money, but it's a promise of money."

Ms. Baker and Collins looked at each other. "We can do that," she said.

"And can you show me the industrial park? I need to see the land to talk about it."

"I can do that," said Collins. "Why don't you follow me, and when we're finished, you can get on the interstate and head back to Birmingham."

"Sounds like a plan," said Ezra. They all exchanged business cards and shook hands and said their good-byes. *First business cards handed out in the new job,* thought Ezra. *Maybe they'll be lucky ones.*

"Thank you again," said Prudence Baker.

Ezra followed Collins, who was driving a white truck with the co-op logo on the side. In ten minutes, they pulled up to the industrial park entrance. It had a brick and metal monument sign and a freshly-paved road going into the park.

"Come get in the truck with me," said Collins, "I'll show you around."

Collins drove them around the park. "This road makes a loop that circles back to the entrance. We have water and sewer to the road. We're ready to run electricity whenever a company locates."

"What about gas?"

"We don't have that and won't anytime soon. The main line is just too far away, and there's not enough demand in this area to run a pipeline."

"Where's the land you want to sell?"

Collins pointed to mostly-wooded property in the distance. Ezra could see the land slope downward. He couldn't see the Tenn-Tom Waterway, but he could see the break in the tree canopy where it ran.

"All that land—about five hundred acres—has flood plain issues, so it has limited use. But the deer don't know that. It has lots of deer. We had a dock down there on the Tenn-Tom, but a barge tore it up, so we used the insurance money to improve the park entrance and run a road and some utilities."

"It would help me in negotiating with the German company if you had the cash in hand to buy the property. Why don't you go ahead and sell that property?" Ezra asked.

Collins said nothing for a moment, and then looked at Ezra. "Did you notice the pickup truck the commissioner was driving?"

"Pretty fancy," said Ezra quietly.

"Several of the commissioners got new trucks like that this year—county trucks. And with the county in bankruptcy. There's a little weekly newspaper in Perigee. It's calling for an investigation. Seems that Commissioner Raspberry filled up his truck with gas twenty times last month. They calculated he would have had to drive almost twelve hours a day, every day that month, to use that kind of gas.

"Cash has a habit of disappearing in Forrest County. Ms. Baker and I want to sell that land down there and buy this land in the same transaction, so there's no cash floating around. We don't want the cash to sit in a county account for even an instant."

"Why do you live here?" asked Ezra.

"I don't," said Collins. "Both Ms. Baker and I live in Tuscaloosa and commute. I work here because the company gave me a promotion to take this job. Ms. Baker's position is paid for by a federal grant to aid the Black Belt counties."

Collins continued, "In some ways, it would be nice to live in a small town like this. It's quiet and peaceful, and you get a lot of house for the money, but I have a family and three kids. The Forrest County school system is the fourth best-funded of the 130-plus city and county school systems in Alabama—they get a lot of federal funds—but their test scores are near the bottom.

"The school system's controlled by an elected school board. Over the past five years, they've had six different superintendents, five different principals, and several vice-principals and football coaches. There's a small private Christian academy here for the white kids, but I wouldn't put my children in that."

They drove in silence for a few minutes back to the park entrance. As Ezra started to open the truck door, Collins said, "I didn't mean to be negative back there. Both Ms. Baker and I believe this place has potential."

"I understand," said Ezra. "I'll do my best to help."

Driving back to Birmingham, Ezra realized that planting seeds and waiting for them to grow into projects in the Black Belt might just take a while.

25

THE GOETHE-INSTITUT

Frankfurt in January was always dark and generally cold, and so it was again. A thin layer of snow covered the ground as Ezra's plane touched down at the sprawling airport south of the city.

To Ezra, Frankfurt was an old friend. The city wasn't pretty—World War II had destroyed seventy percent of it, and they hadn't rebuilt it in the old style. Shown a photo of the Frankfurt skyline, most Americans would think it an American city unless they looked closely at the corporate logos. Germans often called it *Mainhattan*, for its modern skyscrapers and location on the Main River.

It was only the fifth-largest German city, but its airport moved fifty-three million passengers a year and made it the first German city most visitors saw.

Germans also called it *Bankfurt* because it was home to the European Central Bank, the Deutsche Börse, the Bundesbank, and several other large German banks. A job with Deutsche Bank had first brought Ezra to Frankfurt.

About one-fifth of Frankfurt's population were foreigners. When Ezra first moved there, he remembered trying to speak German with waiters in restaurants, only to realize they mostly weren't German.

Ezra had lived in Germany as a kid and had taken German in high school and college, but it was easy to function in Frankfurt without being fluent. Many Germans tried to speak English at every opportunity, and much of the business he had transacted for Deutsche Bank had been in English.

It's said that the best way to learn a language is to have a local girlfriend, and Ezra had done that, but most of those conversations hadn't been deeply philosophical. Now he needed to improve his German to be able to talk philosophy, if necessary. He hoped a month at the Goethe-Institut, with eight hours of class a day, plus homework, would help.

The Goethe-Institut was located on the south side of the Main River in Sachsenhausen, across from the *Südbahnhof*—the South Train Station. The Goethe staff had arranged a tiny efficiency apartment for him about fifteen minutes away by streetcar in *Niederrad*, across the street from an old horse racing track.

Monday through Friday, Ezra would take the streetcar from his tiny flat, switching once to arrive at the *Südbahnhof*. The McDonalds at the train station was his only concession to American life. Most mornings, he would order a Big Breakfast of scrambled eggs, sausage, orange juice, and coffee. Sometimes in the evenings, after class, he would take the streetcar downtown and eat dinner somewhere along the *Hauptwache*, often at a Nordsee or Wienerwald, since he was generally too mentally tired to appreciate anything more expensive.

Ezra had expected the class to have a dozen students, but that first Monday morning, there was just one other classmate—a Croatian high school teacher working on his doctorate in German. After thirty minutes of conversation, Ezra and the Croatian were given voice recorders and sent to the sidewalk outside. Their mission was to interview people who would give their thoughts about the economy in the coming year.

They had one teacher in the morning and a new teacher for the afternoon. Both teachers refused to speak a single word of English the entire month Ezra attended class.

The only rest was during in-class reading assignments. Ezra was not particularly good at memorizing; he preferred to reason things to a conclusion, but much of language-learning was memorization, so he had to work very hard.

During the morning and afternoon *Kaffeepausen*—the coffee breaks—Ezra learned that winter was the low point for language classes at the Goethe. College students taking German rarely chose Frankfurt and never in the winter. Many of the students, especially in the beginning classes, were Asians assigned to work in Germany. If they didn't pass the exams, their companies would send them home.

Most evenings, Ezra was too exhausted to complete his homework, so he would go to sleep and then wake at 4 a.m. to finish the assignments for the coming day. About two weeks into the class, he started dreaming in German.

He ate lunch by himself at one of the neighborhood bakeries, reading and answering emails and catching up on the news.

Both teachers were middle-aged women who took their jobs seriously but also had a sense of humor. After a particularly difficult session, one teacher quoted Mark Twain, who said that learning German is "what eternity was made for."

After being in class together all day, Ezra and the Croatian didn't socialize. Occasionally after class, Ezra and the Croatian and the teachers would walk to the market and purchase food for a group dinner.

It was barely daylight when he started class each morning, and it was dark when he finished. He spent a typical day reading and discussing articles in the *Frankfurt Allgemeine Zeitung, Handelsblatt, Spiegel,* and *Die Welt,* and discussing the works of Goethe and the poems of Rainer Maria Rilke.

They gave Ezra four days to read journalist Peter Scholl-Latour's *Die Welt aus den Fugen* (The World Out of Joint) and to prepare and present a detailed oral book report. He looked online for an English translation, but there wasn't one.

Over time, Ezra had become adept at speaking German in such a way to avoid the more obscure tenses. The teachers quickly found his weaknesses and forced him to answer in the more difficult forms.

The first week, Ezra tried to call the *Finanzchef* of the German paper company in Augsburg to arrange an appointment. They promised to get back with him, and when he made a follow-up call, they told him the *Finanzchef* was traveling on business and afterward on holiday. Ezra should try again in two months.

So much for a meeting during this trip, Ezra thought. In the past, the Silverman Bach name had opened many doors. *Now I'm just a guy in a suit from a poor Southern state.*

***

"Amanda?"

"Ezra? Is that you?"

It was 2 a.m. Frankfurt time and 7 p.m. Birmingham time. "It's me."

"Where are you?"

Ezra was lying in bed. "I'm in Frankfurt. Just finished studying and about to crash. I thought I'd call to see how you're doing."

"I'm fine! How about you?"

"Good. I think this is the first time in a week I've spoken a word of English."

"How is Germany?"

"Cold and dark. Maybe eight hours of light a day. We just had a couple of inches of snow."

"Are you learning much?"

"The classes are brutal. I'm even dreaming in German now."

A pause. "What are you dreaming about?"

"Du, mein Schatz."

"What does that mean?" she asked coyly.

"I'll tell you when I get back."

26

JOURNEY TO MUNICH

On Wednesday of the second week, after a quick lunch, Ezra skipped afternoon class and took the U-Bahn to the *Hauptbahnhof*, where he purchased a first-class round-trip ticket to Munich. As the ICE train glided smoothly out of Frankfurt central station, the snow came down steadily, blurring the outlines of the city.

The car was about half-full. Most of the passengers wore black, the German winter fashion color. Perhaps it reflected the mood, for no race of people loved the sun more than Germans, and few saw it less.

In contrast to the clothing, much of the luggage in the overhead racks were tropical blues, oranges, and reds. *Perhaps Germans purchased their luggage before going on summer holidays.*

A man across the aisle from Ezra wore a Brooklyn Chargers cap. *There's a lot of that in Europe,* Ezra thought. *Cowman jeans, too. If cowboys are cool, then cowmen must be cooler.*

It was three hours to Munich, and Ezra worked on his Goethe-Institut homework. About ninety minutes out of Munich, he began studying the brief emailed him by the Quants.

The Governor and Atlas Ogg, the General Manager of ADIT, were making a recruiting trip through Europe. They had scheduled most appointments with companies that already had a presence in Alabama, a typical itinerary for Governors on such trips. This visit to Europe included a dinner with OberBayern-Chemie, a Munich-based chemical company with an operation in

BUFFALO HUNTING IN ALABAMA

Mobile. ADIT had arranged it through the Alabama plant manager. Mr. Atmani had gotten Ezra an invitation to the dinner.

OB-Chemie was planning a $150 million expansion at one of their U.S. production plants, and they were considering Mobile. They had asked for property and income tax incentives, and the City of Mobile had already agreed to abate most of the city, county, and state property taxes for ten years—a big win for the company. Alabama's property taxes were the lowest in the U.S., but chemical plants were capital intensive, and a large capital investment could still produce a significant property tax bill.

The expansion would only add twenty jobs, which gave the Governor discretion whether to offer an abatement of the state corporate income tax. OB-Chemie admitted the new jobs weren't many but argued the expansion would allow for future expansions, which could employ more people.

ADIT lacked the expertise, access to data, and will to determine if the company was bluffing. Could they locate the expansion elsewhere, or did it *have* to happen at the Alabama plant?

At least there were *some* new jobs. Ezra had heard of projects where large capital investment expansions had resulted in fewer people working at a plant. It reminded him of leadership guru Warren Bennis' famous quote about the manufacturing plant of the future, staffed by only a man and a dog. The purpose of the man was to feed the dog. The purpose of the dog was to keep the man from touching the machinery.

Up to now, new technology had always produced new jobs, but Ezra wondered if that would continue, or was the world facing future widespread unemployment from automation? And what would happen then?

Tuesday evening before leaving for Germany, Ezra and Jack had dinner, and Jack gave him the backstory on Governor Smith and ADIT.

Beauregard Martin Smith was a character, like many politicians. He had been a red-headed, freckle-faced Arkansas high school football star who wanted to follow Paul "Bear" Bryant and play for Alabama. He had done that, playing for the Bear as a left-handed running quarterback with a light passing touch.

After graduating with a degree in journalism, Smith married his Kappa Kappa Gamma sweetheart and played two years for the Green Bay Packers until he suffered a severe groin injury, which ended his career.

He then returned to Alabama. After an industrial products company fired him for "fishing on the job," Smith started his own fishing lure business, which had become highly successful. For many years, he'd had his own nationally-syndicated outdoor fishing show. As bass fishing reached new heights of popularity, Smith had sold the business to a national sporting goods manufacturer and built a marina on Lake Tuscaloosa.

After a few years of fishing and drinking and being fawned over by his adoring fans, he decided to run for Governor. Smith was a shoo-in, having excelled in two of Alabamians' favorite pastimes—football and fishing.

In his inaugural speech, Smith promised to make state government operate like a Chick-fil-A, providing superb service at a reasonable price. State bureaucrats were not overly happy being compared to Chick-fil-A employees.

"I attended the governor's inauguration," Jack had said. "Smith's wife is very religious, and eighty-five percent of Alabamians identify as Christian, so Smith, like many other Alabama politicians, wears his religion on his sleeve.

"They had an actor dressed up like Moses in the inaugural parade. He had a Ten Commandments tablet in each arm, and he sat on the trunk of a white Cadillac Eldorado convertible with his feet on the backseat, like a beauty queen. The intended effect was Charlton Heston, but I kept thinking Monty Python."

According to Jack, in every state, the Governor was the chief business recruiter, and in that respect, Smith had been a mixed bag.

On the one hand, he could charm business prospects with an unending supply of stories and tall tales, and to some, he was a celebrity. On the other hand, he was a staunch opponent of incentives to lure businesses to the state.

"When I started my fishing lure company, I didn't get a damn bit of help from the state. Not a dime! It chaps my ass to give incentives—our hard-earned money—to some of these big corporations to get them to locate in the state. We're givin' away hundreds of millions of dollars. I don't like it worth a damn."

"Governor, the other states offer incentives," his advisors told him. "If we don't as well, we won't win many big projects. We don't make the rules on how to win economic development projects."

Governor Smith frequently referred to his business experience as he discussed economic development. No one would tell him that making rubber worms wasn't the same as manufacturing biotech drugs, luxury automobiles, or commercial jets.

"The Alabama Department of Industry and Trade—ADIT for short—was formed in the 1930s at the urging of DG&L. It's a state agency with the Director appointed by the Governor. The employees are under the state Competence

Plan, which means they're almost impossible to fire, and promotions are mostly determined by seniority," said Jack.

"Nineteen Eighty-Four" terminology, Ezra thought.

"Smith chose Todd Nelson, an old friend, to head ADIT; Nelson's not makin' this trip. The real power in ADIT is Atlas Ogg, the General Manager. He runs the place with an iron fist.

"Ogg, or 'the Major' as he prefers to be called, grew up in Tennessee, went to UT-Knoxville on a ROTC scholarship, and then served twenty years in the U.S. Army, retiring as a Major.

"His wife is from Montgomery, so they moved there, and Ogg started work at ADIT. He climbed the ranks, and after twenty-one years, he's the ADIT General Manager—the top-ranking Competence Plan employee.

"Ogg has managers for Export Development, Project Management, and Marketing. Mark Thornton heads Project Management, which works projects brought to ADIT by site consultants and companies interested in Alabama. Mark's a good guy, and his group does a decent job of winning projects.

"Ogg spends most of his time working with Marketing, who's supposed to generate new projects. They spend a ton of money on print advertising, overseas offices, trade show exhibits, hosting elaborate receptions, attending high-end sporting events—basically anywhere they can spend money.

"Many people believe ADIT's marketing efforts are mostly ineffective, but no one's willin' to push for change, because Ogg's so powerful. No one messes with him. He's one of those bureaucrats who have embedded themselves in government in such an integral way that they have become a source of power themselves. Unlike elected officials or political appointees, the only way to get rid of them is through retirement or death, or if they're caught in a serious scandal. They have job security unheard of in the business world, and even elected politicians ignore them at their peril.

"Be careful with Ogg; he's a mean drunk. If you ever see his eyes start to cross, like he's tryin' to focus on the end of his nose, then watch out because that's a 'tell' he's drunk and *particularly* unpredictable.

"Ogg's done things that would've gotten anyone else fired long ago—even a state employee. Somehow, he stays on, probably because over the years he's taken hundreds of state politicians on overseas prospecting trips, and by simply picking up the phone, important people listen to him.

"Never forget the power of government bureaucrats," said Jack. "Ogg tends to hire ex-military people who follow orders without question. Their actual economic development skills are doubtful. There's not a single person in ADIT who can fluently speak a foreign language except for one of his goons who speaks Pashto—not that we're tryin' to recruit investment from Afghanistan or Pakistan.

"Ogg has probably made a hundred economic development trips to Japan, and he's picked up some nighttime Japanese. If you were in a Tokyo whorehouse with him—not that I would know—you'd think he was fluent, but he has no idea how to hold a business discussion in Japanese or any other foreign language."

"What about the ADIT Director? Why doesn't he do something?" Ezra asked.

"The average tenure of an ADIT Director is about thirteen months. This current one's been there a year, so my guess is he's just holdin' on till he decides what to do next.

"ADIT Directors are typically friends of the Governor, big campaign contributors, or successful businessmen with lots of money. They usually have someone running their company or are retired and don't want to spend all day at home with momma. Many of them have no international experience, and while they function fine in the U.S., overseas, they're like a duck out of water.

"No particular aspect of economic development is that hard, but there are many subjects to master, and new ADIT directors are typically overwhelmed. There's no way they can become halfway competent in less than a year or two—and so they depend on the ADIT bureaucrats.

"Over the years, a couple of ADIT Directors came in with ambitious plans to reorganize and cull dead wood, but they were defeated by the bureaucracy. If you can't fire people and can't reward them for outstanding performance, you really can't manage them.

"When a new ADIT Director takes office, Ogg and the bureaucracy razzle-dazzle him—it's always a 'him'—with prospecting trips. They take him to Las Vegas for trade shows and New York and Chicago to meet site consultants, and they always frequent the best hotels and restaurants.

"Overseas, he gets the Grand Tour—dinner at the Jules Verne in the Eiffel Tower, shopping at the Hugo Boss outlet south of Stuttgart, night cruises in Hong Kong Harbor, lodging at the Park Hyatt in Tokyo, and bargain shopping and custom-made suits in the Itaewon district of Seoul. If you ever go to Seoul with Ogg, you'll learn that all recruiting trips there take at least two full days because the good suits require three custom fittings.

"Except for an occasional prospect, the meetings are mostly with executives of companies already in Alabama, local chamber of commerce officials, or officials in the Foreign and Commercial Service of U.S. Embassies, who are only interested in helping with export development, not foreign direct investment.

"All the meeting participants are polite and diplomatic. They know this is just a little game that government bureaucrats play with elected officials and businesspeople. After all, they've done the same thing in one form or another.

"The smart ADIT directors know they're being played, but most of them don't mind because when you're being wined and dined in grand style, it's easy to rationalize. Some ADIT Directors insist the trips be economical, but I've never heard any gripes over the cost. After all, prospecting travel is hard work and deserves a few perks.

"Most international recruiting trips are made to Europe, Japan, Korea, and China, where world-class companies are located, but if an ADIT director desires something more exotic, then export promotion trips can justify traveling to Brazil, Malaysia, Thailand, Africa—really, any place they want to go. After all, virtually any country is a potential market for Alabama products.

"ADIT bureaucrats know that when they take a new Director out of his natural setting, he becomes very *malleable*. Ten or twelve months of this, and he's generally ready to move on to something else. They memorialize his term with an oil painting that hangs in a hallway along with other past directors. There are a *lot* of portraits.

"ADIT Directors are occasionally experienced economic developers, and they have landed some great projects, but no ADIT Director has been successful in making the structural changes needed for ADIT and Alabama to successfully compete against other states in the future.

"So have fun at the dinner. Listen and learn. If you want to get in Ogg's good graces, call him 'Major Ogg' and ask him to tell you some war stories."

27

DINNER WITH THE GOVERNOR

The wet cold of the Munich winter evening slapped him in the face as he stepped down from the train. At the front of the *Hauptbahnhof*, the taxi queue was short. Completely rebuilt after World War II—mostly in the old style—Ezra had always loved Munich's grandeur and elegance.

As Ezra's taxi drove past Karlsplatz, he could see the lighted ice-skating rink set up for the winter. He remembered skating there with Erika, his old German girlfriend. In five more minutes, the taxi pulled up to the restaurant. *A long way for dinner,* he thought.

The restaurant stood in the fashionable Schwabing district. As he stepped inside, Ezra could see it was furnished as a traditional German *Gasthaus*, with light-brown *Fichte* wood walls and ceilings, and wood tables and white tablecloths, and a chifforobe-sized green ceramic tile stove in the main dining room to keep the place warm.

He was twenty minutes early. At a corner table were five older men, almost certainly retired, who drank their beers and appeared to be old friends at their *Stammtisch*.

Ezra decided to sit at one of the bar tables, where he could keep an eye on the front door. As he sat down, he rapped his knuckles twice on the table, and the old men at the *Stammtisch* smiled.

He had just ordered a Pils when the door opened, and a group shuffled in. OB-Chemie had picked up the Alabama group at their hotel, and they had all driven to the restaurant together.

BUFFALO HUNTING IN ALABAMA

It was easy to pick out the Governor. Smith had been a muscular six-footer as a quarterback, but in late middle age, he had shrunk in height and bulked up a bit. He wore a dark suit with pointed-toe cowboy boots, and he had a big Irish potato head with pig eyes and a nose like a curly fry. *A face made for radio*, Ezra thought, but he had done remarkably well with his televised fishing show.

The guy next to him must be Ogg, Ezra thought. He was a surprise. Ezra had expected a squared away, fit guy with a military haircut and a hard stare, but Ogg was hardly that. Imagine Santa Claus had trimmed his hair and shaved his beard but kept his mustache, wore tortoise-shell glasses, and traded his Santa outfit for grey slacks, a dark blue blazer, white shirt, and a bow tie.

Instead of a soft Santa belly, Ogg's looked hard and round as if all the food and liquor consumed in his life had calcified at his waist. The blazer was a one-button, which, combined with the bow tie, further emphasized his belly.

The Major is hardly a menacing figure, Ezra thought, *but looks could be deceiving.*

The Governor had two security people, one of whom had entered the restaurant ahead of everyone and cased the place as if terrorists were lying in wait.

In all, there were ten or so people in the group. Ezra made his way to the foyer, and as their coats were cared for, he introduced himself to the Governor.

"You're working for Sam Atmani," Smith said it, not as a question. "Sam's a good man. We're glad to have you join us."

Ogg didn't say anything. Up close, Ogg's horn-rimmed glasses sat on a veined nose and shielded beady eyes. *Bad Santa.* Ezra could imagine how those eyes looked when he was drunk, and they started to cross and focus on his nose.

They were led to a private dining room where a large table was set with name cards. Ezra found his place, as far from the Governor as it was possible to sit. A handsome woman in her forties stood to Ezra's left, and one of the Governor's security people stood to his right.

Ezra was surprised. Typically, security stayed in the background. They all sat down, with Ezra helping the woman with her chair. Waiters instantly appeared to take their drink orders. The woman ordered champagne, Ezra ordered a Kir Royale, and the security guy ordered a beer.

"I'm Ursula Kaufmann," said the woman. Ezra introduced himself.

Ezra then introduced himself to the security guy on his right. "Ernest Blunt," the man replied shortly. *Of course you are,* thought Ezra. Blunt radiated enormous physical power. He wasn't overly tall—probably 5'11" or so—but if a pit bull could morph into a man and fit into a suit, it would be Blunt. He had large hands, like giant twin crabs, and his knuckles were thickly calloused.

A man stood and tapped his spoon on his drink glass. "I am Ernst Kaufmann, the *Geschäftsführer* of OB-Chemie, and it is a pleasure to welcome our friends from Alabama. We are especially grateful to have Governor Smith with us here tonight. Our company has had a presence in Alabama for more than thirty years, and it has been a mutually profitable experience. I would like to propose a toast to our long and continued friendship."

They raised their glasses, Ezra and the Germans toasted *Prosit,* and glasses were touched. Ezra found it interesting that the German CEO and his wife sat at opposite sides of the table.

"It's perhaps easier if we all introduce ourselves," said Kaufmann, and they did so. To the immediate right of Kaufmann sat the Governor, then Atlas Ogg. Next was Fritz Meyer, VP of the Americas for OB-Chemie; Bill Lee, the head of marketing for ADIT; then Ursula Kaufmann; then Ezra; then Blunt, the security guy; then a Mr. and Ms. Spitzner. Finally, to Kaufmann's left was the Governor's wife.

After the introductions, Spitzner rose and said, "I manage Mercedes-Benz operations for the Munich area, and we would like to give the Governor a token of our appreciation for his visit here."

Spitzner walked around to the Governor, who stood up.

"Governor Smith, this is a model of the first Mercedes-Benz vehicle, the *Motorwagen,* which we first sold to the public in 1888. Please accept it as a token of our friendship." He held out a model of a three-wheeled vehicle encased in an acrylic cube about a foot square. It looked expensive and well-made.

Taking it, the Governor said, "Well, sir, thank you," and he rotated the model around, looking at it from several angles. "It looks like a three-wheeled wheelchair. Your company has certainly come a long way."

Spitzner looked pale but continued to smile. The Governor passed the model to Ogg and shook Spitzner's hand.

"I also have a gift for you and Mr. Kaufmann," said the Governor, "and I can truly say it comes from the bottom of my heart." He looked at Ogg, who passed him two wood boxes, each about the size of a cigar box. Kaufmann came around and joined Spitzner next to the Governor.

BUFFALO HUNTING IN ALABAMA

"Maybe you know that I made my career—after football, of course—by running a fishing equipment business. It's what I've most enjoyed doing in life, so please—open the boxes."

Kaufmann opened the top of his box and showed it to the group. Inside was a collection of purple and red rubber worms, flies, and assorted other lures.

"These are a collection of my favorite fishing lures. Many of them I designed myself. Maybe your German fish will like them," said the Governor, smiling.

Kaufmann looked genuinely delighted and looked at the others at the table. "I have never been given a gift like this before," he said with a straight face. "My home is near Starnberger Lake, so I must try these out soon. I'm sure our…German fish will find them very tasty. Thank you, Governor!"

The Governor reached his hand in and held up several of the worms and lures. "Don't thank me yet. I've based my whole business career on deception."

"Deception?" The German CEO looked puzzled. "What is *deception*?"

"Eine Täuschung," Ezra quickly translated.

"What do you mean?" asked Kaufmann.

The Governor, holding up the lures, looked at Kaufmann. "My whole business career has been based on making little pieces of wood and plastic look like food."

Kaufmann smiled. "Fooling fish and fooling people are two different things," he said.

"That's for sure, but those fish can sometimes be difficult to fool," smiled the Governor.

They shook hands and sat down, and the waiters brought the first course. OB-Chemie had chosen the menu in advance. Everyone started their soup, and the Governor and Kaufmann continued to talk about the lures, the Governor taking each one out and describing how best to use it.

"Does your husband really fish?" Ezra asked Ursula Kaufmann.

"I'm sure he will after this," she said, smiling.

Ezra knew there were *Forellen*, or trout, in the Starnberger Lake because he had dined there at a lakeside restaurant. He wondered how many trout Kaufmann would catch with largemouth bass lures.

"Tell me, what does the Atmani Foundation do," asked Ursula Kaufmann.

"We're a non-profit foundation," Ezra answered *"eine gemeinnützige Stiftung, oder eine nicht gewinnorientierte Stiftung. Welche Beschreibung ist besser?"*

"Ja, both are good. You speak our language well. Where did you learn it?"

"In high school, at the university, and then I lived in Frankfurt for a couple of years, and now I'm studying for a month at the Goethe-Institut in Frankfurt," Ezra said.

"You honor us by studying our language," she said. "This Atmani name—it's Italian?"

"No, Mr. Atmani was originally Egyptian. He moved to Alabama as a young man and made his career there." Ezra gave a short bio.

"And so, what does your foundation do?"

"We try to help the State of Alabama with certain types of economic development activities. For instance, we know how difficult it is for German university students to find internships in the United States, so we established a program in Alabama to place European students seeking internships with Alabama companies." Ezra didn't tell her the program was limited to children of decision-makers who the Atmani Foundation was targeting.

This excited Ms. Kaufmann, and she started telling her husband across the table about the Atmani Foundation and its intern program. Ezra added details, also in German, as Ezra and Ursula and Ernst Kaufmann talked back and forth.

The Governor looked at them curiously. Ezra could see that Ogg was starting to get pissed, not understanding the conversation, so Ezra switched back to English, and the others followed.

"Perhaps we will speak about this again soon," said Ursula.

"I look forward to it," said Ezra, and gave her his business card.

As dinner progressed, Ezra observed each person and tried to understand the dynamics. The governor's wife was a tall, angular woman with bleached-blonde hair piled on top of her head. The whites of her eyes surrounded her pupils, which gave her a perpetually startled appearance. She drank only water, and while she occasionally spoke with Mrs. Spitzner, there was no flowing conversation.

It was said that Governor Smith feared only one thing—Ms. Smith. She staunchly opposed drinking and smoking—both passions of the Governor.

The Governor was a good conversationalist. He and Kaufmann talked about hunting and fishing, and the Governor promised to take him hunting when he next visited Alabama. "We have these wild pigs in Alabama," said Smith. "They tear up the woods. The hunting season is year-round, and there's no limit on how many you can kill. When you have a 300-pound hog charging you, you're glad to have an AR-15 with a thirty-round clip."

BUFFALO HUNTING IN ALABAMA

Several times Ezra noticed the Governor eyeing the silver salt-and-pepper shakers on the table. There were several sets of them, all identical, and they were shaped like a pair of quail.

"Fräulein, entschuldigen Sie bitte," Ezra said quietly and motioned the waitress to come closer. He whispered to her in German.

"Ich komme sofort," she replied.

By Ezra's reckoning, Ogg was on his fourth scotch-and-water and appeared to be getting crocked. Ezra watched his eyes.

"How long have you been with the Atmani Foundation?" Ursula asked. Ezra explained that he had just started and had just moved from New York and Silverman to Alabama.

"I've been to New York many times. It's an exciting place, and Silverman Bach is a great company. Why did you move to Alabama?"

"It's my home," said Ezra. "It's where I was born and grew up." She asked him what Alabama was like, and Ezra told her about the hills in the north and the beaches in the south and the open spaces and hot summers and mild winters.

"I must visit sometime," she said.

"You're welcome anytime," Ezra replied.

Ezra tried to make conversation with Blunt. "Have you been with the Governor's security detail long?"

"I work for the Major," said Blunt.

"I'm sorry. You look so fit I assumed you were security."

"If necessary, I imagine I could help out a bit."

I imagine you could, Ezra thought. So, this was one of Ogg's goons.

The governor was working his way through the *Schnitzel* and *Bratkartoffeln*, and the Mercedes guy was talking: "When we first produced the M-Class in Alabama, we had some quality complaints, but over the years, the Alabama vehicles have become very, very good. The Tuscaloosa plant is an important part of our company."

"What Mercedes did in Alabama was incredible," Ezra added. "A new vehicle made in a new plant in a country where Mercedes had never built cars before, with employees who had never built cars before. Any one of those 'new' things could have been a showstopper, but Mercedes did them all at once. We're proud of what's been accomplished." Ezra was echoing a phrase from a briefing paper prepared by the GO Team.

"I agree," said Spitzner.

Ezra wished he could speak with Fritz Meyer, the OB-Chemie guy for the Americas, but the seating arrangement made that difficult, and Ogg appeared to be protective.

Ezra talked to the Germans in both German and English. He found it a touchy situation to finesse because while he was comfortable conversing in German, neither the Governor nor any of the ADIT people could speak a word, and so a conversation in German excluded them.

Ezra decided to speak just enough German to be sure the Germans understood his capabilities and then switched back to English, only dropping into German if something needed clarification.

The Alabama people virtually ignored Ursula Kaufmann, so she and Ezra talked freely in German without interference from others. Ezra thought the Alabama people were making a mistake overlooking Frau Kaufmann.

Dinner ended with cognac and cigars. Ezra noticed the governor passed on both, but Ogg took two cigars and didn't smoke either one. *Looks like an after-dinner conversation in the works*, Ezra thought.

The coats were retrieved, and they all shook hands. Ezra spoke to Ms. Kaufmann, "I have class at eight o'clock in the morning in Frankfurt," he said, "but it's been a great pleasure meeting you tonight."

Ezra shook hands with Smith. "Governor, it's been a great pleasure to meet you and have dinner with your group. Please accept this small token of my appreciation."

Somewhere the waitress had found a small white box. The Governor opened it and sitting on white cotton sat a pair of the silver quail salt-and-pepper shakers. Smith's face opened in a broad smile from ear-to-ear, and he said, "Well son, that's very nice of you. I'll treasure these," and he shook Ezra's hand again.

Ogg glared at Ezra as they shook hands.

"Glad to meet you, Major," said Ezra.

Ogg hissed, "You need to go through us before you have any contact with OB-Chemie."

"Sure thing. I'll copy you on any correspondence," said Ezra. *Hope you read German, asshole.*

As Ezra shook hands with Ernest Blunt, he said, "Nice calluses."

"I do a lot of yard work," Blunt replied.

Yeah, I'll bet, thought Ezra. The calluses were on the knuckles, not the palms. Ezra knew they were called *ken-dako* and were formed from pounding a *makiwara* thousands of times. Hardcore Japanese karate. A *karateka* at another dojo had once told Ezra that "a fist with big knuckles is like a .357 Magnum. With untrained knuckles, you cannot break bricks or blocks. A fist with small knuckles is like a BB gun."

As they waited for the cars to be pulled around, Ogg came up to Ezra and said, "Got a second?"

"Sure." Ogg led him to a corner.

Ogg looked Ezra in the eyes and smiled, and anyone watching the conversation from a distance would have thought it genial.

"Your sand nigger got you a seat at the table tonight, but you need to know that I run economic development in Alabama. You hear me?"

"I hear you."

"Fuck with me, and I'll destroy you," said Ogg and walked off.

***

Ezra caught a train to Frankfurt about 10 p.m. His train car was almost empty, and he dictated his report into his iPad, then edited it and emailed it to the Quants.

Ezra wrote, "Ernst and Ursula Kaufmann sat at opposite ends of the table, not because they were mad at each other, but because they work together as a team. I have no doubt Ursula will report the substance of her conversation with me to her husband. We should treat her as a decision-maker and research her accordingly.

"Also, please check on the children of Mr. and Mrs. Kaufmann. I understand they're in university. Find out the universities they attend and their majors. There may be an internship program opportunity for one or more of them."

Ezra then described the private conversation with Atlas Ogg, and then he wrote: "I met Ernest Blunt this evening. He works for Ogg. I want to know more about him."

After writing the report, Ezra purchased a Pils from the restaurant car, returned to his seat, sipped the beer, and thought about the evening.

Ogg was a real enigma. Ezra had typically found military people to be ahead of the general population in race relations. Ogg's use of the n-word had shocked him. He wondered why Ogg hadn't stayed in the military and tried to make Lt. Colonel. He also wondered about ADIT's culture.

Growing up, Ezra had rarely heard the n-word used, except occasionally by rednecks and older folks in rural areas who had no filter. Most Southerners were as appalled by the word as anyone else. *Ogg must feel he has some sort of special immunity*, Ezra thought.

Ezra was back in Frankfurt by 1 a.m. and caught a taxi to his apartment. He was tired but looked forward to the morning. For the next two days, a Swiss national would help him better understand Swiss German. Ezra doubted he would ever speak *Schweizerdeutsch* even half-fluently, but understanding it might be an advantage in a meeting since most Swiss thought only they understood it.

28

LEADING MILLTOWN TO PROSPERITY

Jake Hatfield stared at the calendar hanging on his office wall. February 2014. He couldn't believe twelve months had passed since taking this job. A year ago, he'd wondered if he was crazy for leaving Auburn, and a year later, he still wondered.

The City of Auburn had enlightened leadership who knew how to develop a community. Milltown was a community that wanted to be better but didn't know how.

That was Jake's job to convince Milltown's leadership to do the hard things necessary to be successful. His biggest challenge, according to Mayor Brooks, was not having enough grey hairs. Jake hoped not. *A few years in this job, though, and I'll be white-headed.*

Slightly more than a year ago, Mayor Brooks, the newly-elected Mayor of Milltown, had called Jake asking if he'd be interested in Milltown's new economic development position.

"How big is your economic development staff?" Jake asked.

"Just you," said the Mayor, "if we hire you."

Jake had never visited Milltown; he had to look it up. He found it located about twenty minutes due east of downtown Birmingham, with two exits off Interstate 20 and only fifteen minutes' drive from the Birmingham Airport.

When Jake typed "Milltown, Alabama" into Google, what came up were mostly articles about the town's high school 3A football championships. Milltown was mighty proud of its Blue Tornado football teams.

Reviewing the *Greatschools.org* website, Jake saw that Milltown's schools were mediocre to poor. That would be a challenge. Jake searched for available Milltown buildings and sites on the state's economic development database—he saw none. To companies and their consultants looking for a location, Milltown didn't exist. According to census data, Milltown had only grown seven percent in ten years—not a healthy growth rate. Jake decided to visit anyway.

During the visit, the small downtown's fundamental beauty struck Jake. It had good bones, despite the empty buildings and faded paint. With a lot of work, Jake felt that Milltown could be the small-town Mayberry that people searched for to raise a family.

A textile mill once dominated downtown, but it had closed twenty years ago, bringing decline and decay. *Live by the sword, die by the sword,* Jake thought.

The previous mayor and council had passed zoning laws which essentially prohibited apartment construction. Jake understood the downside of apartments, but without them, you wouldn't lure many young people.

Jake took the job. After spending four years working for the state's best economic development program, it was time to have a town of his own. He knew what needed to be done—he just had to execute.

"We'll miss you," said Duncan O'Neill, Auburn's economic development director, "but we expect you to be successful. Go for it."

Jake knew that Milltown would never be an Auburn because university towns had special advantages. Milltown would have to find its own path to prosperity. He didn't have Auburn's budget, either, but more resources would come if he could get some success started.

Jake had spent much of the first year talking with Milltown's political and business leaders, and school officials, trying to persuade them to support a vision for community success. If they did the right things, Jake told them, success would come. Achievements the first year had been two small business expansions and one new company with fifteen employees—a reasonable start.

During that first year, Jake was the epitome of a purpose-driven person, but he hadn't started college that way. He had grown up in Troy, Alabama, in a comfortable middle-class family. Unlike some of his friends, who had already decided on careers, Jake went to Auburn with no idea of what to do. So he enrolled in the business school and majored in marketing.

Between his sophomore and junior years, Jake had found a summer job with the City of Auburn's Economic Development Department. He had taken the job to stay at school and party, but everything had clicked that summer: He had helped land a company that employed more than a hundred people. It gave him a good feeling and a sense of achievement.

He continued to work part-time for Auburn's economic development department during his junior and senior years and while earning his Master's in Public Administration, and then he worked full-time for four years.

Within Auburn's economic development department, Jake had found meaning and purpose. Helping people live better lives fulfilled him and appealed to his Southern Baptist upbringing. Helping build a prosperous community was a noble calling. He could make a decent living and do good.

The Birmingham Metro area population was 1.1 million, 210,000 of whom lived in the City of Birmingham. The remainder lived in several dozen bedroom communities surrounding Birmingham.

The most prosperous of these—Mountain Brook, Vestavia, Homewood, and Hoover—could compete for quality-of-life with anywhere in the U.S. They were all located in the southern part of the metro. Milltown was one of the other middle- to lower-middle-class communities scattered throughout the metro area.

Most people who lived in Milltown came from families who had lived there for generations. Milltown was just a dozen miles from downtown Birmingham, but it was a world away. Milltown had some small-town retail, a Walmart, a Lowe's, and a few warehousing and manufacturing operations, but nothing that brought significant wealth into the community. As a result, many Milltown citizens worked elsewhere.

Birmingham was seventy-five percent black; the southern suburbs were all at least seventy-five percent white. Birmingham had suffered both white flight and black flight. Birmingham and the suburbs rarely fought, but they didn't cooperate much, either. Milltown's twelve thousand citizens were about sixty-five percent white and thirty-five percent black.

Jake knew that eighty percent of the new jobs in a community came from existing industry expansions. During his first year, he spent about half his time visiting the owners and plant managers of existing businesses to be sure they were happy. He did this until he had met with all of them.

Auburn had specialized in attracting small and mid-sized companies with advanced technology. Milltown was different and would have to chart its own path to success.

Milltown needed product to sell, and the world had to know about it. Other than vacant downtown retail spaces, the town had just two available buildings suitable for manufacturing and warehousing. It had no industrial park and only one parcel of marginal industrial property.

Modern site selection had become automated. Site consultants searching for buildings or sites no longer contacted the economic development departments of each town. Instead, they relied on a state-level or broker database of available buildings and sites. If a property was listed on the database and met the search criteria, it often made the first cut.

It was amazing how often local economic developers got so involved in various community initiatives that they failed to update the site selection databases. It was basic blocking-and-tackling.

Milltown also needed friends. Auburn was one of the few communities that could generate many of its projects, but Jake needed ADIT and DG&L to bring him opportunities. He had his hands full preparing Milltown to compete for projects rather than spend time trying to generate them.

When Jake wasn't talking with existing companies and local officials, he spent time with ADIT and DG&L officials—he was Milltown's evangelist.

He also needed better tools, like a local wage survey, but his budget didn't have the funds. He needed land for an industrial park. Auburn had built its economic development strategy by developing fine tech parks—a fancy name for modern industrial parks—and it had paid off handsomely.

Jake had his eye on a massive parcel of land in the northwest corner of the city where an industrial park, and even a mega-site, might be carved out. Before taking on that challenge, however, he needed to win some projects to solidify his position.

He regularly updated his thirty-second elevator speech and his ten-minute presentation. Being an economic developer could drive a person crazy, trying to make things happen.

And then three months ago, ADIT had brought in a new Mercedes supplier looking for a location, and everything had clicked. The prospect purchased Jake's one parcel of marginal industrial property to build a seventy-thousand-square-foot manufacturing facility employing 110 people. In just over a year, Jake had achieved real success, but it wouldn't continue without product—he was now totally out of sites.

So, he resolved to develop a new industrial park—and maybe more.

BUFFALO HUNTING IN ALABAMA

Creating an industrial park would be a significant challenge; developing a mega-site would be another whole magnitude of cost and risk. Mega-projects were scarce, but so were good mega-sites. If he could get a mega-site in place, Jake felt it would attract a big project, hopefully before the strain of birthing it got him fired.

He knew an economic developer in Georgia whose county commission had paid $30 million for a mega-site, and every day since the developer's life had been hell from the pressure of trying to land a project and relieving the county of the burdensome debt service.

Even after landing a mega-project, the pressure could be intense because buyer's remorse often set in until the project was operating and its advantages more apparent. Governor Folsom had lost re-election in 1994 after bringing Mercedes to Alabama, and Governor Musgrove had lost re-election in 2004 after landing Nissan, Mississippi's first car plant.

USJ Mining owned 6,500 acres of land in northwest Milltown, north of Interstate 20. A faster-growing metro would have developed this land long ago, but the Birmingham metro was about the slowest-growing major metro in the Southeast U.S., and development pressure was low.

USJ Mining, based in Denver, had acquired the property for pennies an acre in the early 1900s for coal mining. With no debt on the property and Alabama's low property taxes, there was little incentive for them to sell it. They could just sit on the property until development eventually came to them.

Jake envisioned a conventional industrial/tech park and a mega-site on the property. He would try to purchase the tech park property but option the mega-site, which would give Milltown the rights for several years to purchase the mega-site property for a specific price. Hopefully, during the option period, they could find a big prospect.

They would call the industrial park a "tech park" because that was the trend. It implied that the companies located there did advanced manufacturing. It was essentially branding; if a prospect wasn't doing advanced manufacturing, they most likely had already moved offshore.

After agreeing on deal points, they would have tests performed to ensure the land was suitable. Coal mining had occurred on a small portion of the property, but sinkholes were a problem throughout Alabama.

They would check for endangered species and environmental issues and would commission a cultural resources study to ensure no Indian burial grounds or other issues existed. Wetlands would be defined to ensure their locations didn't interfere with site development.

Finally, they would have an engineering company sketch a preliminary design for both the tech park and mega-site, proposing road locations, utility infrastructure, and preliminary cut-and-fill calculations. All this work was required before the property was purchased. It was enormously expensive.

Jake, Mayor Brooks, and their consulting engineer made the first trip to Denver. The Mayor was there so USJ would know that Jake had the authority to negotiate for the city.

Cutting a deal seemed impossible. USJ professed only mild interest in selling the property, but Jack Brannon had provided Jake with financial data showing that USJ was in some distress, and they would welcome cash.

It took months of trips to Denver and protracted negotiations to secure purchase and option prices for the property. Jake kept DG&L and Jack Brannon at Atmani informed of his efforts. Brannon had helped him more than once at Auburn.

USJ refused to sell sites adjacent to the interstate and the parallel state highway. These areas had commercial development potential. USJ finally agreed to discuss the possible sale of 2,500 acres of land.

After six trips to Denver and innumerable emails, they agreed on deal points for a three-hundred-acre industrial/tech park and an option for a 2,200-acre mega-site.

***

Milltown's consulting engineer met with Jake and Mayor Brooks and detailed a plan to evaluate, purchase/option the property, and make it ready for use. The cost was eye-watering.

"There's no way we can do this," said Mayor Brooks. "We don't have the cash, and we don't have the debt capacity to issue bonds for this amount."

"We can't bring in new companies if we have no place to put them," said Jake.

"Can we find a private company to develop the tech park?" wondered the Mayor.

"Private industrial parks are popular in some regions, but it's hard for them to compete in the South since so many governments do industrial parks at-cost, or less, to attract companies," said Jake.

"We both know where we're headed," said the Mayor. "We need to talk with Birmingham."

"It's obvious," agreed Jake. *We're just lucky the property is located next to Birmingham,* he thought.

***

It wasn't easy to arrange a meeting with Mayor Burton, given the history of Birmingham and Milltown.

"Why should we partner with you?" asked Mayor Burton. Jake and Mayor Brooks were sitting in the Mayor's office at Birmingham City Hall.

"Mayor," said Mayor Brooks, "I think you and I are about the same age. We were both in high school in the early '60s when Birmingham was the center of the civil rights struggle. We both saw it all. I'm not proud that Milltown was a Klan stronghold."

He continued, "I know that Birmingham and Milltown haven't often seen eye-to-eye, and we've been to blame for more than our share of that—and we've paid the price for our behavior. I know Birmingham can't forget our past differences, but we need each other now. We have an opportunity—not to forget our past—but to work together for our common benefit and good."

Jake interjected, "Mayor, Birmingham's done a slow-burn for years as other cities in Alabama have won mega-projects. Tuscaloosa got Mercedes, Montgomery got Hyundai, Mobile got Airbus. People in Birmingham ask: 'Where's Birmingham's mega-project? When's our turn coming?'

"There's a simple answer: Never, if you have no mega-sites to offer. For a city of your size, Birmingham has few available and ready industrial sites."

"We have lots of land in Birmingham where a mega-project could locate," countered Mayor Burton.

"Mayor, you don't," said Jake. "Companies won't touch brownfield sites that haven't been cleaned up, and dirt without infrastructure is just dirt. Also, dirt that hasn't been thoroughly evaluated is just dirt." Jake went on to list the studies required before prospects would consider a property a legitimate site.

"Mayor, we can help Birmingham win its mega-project," said Jake.

"But this site you're talking about is in Milltown," said Burton.

"Mayor, Mercedes-Benz is located in the tiny town of Vance, east of Tuscaloosa, but everyone views it as being in Tuscaloosa. Hyundai located in the small town of Hope Hull, south of Montgomery, but everyone understands it's in Montgomery." Jake didn't mention that Hyundai was now located within the city limits of Montgomery.

"We'll get one sooner or later," replied the Birmingham mayor.

"Not without a prepared site ready and waiting," Jake replied. "Hope is not a strategy, and mega-projects aren't something handed-out by Washington in a fair and equitable manner. Mega-projects go to the prepared. These days, site consultants won't even look at land for a mega-project unless it's already gone through some type of site certification."

"Why do we even need a mega-project?" Burton half-asked almost petulantly.

"Mayor," Jake said almost gently. "I worked for Auburn's economic development program for seven years. They built three industrial parks from scratch, and I've seen how it's resulted in world-class companies locating there, providing good-paying jobs.

"I understand and appreciate your strategy of offering sales tax rebates to retail companies to locate in downtown Birmingham. An attractive city center is necessary to attract companies, but retail doesn't add to a city's wealth; it only lives on the wealth already there.

"Growing new companies through your incubator *will* add to your wealth, especially if you can keep them, but you also need the capability to attract mature, world-class companies, and you can do that if you participate with us in this project."

He continued. "Manufacturing jobs are still the easiest way for people without a college degree to become middle-class."

"So, you're sure the companies that would locate in this park—they would be good jobs?" asked Burton.

"Most low-end manufacturing has already left the country," said Jake.

Mayor Burton was silent for a moment. "Even if we could put a deal together," he said, "I don't know if I can get the city council to agree."

"To be truthful, I'm in the same situation," said Mayor Brooks. The two mayors looked at each other. Things had to start somewhere.

***

Jake needed a commitment from both city councils to purchase and develop the tech park site and option the mega-site. Bond counsel told them that Milltown had the debt capacity to issue bonds for half the project.

"Jake, you have my vote," said Mayor Brooks, "but it's up to you to win over the city council and the public. You must convince them we're better off doing this than spending money on parks or schools or other things which might benefit them more immediately."

Jake knew he needed help. He had one chance to get it right. He called Jack Brannon for an appointment.

***

"You gotta sellin' job on your hands, Jake, my boy," said Jack. "Let me tell you about this Milltown bunch: You have six city councilors and the Mayor. Your magic number is four. Right now, I figure you've got a 4-3 vote, including the Mayor. That's not much margin.

"I've had my folks prepare bios on each councilor. Let's review them and discuss the best approach for each. We're goin' to be here a while; I'll order a pizza."

The day before the vote, the Sunday edition of *The Birmingham News* reported that during the previous Christmas holidays, the Hoover Police had arrested a Milltown city councilor for a DUI; his second one. Most Milltown citizens had been unaware of this until the news story broke.

29

THE ART OF PERSUASION

The Milltown City Council met every other Monday at 6 p.m. in the general-purpose room of the recreational complex. At one end of the room, the Mayor and City Council sat on a platform raised about a foot above the audience. The citizens sat in rows of metal folding chairs facing the Mayor and Council. There were 150 or so people in attendance, including Billy Jeff Jenkins.

Billy Jeff had met Jake in the Young Men's Sunday School class of the Milltown First Baptist Church. They had bonded and begun having coffee together every couple of weeks or so.

Jake had described to Billy Jeff his dreams for Milltown, and while Billy Jeff would move wherever necessary to earn a living for his family, he hoped to stay in Milltown. Billy Jeff prayed that Jake would be successful.

Along one wall, the town had mounted framed photos of each year's Milltown Blue Tornado football team. There were three rows—fifty or sixty years of photos. In recent years, they had also added each year's marching band and cheerleaders.

The tech park and mega-site were the first items on the agenda. The clerk read the proposed ordinances, and then the mayor asked Jake to speak.

"You've got to find the hook to close," Jack had said. "It's OK to appeal to their minds, but to win, you must appeal to their hearts."

Jake faced the mayor and council. "Mayor, Councilors, I'm here this evening to talk with you about establishing a technology park and a mega-site for

BUFFALO HUNTING IN ALABAMA

Milltown. You're familiar with the investment required; we've gone over the numbers together, so let me tell you what this is truly all about.

"We think we're having our town meeting now, but Milltown's real town meeting is on Friday nights in the fall when we all gather together at the Blue Tornado stadium and watch the flower of our youth play football, play in the band, or lead cheers for the team."

As he talked, Jake slowly moved his hand in an arc that covered all the photos on the wall. The council and audience followed his motion.

"This is what we've done for the last eighty years. Friday nights are when our town is united in celebration of who we are as citizens of Milltown.

"Look at those young men and women; each of them with their whole life ahead of them. They should be our future." And he paused. "Yet, in most cases, they aren't. Look at the photos for the last twenty years. You see kids there who went to college and many who didn't. Regardless, at some point, they all had to make a living and raise their families, and most of the time, they're not working or raising their families in Milltown.

"Look at the Blue Tornado team for the year 2000. The team members are now about thirty-one years old. Only eleven of the sixty-five members of the 2000 team currently live in Milltown. It's not that most wouldn't like to, but they must go where the jobs are. And they're not in Milltown. I'm talking about good jobs that can support a family; good jobs for those with a college degree and those without one.

"Councilor Hayes, I believe you're up there in the 1993, '94, and '95 photos. How many of the people in your 1995 senior year photo live in Milltown now? I can tell you—only eight out of a team of sixty-three people.

"It's not that they don't love Milltown. Who can grow up in this town and not love it? If you asked them, almost everyone would say they have fond memories of growing up here, but they must go where the jobs are.

"What we're talking about building in Milltown is not so much a tech park or a mega-site, but a place that lets the flower of our youth stay in Milltown and make a living and raise their families and enjoy the benefits of growing up in our beautiful community.

"We can't grow our town and have a prosperous community when so few of our youth return here to make their living and raise their families."

Jake looked to the audience. "To those of you who think that Milltown is big enough, I ask you to look downtown at the vacant retail storefronts; at the fact that there isn't a single restaurant in the downtown area. I believe we could do with a few more people in Milltown. Not runaway growth, but new people to replace those of our citizens who have passed on and healthy growth that will help us fund quality-of-life services we need for our community.

"We're talking about bringing the types of jobs to Milltown that will bring additional wealth to the community, so that new retail and service jobs are created as well. So people will rent and renovate the vacant retail spaces downtown and start new retail businesses. So the community will need additional lawyers and bankers and dentists and doctors. We're talking about bringing *all* kinds of jobs to the city.

"The numbers speak for themselves. We'll have to borrow money to build this tech park and fund the mega-site, but when we do that, we'll be investing in ourselves, just as a family would borrow money to buy a house. We should always be prudent with our finances, but we shouldn't be afraid to invest in ourselves.

"What I'm asking you to do tonight is to invest in a prosperous future for our town." He paused, and the room exploded with clapping. After it died down, Jake said, "If you have questions, I'll be glad to try to answer them."

The vote was 5–1 in favor. The councilor with the DUI hadn't shown up. They were now in the tech park and mega-site business if only Birmingham would join them.

Jack Brannon sat in the audience, watching and listening. *I believe that boy has potential,* he thought.

***

Mayor Burton had given the Milltown people a hard time, but not because of its past. He knew that Milltown's young economic developer was essentially correct. Burton had played devil's advocate because he wanted to hear how much thought they had put into their proposal.

A couple of years previously, Burton had attended a national mayors' conference in Philadelphia where Jim Clifton, the CEO of the Gallup organization, had spoken.

Burton had never forgotten what Clifton had said, and he had afterward read Clifton's book, *The Coming Jobs War*. He had framed a quote from that book, and it sat on his desk:

BUFFALO HUNTING IN ALABAMA

Mayors and leaders of every city, town, and village on Earth must realize that every decision they make should consider the impact, first and foremost, on good jobs.
Have your whole city wage a war for jobs. Everybody in charge of everything needs to focus on job creation…The jobs war is what should get city leaders up in the morning, what they should do all day, and what should keep them from getting to sleep at night.

There were too many poor people in Birmingham. The city council hosted "Fun Days" and "Party in the Park" events for the black neighborhoods, but those were just bread-and-circuses. What the citizens of Birmingham needed were good jobs. When that happened, people's lives would improve, and they would have the money to maintain their houses and neighborhoods.

Burton thought about his brother's son, who had dropped out of college and was wasting his life until he got a job with Mercedes. Mercedes hadn't just provided a good job but gave structure to his nephew's life.

Burton had attended an event at the Mercedes plant to celebrate the production of a new car model, and he was surprised to see that half the workforce appeared to be black, and the workforce, not management was running the event. It was damned inspiring.

His brother told him that Mercedes had a day-care facility at the plant where single parents could leave their children and work their jobs without worrying about their kids. *Those are the kinds of jobs we need in Birmingham*, Burton thought. *I know every job can't be a Mercedes job, but we need more of those types of jobs.*

He had called his friend, Hakim, who he trusted, and asked him what he thought about the Milltown proposal.

"Let me check, and I'll be back with you shortly." In a few minutes, Hakim had called back and said that his people thought it was a good proposal, and so did Sam Atmani.

Burton had decided he was going to support this initiative; he just had to get it through the city council.

***

Birmingham had a mayor-council form of government. It often pitted the mayor, who ran the various departments of government, against the city councilors, who controlled the purse strings. Most of the city councilors wanted to be mayor. It was not a "black versus white" situation since the mayor and seven of the nine city councilors were black. It was often not about public service. It was about ambition and raw political power.

When African Americans first got the vote in the 1960s and started electing black political leaders, they expected black politicians to be the saviors of the black community. Instead, many black political leaders turned out to be as greedy and self-serving as the white leaders had been, but with less experience running government, so it was even less efficient than before.

A black mayor and majority-black city council had now run the city for thirty years, and Burton could see a maturing of the black political class. It was still enormously self-serving, but there was hope.

The citizens elected Birmingham's city councilors by districts, and the councilors were often more concerned about their districts than the city as a whole.

Normally, it would be difficult to get the support of the western councilors for a major project in eastern Birmingham, but the city had recently funded several big initiatives in western Birmingham, so the current situation worked in the Mayor's favor. Election by districts allowed the mayor to manipulate the councilors by granting or withholding favors to districts, so he went to work.

Getting five votes for the tech park/mega-site project turned out to be one of the Mayor's easier manipulations.

30

A TECH PARK

Milltown and Birmingham executed the deal to purchase and develop the tech park property and to option the mega-site property.

Milltown funded its half through a bond issue. The Mayor hoped Jake would quickly attract companies to ease the debt-service payments. Birmingham paid their part in cash.

After they signed the contract, they began a 150-day due diligence period, to ensure the sites had no critical flaws. "We've got to make sure these sites are usable before we buy them," said Jake.

Jack suggested they go ahead and list the tech-park and mega-site on the state's buildings and sites database. "You might get lucky," he said.

"There's a local economic developer—I won't mention her name—who listed a fifty-thousand-square-foot shell building on the state's database. The building didn't exist, but when prospects came to see it, she explained its construction had been delayed and showed them nearby sites. She placed four companies in her industrial parks before constructing that shell building."

"What do companies want from a site?" asked Mayor Brooks.

"Businesses hate unknowns," said Jake. "They don't want projects torpedoed or delayed by some site issue. That's why site certification is so popular.

"For an industrial park, they want pad-ready sites with road access and utilities already brought to the site.

"For the mega-site, I've talked with site consultants, and it's three things," said Jake. "First, we must have control of the property. We don't have to own it, but we need an option in place that guarantees the selling price.

"Second, the site must be capable of being served by all utilities. We don't necessarily have to run the water and sewer lines, but we must have engineered plans documented with price tags and schedules. The prospect needs to be able to know—for example—that bringing water to the site will cost $200,000 and take three months.

"Third, the site must be developable, and we must prove that. We must show we've done an environmental Phase 1, delineated wetlands, conducted endangered species and historical resource studies, and have a preliminary drawing showing where a company can construct buildings, parking lots, etc.

"To sum it up, we must show we've done our homework and have a plan in place to identify and mitigate any risks. Prospects and their consultants want to see completed studies, engineered drawings, engineered estimates on costs and schedules, the number of linear feet of pipe needed, and the size pump station required. They want to see it all down on paper."

31

AN ITALIAN STORY

Since he was a young boy, Giovanni Acardi had wanted to be a medical doctor. It started with his grandmother falling and hitting her head, and he remembered the adults lamenting about no doctor in the village. By the time they took her by boat and car to Verona, the concussion and brain swelling had killed her.

So Giovanni studied hard and resolved to become a doctor and one day return to his small village on the edge of the alpine lake in northern Italy and live there and take care of his people for the rest of his life.

In his third year of medical school in Milano, Giovanni learned his town had a new doctor. Giovanni knew his small town could not support two doctors, and he was already interested in doing medical research, so he shifted his studies in that direction.

He would frequently come back to visit his family, and one day he was sitting in his father's butcher shop, his sixty-five-year-old father working as hard as ever cutting meat. He looked at the white marbling in the meat, and from his studies, he knew how much it contributed to heart disease. And in walked Mr. Mario, his third or fourth cousin, at least eighty-five years old and still hale and hearty, and he ordered a big slab of that fat-marbled meat.

And then it struck him! He had never known of anyone in his village who had a heart attack. He visited with the new doctor, who was a nice guy, and asked him if he'd ever had a patient in the village with heart disease or a heart attack.

"I can't remember one," said the good doctor.

By this time, Dr. Acardi was doing research at Munich's prestigious Ludwig-Maximilians-Universitäts Medical Research School. He decided to focus his research on trying to understand why the people in his village didn't have heart attacks.

Like many Northern Italians, Dr. Acardi looked nothing like the dark and curly-haired American stereotype of an Italian. Most Italian immigrants to the U.S. came from Sicily and Southern Italy, while Dr. Acardi and his ancestors lived near the Austrian border.

Dr. Acardi had a light complexion with aquiline features and longish straight hair with blonde highlights. Many northern Italians had these features, but in Dr. Acardi's case, there was something extra. Tradition said that one of his ancestors came from Sweden more than eight hundred years ago and settled in the small Italian village.

Until recent times, winter snows closed off the passes and isolated the high alpine villages for many months each year. Inevitably, the villagers intermarried, and Acardi married Acardi, though they had strict rules against first cousins marrying each other. The inbreeding, however, resulted in each community having its peculiarities. One village was known for having unattractive people, another for everyone being frugal, though that was probably behavioral, rather than genetic.

In Giovanni's village, many of the Acardis and their neighbors lived well past ninety. And when they finally died, it wasn't from heart disease.

Growing up, Dr. Acardi didn't notice this. One rarely notices the absence of something. Only when he returned to his village as a doctor and noticed the lack of heart disease did he begin to realize that the isolation of his community over the centuries had produced unique genes.

Dr. Acardi conducted a research project in his hometown, and the first person he examined had an HDL of seven, which was dangerously below the normal level of forty. His triglycerides—other blood fats linked to heart disease—were 319, more than twice the norm. Despite these abnormal signs, further examination proved the man's arteries were clear.

Dr. Acardi eventually screened all eleven hundred residents to see if others had the same blood profile. He found 117 people, who he traced to common ancestors born in the late 1700s. Their HDL averaged less than twenty, half of normal for men and women.

He studied the blood samples in greater depth and found the villagers had a mutation in HDL's biggest protein, apoA-1. He dubbed the mutant version apoA-1 Acardi.

At the ripe old age of thirty-four, Doctor Acardi found himself on the edge of a significant medical advance. Through gene therapy, it might be possible to reverse heart disease.

The challenge was, could they synthesize apoA-1 Acardi in large quantities, and if they administered it to patients with heart disease, would it help them? And would it be safe with no significant side effects?

Giovanni felt if he could give this gift to the world, it would be a wondrous thing. His partner, Hans, who had helped with the research project, convinced him it would also be wondrous if they could both become wealthy doing it. They formed a company and patented the discovery.

Munich was a hotbed for biotech companies, and in a short while, their little company came to the attention of OB-Chemie, a large Bavarian chemical company that wanted a greater involvement in the life sciences and who paid them a ridiculous amount of money for the rights to the discovery. OB-Chemie formed OB-Bio to exploit the discovery.

As development progressed, OB-Bio realized the total cost of developing the drug would be very high. Developing the recombinant technology to produce large quantities of the protein would be very expensive. Even a pilot production plant would be costly. And then there were the pre-clinical and clinical trials, which also promised to be expensive.

OB-Bio had not fully realized the investment that would be required, so they looked for an experienced partner with access to additional financing.

The Manchester U.K. region was home to four universities and 250 biotechnology companies that employed more than twenty thousand people. Rochdale Bio, a Manchester-area company, proved to be a partner with financing and biologic pharma manufacturing experience.

If they could get the product through clinical trials, it would be a blockbuster.

Drugs that lowered cholesterol and other blood fats were the world's biggest sellers, with sales of $20 billion in 2012. Lipitor and other statins, even by the most optimistic studies, only cut heart attacks and strokes by one-half, and even in high doses, statins alone couldn't undo artery disease.

Project Victory, the joint venture of OB-Bio and Rochdale Bio, promised a drug that would help clear artery-clogging LDL cholesterol from the body and plaque in artery walls. Clinical trials showed the drug was substantially better than any cholesterol drug on the market.

Their drug would actually *reverse* heart disease, if only they could get it approved for manufacturing.

32

FIRST DAY ON THE JOB

Spring had come to Alabama while Ezra was in Germany. Yellow daffodils were blooming, and dogwood and redbud trees displayed their white and pink blooms under the tall pine canopies which lined highways and interstates.

Back in Alabama, Ezra took a couple of days to get situated. He needed a car and a place to live. Amanda had found him a six-month sub-let on a furnished condo downtown. A professor friend of hers was teaching overseas for a semester. Ezra unpacked his few possessions and made himself at home. Six months would give him time to decide if Alabama was going to work.

Ezra's first thought was to buy an old sports car, but he needed something reliable, so he purchased a two-year-old Ford F-150 truck. The vehicle "more millionaires drive than any other," said the salesman, and he checked on Google and found it to be true. The typical millionaire was a plumbing or electrical contractor or house builder. Ezra had never owned a pickup truck before, but it felt appropriate, moving back to Alabama. *Hell, I might even buy a pair of overalls.*

***

It wasn't his first day on the job, but it *was*.

Ezra arrived at Atmani Headquarters at 6:45 a.m. and entered his code to open the entrance gate. After parking, he found the front door locked. He sat in his truck until 7:15, when Mrs. Avery showed up and unlocked the door. *Different culture*, Ezra thought. *Their life doesn't revolve around the market opening and closing.*

"We all work odd hours, but that's what laptops and iPads are for," Simon later told him. "Most of your work won't be done at your desk."

Mrs. Avery guided Ezra to an office with a glass wall overlooking the lake. Flowering trees framed the view. It was much like Mr. Atmani's, only a fourth the size. Still, *even a Silverman managing director didn't have an office like this*, Ezra thought.

Ezra sat his backpack down. The desk was empty, except for a single sheet of paper:

GO Team meeting at 9 a.m. Conference Room A.

Mrs. Avery handed him a key to the front door. "You already have the gate and alarm codes. First one at work each morning unlocks the front door and disables the alarm. Last one out locks and alarms. Welcome to the Atmani Foundation. Have you met Augustus?" she asked.

Ezra hadn't.

"He'll equip you," she said and led Ezra downstairs. She knocked on a door, and a middle-aged man with longish hair answered.

"This is Augustus, our IT and hardware guy," said Mrs. Avery. "Mr. Atmani sometimes calls the GO Team the 'tip of the spear,' so we started calling Augustus 'the armorer.' He'll help you with hardware and software needs, except for the databases, which the Quants handle."

"A pleasure to meet you," said Augustus, and shook Ezra's hand.

"The basic equipment for a GO Team member is an iPhone, an iPad, and a laptop," said Augustus. "For laptops, we prefer Thinkpads; they're rugged and reliable. You'll use the iPad for reference, training, and probably at least half your presentations, so you get one with all the bells and whistles."

"Sounds good," said Ezra, and he reflected that Chinese factories manufactured all three of his primary tools.

Augustus handed him several boxes of electronics. "The iPad has about thirty gigs of PDF files and presentations already loaded. Collectively, you'll hear those regarded as *The Book*. Simon will explain."

"Download any iPhone and iPad apps you want, but I approve any PC software, and no outside flash drives allowed before I check them out. Here are your passwords." He gave Ezra a sheet of paper. "Questions?"

"Nope," said Ezra and thanked Augustus. As Ezra walked upstairs, he reflected that Silverman had the same flash drive policy.

Ezra returned to his office to find Simon waiting. "I want to introduce you to Hakim, the President & CEO."

In the office next to Mr. Atmani's, a tall, slim, very fit black man, perhaps forty years old, in a suit, stood up and reached over his desk to shake Ezra's hand. He was at least six-and-a-half-feet tall.

"Welcome to Atmani Enterprises. I'm Hakim Adbelkarim. Please sit down." He looked exotic but spoke English with no accent. Ezra and Simon took seats.

"I see you worked for Silverman. I worked there too for several years after school. Thoroughly enjoyed it. They liked my algorithms. People criticize them, and occasionally some of the criticisms are justified. After all, free enterprise is competitive, and occasionally people cross the line. But they're a good company."

"I've always thought so," said Ezra.

"I'm sure Mr. Atmani told you his story, so I will tell you mine because it will help you understand us. When Mr. Atmani lived in Ethiopia, he became good friends with my father, who was a young man at the time.

"After Mr. Atmani moved to America, he arranged for my father to follow him. My father was an Ethiopian Jew. Have you heard of us? According to legend, we are the descendants of King Solomon and the Queen of Sheba.

"As you can imagine, there were very few black Jews in Birmingham in the 1960s—exactly none—so while my Father was very devout, he was also a man, and when he met my Mother, she won his heart. So, a black Ethiopian Jew married a Southern American black woman of the African Methodist Episcopal faith.

"I am the result—the luckiest person in the world. I had two parents who loved me and a godfather—Mr. Atmani—determined to help me reach my potential. He sent me to MIT for my undergraduate degree, then to Wharton, and then back to MIT for a doctorate. After a few years with Silverman, I came back to work for him. Perhaps you and I are a little alike.

"In addition to managing the holding company, I give guidance to the Quants and help them by writing a few algorithms and keeping them focused. For my area of interest—manipulating large amounts of messy data—the world has become a huge cookie jar."

As they left the office, Simon said, "Hakim is Mr. Atmani's right-hand man. There's no one closer to him, especially since Hakim's father died."

***

"Ezra's a German-speaker," said Simon to the group, "so he's going to pick up much of what I've been doing in Europe. He has project finance background, so he's our expert on ways to get projects financed. In terms of industry specialization, we want him to learn about the bioscience industries.

"He must quickly learn a lot; I want each of you to be his teacher. I'll be emailing you a listing of training responsibilities. Fit the training in with your other work.

"We don't often have a new team member, so let's use this opportunity to review our mission and goals," said Simon, who sat at one end of the table.

"Our job is to get Alabama on the shortlists of companies looking for sites. We get to the companies before they start an active site search and before they retain a site consultant or real estate broker. We build relationships with the decision-makers and persuade them to consider Alabama for their expansion or relocation plans. When the active site selection process begins, if Alabama is included, we monitor the project to make sure everything goes well.

"We don't work the active project; Alabama economic developers do that, and our involvement at that stage is just a source of conflict. We *do* understand—since we built the relationship and got the prospect interested in Alabama—that the prospect may want some hand-holding, and that's only natural.

"Each of you is highly competitive, or you wouldn't be here. Remember, we're *not* to be competitive with the rest of the economic development community. We're here to build friends, not enemies."

He continued, "Remember, no one single-handedly wins an economic development project. Teams win projects, not individuals.

"The Atmani Foundation is a recognized part of the economic development community, but only because of Jack and Mrs. Avery. As far as most of the economic development community is concerned, the GO Team doesn't exist. We stay below the radar. We try to avoid contact with site selectors and brokers, with local economic developers, and with the state-level people.

"When we recruited Ezra, most of you were traveling, so let's go around the table and introduce yourself. No speeches; just a few sentences."

BUFFALO HUNTING IN ALABAMA

In addition to Ezra and Simon, there was another guy and two girls in the room. The guy spoke first. He looked about thirty-five years old, solidly built, and well-dressed with a five-day-old beard.

"I'm Marco Hill. I came from Bain, where I consulted with companies about their logistics challenges. I've been here about a year, and my territory is primarily the Midwest, the Southwest, and Spain since I'm a Spanish-speaker. In addition to supply-chain issues, I've been learning about the metals industries and nanotechnology. Welcome to the team."

An Asian girl of medium height spoke next, her glossy black hair reaching to the middle of her back.

"I'm Lisa Chen," she said. "I was born in Hong Kong. My parents moved us to Vancouver in the late '90s, before the Chinese government took over. In 2001 we moved to Alabama, where my father is an engineering professor. My parents taught me Mandarin as well as Cantonese.

"I went to Stanford for my bachelor's and master's in electrical engineering and then worked at Apple for a while. I've been here about nine months. My territory is Silicon Valley and California; also the medical device industry, which has a concentration in the Minneapolis area."

Next to her was the tall, striking blonde that Ezra had met on his previous visit.

"I'm Ella Larsen. I grew up in Alabama and went to Auburn University, where I swam butterfly. I earned a bachelor's and master's in Accounting and then went to Wharton for an MBA. I then worked at McKinsey for several years. I'm learning about the aerospace industry. My parents are Swedish, but I was born in Alabama. My father headed a Swedish manufacturing plant here. My Swedish is OK, but that's a development goal."

"She also won a bronze medal in the Olympics," said Lisa. Ella looked a bit embarrassed.

It was Ezra's turn. "I'm Ezra Drake. I grew up in Alabama and went to Harvard. After that, I worked for Deutsche Bank in Frankfurt and then Silverman Bach in New York. My German has recently gotten better, thanks to a month at the Goethe-Institut in Germany. I'm glad to be back in Alabama, and I look forward to working with you."

"So that's us," said Simon. "We're the tip of the spear. Sean Smith and the Quants provide us with the information we need to do our jobs, and Jack

Brannon and Mrs. Avery run interference for us with the communities, politicians, and economic developers.

"We have a team dinner tonight at Hot and Hot. Be sure and arrange to get home afterward because there *will* be drinking.

"Ezra, you have an appointment with Sean for much of the rest of the day. All our efforts begin with data because as Sean will tell you, without data to guide us, the GO Team are just fools wandering around talking to whoever will listen to us."

33

BIG DATA

"I'm here because of Hakim," said Sean. "He convinced me the Atmani Foundation was serious about data science. For many economic development organizations, data science is their Rolodex file. Most local economic developers don't have the resources to do data-based prospecting. If it's done at all, the states or utilities usually do it."

They were sitting downstairs, talking at Sean's desk over coffee.

"Our team writes algorithms and applies them to databases. That lets us point you guys—the GO Team—where you can be most effective. We started with a database of every company in the U.S. and then narrowed it down to a target group."

"Where'd you get a database like that?"

"The Census Bureau's Longitudinal Business Database would have been ideal, but it's only available to qualified researchers, and business recruiting doesn't qualify, so we looked elsewhere. You familiar with Dun & Bradstreet?"

"Generally."

"Dun & Bradstreet's databases include more than 240 million companies and a hundred million contact names across two hundred countries. Every business at every location has a DUNS Number and data file. If a business has a headquarters, three regional sales offices, two warehouses, and a manufacturing plant, it has seven establishments, seven DUNS Numbers, and seven data files.

"D&B info is great, and their reports have a company history component, but we need more in-depth historical data: How fast has a company grown in revenue and employees in the last three years? Five years? When and where has it expanded geographically?

"Fortunately, some years ago, a company called Walls & Associates worked with Dun & Bradstreet to create the National Establishment Time Series Database—NETS for short. They used D&B archive information to create a database of more than fifty-four million business establishments that existed some or all the time between January 1990 and recent times.

"If a particular establishment has existed the entire time, NETS has more than 350 fields of information, including the number of employees each year at each location, whether the firm added or changed business locations, and much more."

"I've never heard of this database," said Ezra.

"It's mostly used by academia, but we licensed it to drill down to the one-in-a-thousand companies that interests us."

"One in a thousand is still, what—fifty thousand companies?"

"Less than that. One business can have many establishment locations, but you get the idea. First, we eliminated all the companies with less than five employees. That's most of them. Then, we eliminated the non-traded companies. Do you know the term?"

"No."

"Historically, economic developers have focused on attracting manufacturing companies, but they make up just four million of the fifty-four million establishments in the NETS database, and most of them aren't growing.

"A better strategy is to target traded companies, which import wealth into a community. Non-traded companies live off a community's existing wealth. There's a saying that auto plants bring Walmarts, but Walmarts don't bring auto plants. If we attract traded companies, the non-traded companies will start-up or establish a presence.

"For instance, Apple is a traded company and employs about twelve thousand workers in Silicon Valley, but it generates more than sixty thousand additional nontraded service jobs in the area.

"There are 1,088 different 6-digit NAICS codes used to classify U.S. companies. Traded industries account for 778 of those and directly account for about thirty-six percent of total U.S. employment.

BUFFALO HUNTING IN ALABAMA

"Drilling down further, we're not interested in all traded companies, just the ones that are good fits for Alabama. We're not interested in salmon fishing and uranium mining, for instance.

"Also, we're only interested in *growing* companies. If a company's not growing, it won't be adding business locations, and if it *does* try to relocate, that's often a desperation move. We eliminate companies that haven't experienced a recent healthy rate of revenue growth.

"Finally, we eliminate companies who already have a headquarters or manufacturing operation in the Southeast. Unlike California companies who move to Nevada, we're not typically going to attract a company to move from Georgia to Alabama. If a traded company just has a sales office or warehouse in the Southeast, we keep them in the listing.

"To summarize: We look for traded, growing companies who are a good fit for Alabama and who don't have a significant Southeast U.S. presence. We started with more than fifty million business establishments, and we've narrowed it to 10,000 companies—the needles in the haystack. Through this process, we eliminated 99.98 percent of all the companies in the U.S. from consideration as targets."

"Impressive," said Ezra.

"That's the easiest part of the process. "Your job is to contact these companies' decision-makers and build relationships with them. For most economic developers, this type of prospecting is perhaps one percent of what they do. For you, it's almost one hundred percent.

"We identify the target company decision-makers by giving Dun & Bradstreet the DUNS Numbers of the target companies, and they provide us with the names and basic info about the companies' officers.

"So we've identified the target companies and the decision-makers. That's not nearly enough. If you try cold-calling them, you'll have almost no luck.

"You must find a hook—something to let you make contact and build a relationship. The more you know about the decision-makers, the greater the chance of finding a hook. We help you with this.

"We begin by building extensive profiles of each decision-maker. Obviously, with ten thousand target companies and thirty thousand decision-makers, we can't build these profiles manually, so algorithms do most of the work.

"We created a database we call the 'decision-maker profile.' It includes data fields for a wide variety of information about each decision-maker: When and where were they born? Who were their parents? Who were their brothers and sisters? Do they have famous relatives? Where were they raised? What schools did they attend? What's their work history? On what boards do they serve? Did they serve in the military? If so, when and where? Are they married? Do they have a partner? Do they have children?

"We gather information about their beliefs, passions, and social life: What associations do they belong to, and on what boards do they serve? What charities do they support? To which politicians and PACs do they contribute? Who are their friends? Do they exercise? Where do they like to go on vacation? What are their hobbies? What are their passions?

"In short, we try to collect any kind of information we might use as a hook.

"We *do not* illegally gather information in any way—no hacking credit card records or emails. We collect everything legally. Lucky for us, people today seem more than willing to divulge almost every detail of their lives on the web.

"We use algorithms that scrape the web for information about the decision-makers. They search structured databases like LinkedIn and unstructured databases like Wikipedia, Facebook, and Lexus/Nexis. Information that's gathered is automatically inserted into the appropriate database fields in the database profiles.

"We also search all kinds of very specific databases, such as federal election campaign records, to determine who decision-makers support politically; charity databases to find out what causes they support; non-profit foundation 990 forms to see on what boards they serve. At this stage, some of our algorithms are sophisticated because the data being searched is generally messy."

"It sounds like you manipulate an enormous amount of data," said Ezra, trying to be complimentary.

"It's not so much. Have you ever heard of Dataminr? They sort through five hundred million tweets *each day* to find news that could affect the markets before the news services broadcast it. Dataminr's algorithms categorize and analyze every single tweet in *real-time*, weed out the spam, and compare information against newsfeeds, market prices, weather patterns, and other data to determine its significance. Their algorithms also check whether a source has been reliable in the past.

"They built their whole business model on the idea of giving their clients important news ten to fifteen minutes before anyone else hears it. Fifteen minutes can be forever in the stock market. Dataminr's systems gave advanced notice of the Boston Marathon bombing and the Home Depot data breach. *That's* Big Data.

"If a decision-maker has an Alabama connection, that's one of the best hooks for us because they may look more favorably on Alabama. There are thousands of target company decision-makers with Alabama connections. Tim Cook, the Apple CEO, is perhaps the most famous.

"We want to find out if a decision-maker was born in Alabama, grew up in Alabama but attended college in another state, if their spouse is from Alabama, or if their children have attended an Alabama university.

"If they previously worked for a company either based in Alabama or with operations in Alabama, that's gold. If they served in the military and were stationed at one of the military bases in Alabama, that's also gold.

"We even want to know if they attended Space Camp at Huntsville—don't laugh! Many prominent Silicon Valley execs attended Space Camp as a child.

"One of our goals is to know about every person with an Alabama connection who is a decision-maker in business and government.

"We try to find Alabama hooks in two ways: First, we have built or acquired databases of people with Alabama connections that we cross-reference with the listing of target decision-makers. Have you talked with Mrs. Avery yet?"

Ezra nodded.

"We built the program she markets for high school reunions. We're also building a database of everyone who's graduated from Alabama colleges and universities in the last forty-five years. We're about eighty percent finished.

"Foreign students who attend Alabama universities are particularly interesting. Many of them fondly remember their Alabama experience. Some stay in the U.S. and work for American companies; others go back to their home countries. Either way, they're interesting to us. Need a good contact in Seoul, Korea? The Vice-Mayor is an Auburn University graduate.

"We're also building a database of everyone who's been stationed at Alabama's four military bases because we believe that creates a hook. For instance, Fort Rucker in South Alabama trains Army and Air Force helicopter pilots, conducts aircraft testing, and is the home of the Warrant Officer Candidate School and Warrant Officer Career College.

"The Air War College in Montgomery recently graduated 245 students, including forty-four international fellows from forty-one countries. Since 1947, the Air War College has graduated over seven thousand international military officers. Whether these people stay in the military or move to industry jobs, they're potentially useful contacts.

"Another way we find Alabama hooks is by using what we call the Alabama Attributes Database. It's a listing of people, places, and things associated with Alabama. Nick Saban, Cam Newton, Bo Jackson, Harper Lee, NASCAR, Indycar, motorcycle racing, golf, deer and turkey hunting, and so on. We have more than three thousand attributes in the database. We cross-reference this database with the decision-makers' profiles to see what hits we get. We're looking for commonalities between the decision-makers and Alabama.

"Sometimes we turn up interesting connections such as the CEO of a California biotech company whose grandfather was a Tuskegee airman. Or a CEO in Chicago who is a huge Bo Jackson fan. You send that CEO a football autographed by Bo Jackson and ask for fifteen minutes of his time, and it's hard for him to turn you down.

"Did you know that Facebook's Mark Zuckerberg is a big hunter?" Sean asked. "Hunts game and cooks and eats it. Don't you think Zuckerberg would find it fun to hunt twelve-foot alligators in Mobile's delta?"

"Has he?" asked Ezra.

Sean just grinned. "A lot of these attributes are low probability hits, but by using algorithms, the labor cost is manageable.

"We collect all kinds of information about the target companies. Many are public, which makes it easier since public companies have extensive financial reporting requirements. In addition to scraping the web regarding the financial condition and plans of each company, we get our friends at Stein Stewart to help us. You would be surprised to learn what public companies will divulge at quarterly earnings calls.

"Most economic developers have difficulty making meaningful prospect appointments. They decide to visit New York or Chicago or California and try to make appointments with company decision-makers and generally get poor results. They mostly fail for several reasons.

"First, they often don't have a hook, so getting an appointment with a decision-maker is extremely difficult.

"Second, at any given time, many target companies don't have an expansion project upcoming, so they don't have time to chit-chat.

"Finally, successfully making appointments is a numbers game. You want lots of appointments? Then you need lots and lots of prospects.

"It's like the story about the guy who goes to bed with a different girl every night. 'How do you do it,' his friends ask. 'Easy,' he replies, 'I just walk down the street and keep propositioning girls until one says yes.' That's why we work the numbers. When we have thirty thousand target decision-makers, we're going to get appointments."

"How do I manage all this information?" asked Ezra.

"We have software tools to help you. For instance, for each geographical location, our software automatically ranks target company decision-makers by hook strength. If you're making a prospecting trip to Boston, you can easily review the top fifty decision-maker profiles in that area, ranked by hook strength."

"I like that," said Ezra.

"You're a salesman, and salespeople don't like paperwork, but our efforts depend on information like no other economic development organization, so we have some pretty rigid reporting rules. Most important is to document decision-maker meetings. We need your contact report ASAP after a meeting.

"We make it easy for you; just dictate your report into your iPhone and email it. The computer will parse it up, filling in various fields of information. It's your responsibility to review what the algorithm has done and make corrections.

"I understand your focus will be Europe. Unfortunately, there's no NETS database for companies outside the U.S. Also, some European countries have strong privacy laws, so it's harder to compile information about the decision-makers. Still, we have other ways to help you generate prospects. Simon will explain. Any questions?"

34

GO-GO-GOING

The GO Team, minus Simon, grabbed lunch at a deli in a nearby shopping center. Outside the Atmani Foundation's heavily forested acreage, the area felt like typical suburbia.

"How was German school?" asked Ella. "Simon wants me to do language school in Sweden."

"Lots of work, but it helped," said Ezra. He went on to describe the dinner with the Governor and the chemical plant prospect. He didn't mention Ogg.

"What's your sport?" asked Marco.

"Karate," Ezra replied.

"I mean a sport you can use to bond with a prospect."

"Sporting clays?"

"Keep going. We're all pretty good with guns. What else?"

"I used to play a lot of tennis, but haven't lately."

"Good. Start practicing again. You'll be our tennis guy. Lisa's not bad if you need a partner. Do you play golf?"

"Some."

"You might work on it. Golf's popular here. There's no law in Alabama against recording a conversation as long as one party knows it's being recorded, so lots of people do business on golf courses."

"We have people who play the piano, harmonica, violin, and guitar. Do you play an instrument?" asked Ella.

Ezra was starting to feel inadequate. "No," he said.

BUFFALO HUNTING IN ALABAMA

"OK, you'll be a karaoke guy," said Marco. "Better start practicing."

"When we all gave our bios, Simon didn't give his," said Ezra.

"I'm sure he'll fill you in some time," said Ella. "We just think of him as the reincarnation of Sir Richard Francis Burton."

Ezra had heard the name before but made a mental note to look it up. "What's something important that I don't know yet?"

Marco spoke up, "Probably that no one but us wants us to be successful."

"What do you mean?" Ezra asked.

"Well, the general public doesn't know we exist, DG&L and ADIT fear a loss of power if we're successful, and the states we're competing against—if they know about us—certainly don't want us to succeed."

"Does ADIT even know we exist?" asked Ezra.

"Oh, they know. It's hard to keep secrets in the economic development community. For the last six months, I've been building a relationship with a company near Chicago that 3D prints metal parts for the aircraft industry, and then last week, one of ADIT's guys met them at a trade show and heard I've been talking with them. He called me up all pissed off and told me to back off."

"Did you?"

"We don't want infighting in the state, so I called the prospect and told him I was letting ADIT be his primary contact, but the prospect insisted I stay in touch. Not sure yet how I'll finesse it, but we'll make it work."

"Surely ADIT understands that if we're successful, they'll have more projects, and the state will benefit?"

"I don't think they look at it like that," said Marco. "They care more about maintaining power and control than getting a win for the state."

"Maybe if we keep trying, they'll eventually accept us as partners," said Ezra.

"Maybe," said Marco, raising his cup in a salute. "Blessed are the peacemakers."

"Have they showed you the goody vault yet?" Lisa asked, changing the subject.

"The what?"

"The goody vault. Mrs. Avery is the gatekeeper. Have her show you the hundred footballs signed by Nick Saban."

"Or the twenty-five signed copies of *To Kill a Mockingbird*," chimed in Ella.

Lots of new things to absorb. "So why are we called The GO Team?"

"I've heard it's because we're go-go-going all the time," said Ella.

35

SIMON'S CHARGE

"How's the day so far?" Simon asked.

"Good," said Ezra. "Lots to learn. Great people."

"For the next few months, you'll be training but also setting up appointments for your European recruiting trips.

"What we do is hard. There's no sugar-coating it. There are a thousand easier things in economic development besides trying to meet with and persuade decision-makers, but that's *all* we do. No site development, no fundraising, no meetings with mayors listening to their agendas, no economic gardening.

"We just grind it out *all* day *every* day, proactively finding, meeting, and persuading prospects."

Ezra thought of Amanda's running shirt, which said, *My sport is your sport's punishment.*

"It takes a special sort of person to do this. The shrinks said you qualify; that's why we hired you. You're the tip of the spear, and it's up to you to make things happen.

"As we've discussed, our biggest challenge is Alabama's poor reputation. When an Alabama politician does something stupid, the American public thinks 'That's Alabama!' even though politicians do stupid things everywhere. And the media likes to take cheap shots.

"Our poor reputation has many consequences. One is slow population growth, which makes it more challenging to have the necessary skilled labor or to recruit people to move here.

BUFFALO HUNTING IN ALABAMA

"Another is that site selection is all about eliminating sites until one is left, and it's often an easy call to cut Alabama because of its reputation.

"We can't change the state's reputation in the short term. So we put in front of corporate decision-makers truly excellent people who represent and personify Alabama.

"One reason we focus a lot on international companies is that their decision-makers haven't typically grown up in the U.S. and been bombarded by negative press about Alabama.

"I've been handling Europe, but I want you to handle it, except for Spain and Sweden. Lisa and I will handle Asia," said Simon.

"Sounds good," said Ezra.

"By the way, Ogg tried to complain to Mr. Atmani about your being at the Munich dinner. Jack took the call and told him the Governor extended the invitation and to take it up with him."

"Should I have done anything differently?"

"No. Ogg just doesn't want you around. Mr. Atmani will run interference for you with the Governor. Just use good judgment and take care.

"As Sean explained, we have limited data tools for working international companies, but in Germany, Switzerland, Austria, and the U.K., you speak the language, and you can give testimony as someone who has grown up in Alabama. That often piques decision-makers' curiosities and gives us a hook.

"FYI, our challenge hasn't been finding foreign-language speakers; it's finding them with the other skills we need.

"The most critical moments of your job are when you're meeting with decision-makers. You should plan those moments as carefully as any general plans a battle; don't waste a single word. Give prospects the correct information; don't make anything up, and don't exaggerate. If you make a mistake, admit it immediately and move on. If you don't have an answer, find it quickly. Be upfront and direct.

"It's essential that you're well-informed about the state. You should know about historical links between Alabama and the countries you're targeting.

"You need to know about the early German settlements in Alabama, like Cullman and Elberta. You need to know *all* about Huntsville and von Braun and the German rocket team, and the ambivalence in Germany about von Braun. You need to be able to tell others how Mercedes came to Alabama and what it's meant for the state.

"For French decision-makers, you need to know that Mobile was the first capital of French Louisiana, that America first celebrated Mardi Gras in Mobile, and why the capital was moved to New Orleans. You need to know that Napoleon's soldiers tried to establish a vine-and-olive colony in Alabama and how Marengo County was named for one of Napoleon's famous victories. You need to absorb these stories so you can use them at meetings and dinner parties to help build relationships.

"You also need to be well-informed about the American South because you have to sell the South before you can sell Alabama.

"There's an extensive reading list of articles in *The Book*. Best get started. Let me know when you're ready to be tested.

"Here are some other things I want you to do," Simon was reading from his iPad. "They're in no particular order.

"First, you know about the IHK organizations in Germany?" Ezra nodded. "Good. I want you to visit all seventy-nine of them and try to become a regular speaker at their export seminars. You'll need to start scheduling those appointments almost immediately."

"Will do," said Ezra.

"Second, I want you to develop relationships with the decision-makers of Tier Two and Three European auto suppliers who don't yet have U.S. production. We want them to call on you when they're ready to consider the U.S. Marco has done the analysis work on this, so get with him.

"Third, Alabama has been making cars for more than fifteen years, but we still mostly just assemble parts designed and engineered elsewhere. Whenever possible, try to build relationships with auto executives to try and steer some of their design-and-engineering functions to Alabama.

"Fourth, consul generals don't bring us projects, but they can get us cut from projects. Make appointments with the relevant ones and introduce yourself. It's worth a trip or two to Atlanta to meet them.

"Likewise, go and visit the U.S. embassies in your target countries when it fits your schedule. Visit the Foreign and Commercial Service Sections of each embassy and see if there are allies with whom you can work. Mostly these people are interested in promoting U.S. goods abroad, not attracting foreign investment to the U.S., but it's worth checking out.

BUFFALO HUNTING IN ALABAMA

"Fifth, as you know, you're to learn about the biosciences industry segment. We're hopeful this can become an industry strength in Alabama. If you need to talk to experts or go to conferences and trade shows, then go."

"Yes, sir."

"Sixth, I want you fluent in French in two years. We have a tutor for you in Birmingham. When you're in Europe and have downtime, try to spend it in France and work on the language.

"Finally, we're a young organization and still building our culture. You can help because we want to copy certain elements of how Silverman gets highly competent, very competitive people to work together for a common goal."

"So, what *is* our culture?" asked Ezra.

"It's still developing, but here are some key points: We're highly competitive, but we compete against our opponents, not our partners. Our partners are not just the Atmani Foundation people, but the other economic development entities in the state. In some states, economic developers spend more time fighting each other than competing with other states. It's *never* better for a city or town in another state to win a project over a city or town in Alabama.

"Teamwork is critically important. We work together, but we also party together.

"We give you lots of freedom, but we also push you. We can't ask you to build relationships with entrepreneurs and CEOs and then treat you like low-level employees.

"At the same time, we push each other regarding accountability and achievement. Even high-achievers need a kick in the ass occasionally. Things won't always go smoothly because friction is natural in high-achieving teams.

"One other thing about our culture: We believe in testing. We don't take it for granted that you know or have learned something. We test you, to make sure you know it."

Very Reaganesque, Ezra thought.

36

DINNER AT HOT AND HOT

"This place used to be a dump," said Amanda. "At one time, it was a beer bar called The Upside Down Plaza."

It was Tuesday evening, and they were sitting in the Hot and Hot Fish Club in the Highland area of Birmingham. The restaurant building looked like a thick wedge of pie tacked on to a larger building, but inside it was fitted out nice and cozy. Sitting around the table were Simon, Lisa, Marco, Hakim, Ella, Ezra, Amanda, and Sean. Ezra had come alone after work and been surprised to learn they'd invited Amanda.

"Never hurts to have a doctor at our parties," joked Marco.

"We work our schedules to be in the office together a few days each month," said Simon. "Even though we mostly travel alone, it's important we work together and play together. At least once a month, we try to have dinner together."

So they talked and drank, and Amanda gave Ezra detailed recommendations regarding the food. For an appetizer, he settled on the Wagyu Beef Tartare with Quail Egg. For the Entrée, he chose the Wood Fired Mangrove Snapper with Chinese Forbidden Black Rice.

During dinner, they talked about work and travel and the latest happenings in Alabama, and there was much laughing and drinking. Ezra noticed that Ella and Hakim appeared to be something of a number. Maybe the same with Simon and Lisa. He couldn't be sure.

BUFFALO HUNTING IN ALABAMA

As the waiter removed the plates, and they ordered another round of drinks, Simon said, "So two questions and a word game tonight."

"This is something of a tradition at our dinners," whispered Ella to Ezra. "I think he wants to see how sharp we are when we've been drinking."

"Two questions tonight," Simon repeated. "First, who is the most famous and important Alabamian?"

That drew endless discussion. Currently most famous or throughout history? Famous or infamous? *Important* and *famous* were two entirely separate things, some argued.

Various people were offered, including Tim Cook, Charles Barkley, Condoleezza Rice, biologist A.K. Jackson, Joe Louis, Harper Lee, Bo Jackson, Willie Mays, Hank Aaron, Jesse Owens, Bear Bryant (though he wasn't born in Alabama), Tallulah Bankhead, and Jim Rogers.

They never reached a consensus—though a majority thought Harper Lee or Tim Cook should be the answer.

Simon moved on. "Second question: What entity has done the most to promote a positive image of Alabama?"

"Entity?" asked Marco.

"Person, place, or thing," said Simon. Again, it drew vigorous discussion.

"Mercedes—the fact that Alabama makes beautiful, luxury cars driven by CEOs and the wealthy."

"Airbus. People fly miles above the ground and trust their lives to planes made in Alabama."

"Frank Stitt. He created a fine-dining culture in Birmingham."

"Harper Lee. She was the South's conscience, and maybe the nation's."

"Huntsville and NASA. Man went to the moon on the backs of Alabamians."

"And Germans!" added Ezra. They all laughed.

"How about the song, *Sweet Home Alabama*?" said Lisa. "I hear it wherever I go in the world, and it presents a positive image of the state."

In the end, they all agreed that *Sweet Home Alabama,* by Lynyrd Skynyrd, was Alabama's best marketing gift.

"Now for the word game," said Simon. "For the benefit of Ezra and Amanda, we're looking for words that are hard to translate into English. It should ideally be a word, not a phrase. I'm the judge, and the winner gets this!"

And he pulled a bottle from a brown paper bag. "Kessler Sekt, from the oldest champagne factory in Germany.

"Lisa, you begin." They all focused on her.

"OK, there's a Chinese word, *shān zhài*. It means 'mountain fortress' or 'mountain village,' but people use it to refer to the cheap knock-off goods you can find everywhere in China. If you know what you're doing, it's a great way to get good stuff cheap. People usually translate *shān zhài* as 'bootleg' or 'knock-off' goods, but it's also used for anything fake like *shān zhài* politicians and *shān zhài* movie stars."

"Marco?"

"*Pardo*. It's a Spanish word that describes a color between gray and brown."

"Maybe beige or taupe?" asked Ella.

"Maybe," said Marco.

"Hakim?"

"I don't know enough Ethiopian Amharic to play this game, but I do know some French. How about *Espirit d'escalier*? It's when you're in a conversation with someone, and you think of the perfect verbal comeback, but too late. Literally, it means the 'the wit of the staircase,' like you're walking away when it comes to you."

"A good word," said Simon. "Ella, your turn."

"As a kid, I spent summers with my grandma in Sweden. She lived in the country in a house near a lake. There is a Swedish word, *Mångata*, that describes when the moon is shining on water at night and makes a long, wavy shape like a road. It translates as 'moon-road.'"

"That's beautiful," said Lisa. Ezra could see that this group savored interesting words like others savored fine wine.

"Your turn, Ezra," said Simon.

"OK, how about *Backpfeifengesicht*?" said Ezra, a little smugly. "It's a German word that describes a face badly in need of a fist."

"It's been used before," said Simon. "Try another one."

Deflated, Ezra thought furiously. "How about *Handschuhschneeballwerfer*? It's a word used to describe a coward. It means 'someone who wears gloves to throw snowballs.'"

"Is that a sentence or just one word?" asked Hakim.

"It's German—just one word," said Ezra.

"Not bad," said Simon. "My word is *Komorebi*. It's Japanese and refers to the scattered, dappled light effect that happens when sunlight shines through trees."

"Very nice," said Ella.

Lisa's turn again. "I've been working on Arabic. I've found it to be a fascinating language. They have a word, *Ya'aburnee*. It translates as 'you bury me,' but it's used to declare your hope that your lover will outlive you because of how unbearable it would be to live without them."

"We don't exactly get that perspective on the Arab culture from the national news," said Sean, who had been quieter than most of the rest of the group.

"Marco?"

"Spanish sometimes has more specific words than English. For instance, *Manco* is a one-armed man, and *Tuerto* is a one-eyed man. There are no words like that in English."

"Far out," said Sean. Ezra decided that Sean was either drunk or stoned.

"Hakim?"

"How about *Dépaysement*? It's a French word that describes the disorientation and bewilderment you sometimes feel when you're in a completely foreign environment—it's how I felt the first time I went to Japan. It can also be used to describe a changed mental state, like if something major happened in your life."

"I like it," said Ella.

"I do, too," said Ezra. "It's the word I've been searching for since I joined this outfit." Everyone laughed.

"Ella?"

"How about *Buksvåger*?" she said with a little grin. "It's Swedish. It's what two people are to each other if they've both had sex with the same woman. It means 'Belly-in-law.'"

There were embarrassed laughs, and Ezra tried to interpret the glances being flashed around the table.

"Next," said Simon.

"*Treppenwitz*," said Ezra. It's German and means the same thing as *Esprit d'escalier*, but the Germans are more efficient and use one word."

Simon followed. "My second word is *Arigata-meiwaku*. It's a good example of the huge cultural differences between Japan and the U.S. It means an act someone did for you that you didn't want them to do and tried to avoid having them do, but they went ahead anyway, determined to do you a favor, and then bad things happened and caused you a lot of trouble. Yet, in the end, social conventions required you to express your gratitude."

Everyone just sat there for a moment, trying to absorb the meaning of the word. Ezra decided that most everyone was too drunk to absorb such deep thoughts. *If this was Simon's test, they probably all failed.*

Amanda hadn't been playing the word game since she wasn't fluent in other languages, but now she spoke up. "I'm impressed by all the foreign words y'all know, but there are many Southern words that are just as difficult to translate into standard English."

A slight smile formed on Simon's face. "Such as?"

"Such as *Bless your heart*," said Amanda. "It can be a sincere expression of sympathy, or it can be used to congratulate someone for doing something good. It can be said to someone who doesn't understand something that's obvious to everyone else, or it can be used to dress up an insult. It can also be the most Southern 'Fuck you' there is."

***

As they rode home in the cab together, Amanda leaned on Ezra's shoulder and said, "I understand why you've joined this group."

Ezra smiled but said nothing. The lyrics of *Sweet Home Alabama* were playing in his head. He looked over and saw that Amanda had the bottle of Kessler Sekt snugly cradled in one arm.

37

DEATH IN THE FAMILY

Marco was tired; the dinner and three beers had relaxed him. The night air was chilly—bordering on cold—but was fine for riding leathers.

The twists and turns of Grants Mill Road were perfect for motorcycling, but the road was often too busy, as people used it for commuting. But not at 1:20 in the morning. Just him and a solitary vehicle approaching from behind. The headlights were high, like a truck or van. A straight section of road lie ahead, and the vehicle appeared to want to pass. Marco wasn't in a mood to play games, so he let him. A white panel van pulled even on the left, the driver looked at Marco and suddenly jerked the steering wheel to the right and slammed into him. Marco felt his bike go airborne, a white flash, and then nothing.

***

The buzzing awakened him. Ezra blearily saw he had three text messages. The first said:

Come to the office NOW. Be watchful for personal security threats. — Simon.

The other two said the same thing. 4:13 a.m. *What the hell?* he wondered as he struggled out of bed. He powered on the coffee machine, hoping to grab a cup for the drive to work.

After a two-minute shower, he threw on some clothes.

Slightly paranoid and wary, Ezra walked down the condo corridor, took the elevator to the first floor, and exited the building. He had parallel-parked his truck at the curb nearby.

With no traffic, it was a ten-minute drive to the office. Pulling in, he saw cars already there. As he entered his door code, he saw a sign taped to the glass door that said: *large conference room*. Entering the room, he saw Simon and Lisa, and Ella and Hakim, and Jack and Sean. They all looked like he felt.

Simon stood up and spoke. "Ms. Avery's out of town, so this is all of us for now." He paused. "It's my sad duty to tell you that our dear friend, Marco, died earlier this morning."

Everyone stood silent for a moment. "What happened," Ella gasped.

"He was driving his bike home from our dinner." Ezra had heard that Marco lived somewhere east of Birmingham.

"What happened?"

"We haven't received an official report, but he was driving on Grant's Mill Road when he wrecked. If you know that road, there's a section that cuts through the hills with rock walls on each side. He appears to have lost control of the bike and crashed head-on into one of the walls. Broken neck."

"Any other vehicles involved?"

"Not that we know of."

Everyone sat there, saying nothing, lost in their thoughts, and trying to hold it together. Ezra felt out-of-place, not knowing Marco well.

Finally, Ezra said, "What was the security warning about?"

Simon said, "We have no evidence of foul play, but we always want to be extra cautious in a situation like this."

"He didn't seem to drink much at dinner," said Hakim.

"Marco's an expert rider; he could ride better drunk than I can sober," said Lisa. "He taught motorcycle riding at Barber on weekends; he taught me to ride." Her face cracked for a moment. "Maybe he lost control," she sniffed, "but I doubt it. I'm betting a car ran him off the road."

"We don't know," said Simon, "and until we do, it's always prudent to be cautious and keep an eye out. That's all we know now. Go home and try and get some sleep. I'll let you know more when we know more."

As they broke up, Simon asked Ezra to stay for a moment. When they were alone, Simon said, "You've met Ernest Blunt. What's your impression of him?"

Ezra remembered Blunt's fitness and those knuckles. "He appears to be a tough customer. What does he have to do with this?"

"Recently, Marco and Blunt got crossed over a prospect. Marco backed off because it's our policy not to get crossed with other economic development groups, but the prospect wanted Marco to stay involved because of his logistics expertise. Marco told me Blunt wasn't happy about his involvement."

"Maybe not, Simon, but shit, we're economic developers, not spies; we don't kill our competitors. I can't imagine Blunt getting mad enough to harm Marco."

"You can't?" Simon gave Ezra that intense look he remembered when they first met. "Read the news. People kill each other over a pack of cigarettes these days."

"But not educated people," said Ezra.

"Not typically," said Simon. "Educated people generally kill for power—or *lots* of money."

As Ezra drove home, he thought about his first day—the people he had met, all he had to learn, the dinner party, and then the dark ending.

He was glad to be driving a heavy F-150 truck. He periodically glanced into the rearview mirror, checking for headlights, and then Ezra saw the eyes of Atlas Ogg in the mirror staring at him, and in his head, Ezra heard "Fuck with me, and I'll destroy you."

38

THE GOODIE VAULT

The office felt strange. Everyone acted distracted, perhaps wondering, like Ezra, what they had gotten themselves into. During lunch, Ezra visited a firearms shop, and after waiting fifteen minutes for the federal background check walked out with a Beretta nine-millimeter, a Smith & Wesson .38 Special with a laser sight, and holsters for each.

He then spent an hour at the sheriff's office, filling out an application for a concealed carry permit. It would be a couple of weeks before he could pick it up.

After work, he spent two hours at a Hoover indoor shooting range until he felt comfortable with the weapons. The Beretta was accurate for a pistol but a little large to conceal-carry. He would keep it in the truck. He knew his New York and German friends would have a fit about the guns, but *fuck them*—this was Alabama, not New York or Germany.

***

Ezra tried to focus on all he had to learn. Eventually, he found time to ask Mrs. Avery about her goodie vault.

"We've collected and stockpiled small mementos and keepsakes to aid in relationship-building. Many of them are sports-related since many decision-makers identify with sports. A few are literary. Some are business or career-related. All are tied to Alabama in some way."

BUFFALO HUNTING IN ALABAMA

She unlocked a door and showed him in. The room was probably twenty-five feet square, with shelves stacked to the ceiling with boxes. She showed him around.

"Here's about sixty footballs autographed by Nick Saban. I think we started with a hundred. It's a popular item. Here are about forty footballs autographed by Gus Malzahn. We have four footballs with Bear Bryant's signature, but the decision-maker must be very special to get one of those.

"Here's something very nice, which would mean a lot to certain decision-makers. We have twenty-three copies left of Harper Lee's *To Kill a Mockingbird* that she autographed for us. We'll give these away sparingly because she's elderly now, and we may not be able to get many more."

In one corner was a table with wrapping materials and a small machine. "Gift-giving is a formal process in Japan and many countries, and the wrapping is important, so we have a wrapping station here. If you want gifts wrapped, let me do it, since I know how to wrap them properly for each country and occasion."

"Will do," Ezra said.

Small model helicopters in boxes sat stacked on one shelf. "What are those?" Ezra asked.

"Perhaps Sean told you about our program to track people who've served at Alabama military bases. When a GO Team member tries to meet with a decision-maker who took helicopter training at Ft. Rucker, along with the request for an appointment, we send them a model of the helicopter they trained on. Engraved on the base are their name and graduation date."

Mrs. Avery pointed, "Next to the wrapping station is an engraving machine so that we can engrave in-house and with fast turnaround.

"Here are about thirty baseballs and forty footballs signed by Bo Jackson. Very popular. Here are five models of the latest M-Class Mercedes, signed by the current and past heads of the plant." Ezra turned the model around and could see the signatures of Andreas Renschler, Bill Taylor, Ola Källenius, Markus Schäfer, and Jason Hoff.

"A gift should always be appropriate to the stage of the relationship. For instance, there are many Alabamians on major-league baseball teams around the country. If you're working a company in San Francisco, and the profile shows the decision-maker is a Giants fan, you might want to give him or her a baseball signed by Giants pitcher Matt Cain, who is from Dothan, Alabama. It's a nice, thoughtful gift, but not so extravagant that it's inappropriate."

"Do you have an inventory of the gifts available?"

"It's loaded to your iPad and updated regularly. You need to know what we have, so when you're studying the decision-maker profiles, you're aware of gift possibilities."

"Do you have gifts related to von Braun and the German rocket team?" Ezra asked.

"We've acquired some memorabilia off eBay. We also have this for Space Camp alumni," and she showed him a small model of a Saturn 5 rocket, roughly eight inches tall, vertically-mounted to a base. "Like the helicopters, we can engrave the prospect's name and the year they graduated from Space Camp.

"I'm sure they've told you that site selection is an emotional process. Relationship-building is *certainly* emotional, and we pay attention to the small details. In this regard, we're totally shameless," she said.

***

Jack saw Ezra and waved him to his office. "How was your visit to Forrest County?" he asked.

Ezra gave him a short account of what had happened.

"A good start," said Jack. "Remember, though, a successful economic development effort is like a chain; every link has to be strong. Don't be surprised if ten years from now that industrial park is still vacant. Some people think of Alabama as The Third World, but in some ways, the Black Belt is Alabama's Third World. It has a lot of weak and broken links. You're tryin' to weld together just one of the many links necessary to win a project."

***

Jimmy was in town from New York and invited Ezra out for drinks. They met at Avondale Brewery, got their beers, and sat outside. Avondale had a large fenced-in, grassed area behind the brewery with tables and chairs, an outside bar, and a covered stage for a band.

Though it was still winter, the temperature was mild. Ezra's phone said sixty-seven degrees, and the sun had already gone down. A full moon was rising in the west.

Jimmy looked around while drinking his beer. "Look at all these trees and plants," he said. "I love it."

BUFFALO HUNTING IN ALABAMA

Ezra smiled. Jimmy was about to crank up his "I hate New York" *spiel* again. It always started like this.

"There are trees and plants in New York," said Ezra, playing along.

"But mostly in the parks," said Jimmy. "Parks are like zoos for trees and plants. I want to see trees and plants everywhere," he said.

There's something profound there, Ezra thought.

"I just read there's more species of crawfish in Alabama than anywhere in the world," Jimmy said.

"I'm sure the people in New York don't give a shit," said Ezra.

"That's their loss," said Jimmy. He changed the subject. "So, how's it goin'?"

"I'm not sure," said Ezra truthfully.

"Wish you'd gone with DG&L?" Jimmy asked.

"No," said Ezra.

"God, feel this weather," said Jimmy. "In New York, even when it's not snowin', the cold wind blows like a fuckin' hurricane between the skyscrapers and sucks all the sunshine out of my bones. Hell, I have to come home at least once a month just to lay out at the lake and suck up enough sunshine to make it a few more weeks up there."

"It gets cold in Alabama, too," said Ezra.

"Not like New York," said Jimmy, as he lifted his plastic cup of beer. "It gets so cold there I almost stop drinking beer in the winter. Almost."

"What about summer?"

"Oh, it gets hot as hell there, too—only there's less air conditioning.

***

Two days later, Mr. Atmani's Gulfstream flew them to Mobile for Marco Hill's funeral. Ezra was surprised to learn that Marco was from Alabama.

39

BIO, BASEBALL, & BEER

"See that third-base player?" asked Jack. They sat in the stands at Regions Field downtown watching the Birmingham Barons play the Chattanooga Lookouts. "He's really good. They're going to bring him up to the White Sox soon." Around them, hipsters, empty-nesters, curious suburbanites, and corporate supporters packed the seats.

Jack looked at Ezra. "That's the challenge we have with tech startups in Alabama. We start some good companies, but then they're lured away to the majors."

Earlier that afternoon, Jack had stuck his head in Ezra's office and said, "Let's talk about your bioscience studies." He held up two tickets and whispered, "Regions Field—4 p.m.—Barons versus the Lookouts."

The new stadium downtown was the best minor league stadium built in the U.S. in many years, and Birmingham citizens were supporting it with capacity crowds.

"Biocryst was our great bio hope in 1986 when they formed as a spin-off from UAB," said Jack. "They went public in 1994, and we were all very proud. They put us at the forefront of a new way to design drugs. In 2010, after twenty-four years in Birmingham, they moved their headquarters to North Carolina. Vaxin began as a UAB spinoff in 1997. In 2012, they consolidated operations in Maryland. TransMolecular began from research done at UAB, but in 2005 they moved to Massachusetts. SurModics specialized in drug delivery and medical diagnostics. They moved to Minnesota to be closer to the medical device industry.

"Tech companies startup, sometimes with local government help, and then along comes a big company or venture capitalist who flashes some bucks and poof!—they move away. It's happened more and more in recent years as pharma companies find it easier to buy companies than to do their own research. Some startups even have a goal in their business plan to be acquired and likely moved away.

"Occasionally, there's someone truly committed to a community, like Jim Hudson in Huntsville. He founded the biggest bio startup in the state—Research Genetics—and sold it to Invitrogen in California. Instead of just walking away, Jim used his money to start the Hudson-Alpha Institute, which will probably end up producing more and better bio companies than UAB. Huntsville doesn't have nearly the level of bioresearch as Birmingham, but it has more of what counts—entrepreneurship.

"So, as you work on your bioscience studies, here's something to think about: What should be the balance between helping bio companies startup and grow—only to have most of them fail or move away—versus attracting a billion-dollar pharma plant or a huge medical device plant where the company can't just pack up a few computers and leave town? And where people with a wide variety of skills are employed, not just researchers in labs."

"Good question. I don't know," said Ezra.

"Also, chew on this: UAB is the largest economic entity in Metro Birmingham. As a university, it attracts students from elsewhere. As a regional medical center, it attracts patients from elsewhere. As a regional and national research center, it attracts federal, state, and industry research funding. It brings us enormous benefits.

"It's also a great research institution, but most researchers have little interest in starting companies. If they wanted to start companies, they would have gone to business school. They're mostly research nerds happy fiddling in their labs and writing papers. If they happen to discover something with market potential, they're likely to license it to the highest bidder, whoever and wherever they may be, and the benefits of that discovery are largely gone from Alabama.

"I'm not sure it's reasonable to expect UAB to be the source of large numbers of startup companies. As you dig into your bioscience studies, check around. I'll bet you'll find that's true of most research universities."

"Should we give up on bio startups?" asked Ezra.

"Not at all," said Jack, "but we need to figure out how to keep more of 'em."

***

"What did you learn today, grasshopper?" Jack asked in a sing-song Oriental accent. They were drinking beer at Good People Brewery after the game.

Ezra liked Jack's pop phrases from the ancient past, and he made a mental note to look up the "grasshopper" reference.

"Has Lisa heard you talk like that?" Ezra chided jokingly.

"Many times," said Jack in his normal voice. "Puts her in stitches. Then she gives me her impression of a Southern redneck talking. We're not so politically correct in the Atmani Foundation. We're a good team, and everyone has each other's back."

Ezra raised his glass of beer, so light from a nearby window shone through it. "Did you know that making biological medicines is a lot like making beer?" he asked.

Jack's eyebrows lifted. "Oh, do tell," he said. Jack was on his second or third beer, not counting what he had drunk at the game.

"With beer," said Ezra, "the brewer puts yeast in a soup of water, barley, and hops—or wheat—and allows it to ferment, and the yeast grows and converts sugars in the mixture to alcohol. After fermenting, the brewer filters the mixture, and a beautiful glass of beer—like this—is the result. If the brewer makes a wheat beer, it's filtered less, so the beer is cloudy.

"With biological drugs, scientists first discover a protein that acts to inhibit a disease. They need to grow a lot of the protein, so they insert a gene—one they've created by splicing DNA together—into the nucleus of a harmless cell that will multiply and produce the protein. Once the cell is producing the protein, scientists encourage cell growth with enzymes until billions of copies of the original cell develop. This is called a bioengineered cell line. They freeze this cell line in dozens of test-tubes, and it serves as a cell bank for producing future batches of the drug. Think of a bioengineered cell line as the brewer's yeast.

"Then they create a mixture of nutrients, like the barley and hops mixture, unfreeze a test tube, and let the bioengineered cells grow and multiply.

"After some time, when the cells have multiplied and produced a large quantity of protein, they filter and purify it. They only need the protein, so they filter off everything else using centrifuges and specialized filters. Then they either freeze-dry or suspend the protein in liquid.

"Just like a brewery, a biological production plant uses healthy amounts of electricity and gas for the fermentation and purification, so that should interest our DG&L friends."

"So why are these drugs so expensive?" Jack asked.

"First, it's costly to do the research necessary to discover proteins that inhibit diseases. Second, they must find a way to grow the protein. Third, they must go through years of testing to be sure the protein is safe, it's effective, and what's the proper dose. Too much of anything is a poison—even water. These are the Phase I, II, and III clinical trials. Less than twelve percent of drugs that enter clinical trials win regulatory approval.

"Since 1998, pharmaceutical companies have developed over a hundred Alzheimer's disease drugs, but the FDA's only approved four. There have been some real nightmare cases where drugs have caused unintended side effects. Search 'Thalidomide' on Google."

"I remember when that happened," said Jack quietly.

"While they're doing the clinical trials, they're also trying to figure out how to scale up production so they can manufacture the medicine for large numbers of people. With beer, a certain amount of care is necessary to be clean and sanitary, but the alcohol produced helps with that. Absolute cleanliness and sanitation are crucial when making bioengineered drugs that go into peoples' bodies."

"Well, cheers," Jack tapped his glass against Ezra's. "Let's drink our medicine."

"I'm not finished," interrupted Ezra. "You asked, so I'm explaining, and you're just going to have to listen."

Jack smiled.

"Let me give you an example. Up until the last few years, the only real treatment for Psoriasis was to put tar on people's skin. The treatment was almost worse than the disease. Then, scientists discovered a protein that could inhibit the disease. They used recombinant technology to insert this protein into Chinese hamster ovary cells so those cells would act like miniature factories, floating in nutrient, and pumping out proteins in a bioreactor."

"Chinese hamster ovary cells?" asked Jack.

"Sounds crazy, I know, but scientists have used Chinese hamster ovary cells for medical research since the 1940s.

"It's like this sourdough starter mixture my mother had. She fed it, and it continually made new sourdough. She claimed one of our ancestors started it in the 1800s with wild San Francisco yeast, and each generation has passed down the mixture.

"The same is true for cell lines. Once scientists develop a particular cell line, they know its characteristics and keep using it for different experiments.

"Chinese hamster ovary cells are used in many different studies, and they're the most common mammal cells used for industrial production of recombinant proteins. They multiply rapidly in a nutrient culture, make large amounts of proteins, and produce few side effects."

"Cheers to Chinese hamster ovary cells," said Jack as he lifted his beer and took another gulp.

"I'm still not finished. I've been learning all this shit, so you've got to listen," said Ezra. "Enbrel, and biologic drugs like it, represent a major scientific advance for psoriasis treatment."

"I'm impressed. You've been studying."

"There's no room for slackers in this outfit." Ezra then changed the subject. "So, am I the grasshopper, and you're the ant?"

"Nope. Try Googling Kung Fu."

40

FOREIGN INVESTMENT

"The accident report is inconclusive," said Simon. "There's damage to both sides of the motorcycle, but that could have happened from the bike tumbling. They couldn't determine whether Marco lost control or whether another vehicle bumped him.

"I visited the accident scene. It happened on a straight stretch of road where it's hard to see how he would lose control. It's easy to imagine how a passing car might bump him off the road, especially if Marco was caught by surprise. We'll probably never know what happened."

And what we're all wondering—if another vehicle bumped him—was it malicious or accidental? Ezra thought.

Simon and Ezra were driving south on Interstate 65 toward Birmingham. They had attended the ground-breaking for a Japanese electronics plant in Cullman, a small town located halfway between Birmingham and Huntsville. Cullman had an excellent economic development team, good industrial parks, and three interstate interchanges. Simon had made "first contact" with the company.

After a period of silence, Ezra asked, "I enjoyed the ground-breaking, but I wondered how Alabamians feel about foreign investment in the state?"

"People are mostly interested in good jobs," said Simon. "They don't much care who owns the plant. Over the last decade, lower-wage manufacturing jobs—like textile plants—have gone offshore, while higher-skill, higher-wage manufacturing has located here from abroad. The more foreign investment we attract, the more Alabama's household income rises. The loss of U.S. manufacturing jobs in the past couple of decades would have been much worse if foreign-based companies hadn't established manufacturing here."

"Is there such a thing as too much foreign investment?" asked Ezra.

"Maybe, but we're nowhere near that level. In Alabama, five to six percent of private employment comes from foreign-owned companies, ranking us sixteenth among U.S. states. More importantly, Alabama ranks eighth in the percent of foreign investment jobs that come from new facilities, versus acquisitions. That's important because when a foreign company acquires an existing U.S. company, they may expand it or consolidate its operations elsewhere, but when they construct a new plant, that *always* means additional jobs.

"Nationwide, foreign-owned companies in the U.S. employ more than five million workers, including over two million in manufacturing and 1.4 million in advanced industries.

"Foreign-owned operations in the U.S. also tend to be traded industries, which we target. More than thirty-eight percent of foreign-company employment in the U.S. is in manufacturing, compared to less than eleven percent for the general economy.

"Foreign-owned operations employ more than eighteen percent of all U.S. manufacturing workers, and they account for more than twenty percent of U.S. goods exported. In 2013, Honda imported 89,000 vehicles from Japan but exported 109,000 U.S.-made vehicles. BMW exports more than seventy percent of the vehicles they make in South Carolina, and Mercedes-Benz exports more than half the vehicles made in Alabama to 135 different countries.

"The positive impact of traded industries is easy to see if you visit the dozen or so small South Alabama towns with Hyundai suppliers. New wealth is pouring into those towns, instead of the existing wealth just being recirculated.

"Foreign-owned companies help raise Alabama's median income. Foreign firms paid an average of $77,000 per worker in 2011, compared to the U.S. average of $60,000. They also spent more than twice the private sector average on worker benefits.

"There's also a skills benefit: Alabamians who work for foreign companies like Honda and Mercedes learn advanced skills useful for the rest of their lives.

"Finally, foreign-based companies have given Alabama a chance when many American companies haven't. Detroit passed us over, but Mercedes came in and said, 'We think Alabama is a good place to build automobiles,' and Alabamians appreciated that. After Mercedes began making cars here, some Alabamians who had traditionally bought Buicks and Cadillacs started buying Mercedes, and not just Mercedes made in Alabama, but E-Classes and S-Classes made in Germany. Alabamians appreciated Mercedes' investment in the state.

"So chasing foreign investment is a high priority for us. Fortunately, we don't have to travel the entire world to do it. Most foreign investment comes from just a few places within a few countries.

"Almost half of all U.S. jobs in foreign-owned companies have parent companies based in just ten global city-regions. Since 2010, more than eighty percent of new foreign investment has come from seven European countries plus Japan, Canada, Australia, and Korea.

"Sometimes, people worry about 'foreign ownership,' but what does that mean? We think of Mercedes-Benz as being German. They're headquartered in Germany, but they're owned by investors all over the world. German investors own thirty-six percent of Daimler, Mercedes' parent company, but non-German Europeans own twenty-nine percent, and U.S. investors own twenty-four percent. Kuwait owns seven percent, and Asians own three percent. The current head of Daimler is German, but the next head will probably be Swedish.

"There's a brief about all this in *The Book*. Study it, and I'll give you the test in two weeks."

***

As they walked toward the front door of the Atmani Foundation's offices, Simon reached over and picked a full, reddish-pink flower from a leafy bush, holding the stem between his thumb and forefinger.

"Do you know what this is?"

"A flower."

"It's not *just* a flower; it's the official state flower of Alabama—the camellia. The state adopted it in 1959, replacing the goldenrod. Do you know what else is special about it?"

"Again, I feel stupid," Ezra said.

"They're foreign. They're native to eastern and southern Asia but are now cultivated in the Southeastern states in many different varieties and colors."

41

TRAINING

"We have to stop meeting like this," Ezra panted, flat on his back and breathing hard. Ella's damp blonde hair hung in his face. "Uhhh," grunted Ezra as Ella jammed her shoulder further under his chin while she cranked his extended arm, so the tendons were about to pop.

"Submit," she commanded, and he tapped out immediately. Ella was the strongest girl he had ever met, but it was more than that. She had taken him down with a leg sweep and then finished him off with her superior knowledge of jiu-jitsu. His hesitation about learning it vanished.

He lay on the mat, exhausted and sweaty, and thought about how he had ended up like this.

***

"We ask you to travel alone, so we train everyone to be competent in self-defense. I take personal charge of that. Unless you hear otherwise, let's plan to work out in the gym every day from 3:30 to 5:00," Simon had told him.

The first day had been purely boxing with gloves and headgear. Without the protection of kicks, Ezra realized he wasn't that good a puncher. His head seemed to easily find Simon's glove. "You've got to move your head more," Simon said.

They did this for two more days, and just when Ezra felt he was becoming a better puncher, they switched to nothing but kicks. No use of the hands, except to push off and block.

BUFFALO HUNTING IN ALABAMA

"Kicks take longer to develop, so you've got to disguise them or distract the opponent," Simon said as he pushed Ezra violently with both hands. Off-balance, Ezra took a roundhouse kick to the head and went down. If not for the headgear, it would have put him out.

"Hey, I wasn't expecting that!"

"You need to expect anything anytime," Simon countered.

The next day, they switched to sparring with hands and feet—conventional karate—and most of the time without pads or gloves.

"I took karate mainly for exercise, not self-defense," said Ezra, as they were toweling off at the end of a session."

"That's nice, but now you've got to learn to protect yourself."

The next day they continued with karate. Simon's movements were uncannily smooth, like an industrial robot on an assembly line. No wasted motion; everything fast and efficient.

As they sparred, Simon said, "Your karate is pretty good. The problem is, most fights end up on the ground," and he slammed his head and shoulder into Ezra's midsection, hooked his hands around Ezra's knees, and took him to the ground. In two seconds, Ezra found his arm twisted into an unnatural position, and he had to tap out.

For the rest of the session, they sparred, with Simon taking him down at-will and locking his arm or leg in a position where pressure, if applied, would break it or tear ligaments and tendons. Ezra tried to keep from being taken down but was rarely successful.

"You must be careful even practicing this one because it's easy to tear up a knee joint." They were prone on the mat, and Simon had clamped Ezra's right leg between both of his. Simon used the power of his shoulder and bicep to apply a gentle twisting motion to Ezra's foot. Ezra could feel his knee joint strain.

"It's called the heel hook, and its brother, the reverse heel hook, is even nastier. Don't even practice it with anyone else but me, until I tell you it's OK."

"So how'm I doing?" asked Ezra after a week or so.

"Right now, Ella would beat you in a fight."

"That'll be the day."

***

He lay there on the mat, exhausted, fully aware of the irony of it all. His previous employer had threatened to fire him for taking martial arts. *Be careful what you ask for*, he thought. He couldn't help but smile at the absurdity of life.

As Ella started to get up, he said something smart, and she grinned and kneed him in the ribs. "You're a slow learner," she said.

***

On days when Simon was traveling, a sensei from a local jiu-jitsu dojo was there to train him. Ezra's primary deficiency was grappling, and Simon was trying to correct that as quickly as possible.

Ezra sat on the tile bench in the shower at the end of a session, too tired to stand up, hot water beating on his head and shoulders.

"You might want to do some running or bicycling on weekends to improve your endurance," said the sensei.

***

Most of Europe was seven hours ahead of Alabama, and Ezra typically spent his mornings making calls to officials at the seventy-nine *Industrie- und Handelskammern (IHK)*, or local chambers of commerce, located across Germany. Unlike the U.S., most German companies were required to join one.

The IHKs supported German companies and their employees in multiple ways, from sponsoring worker training to fostering technology transfer. Exports were always promoted. With less than four percent of the U.S. land area and a fourth the population, Germany exported almost as much as the entire United States, and exports were critical to the German economy.

Ezra's goal was to become a regular speaker at IHK export seminars. This would give him exposure to thousands of German companies. Simon sat with him for the first morning of calls and occasionally made a comment between calls, but after that first morning, Ezra was on his own.

Ezra had French lessons five days a week. Two of those days consisted of lunch with his French teacher.

"Many meetings happen over lunch or dinner. You must not just be a French speaker, but a student of French cuisine and dinner conversation," said Mme. Laforêt. The other three days of the week, she met him at the Atmani Foundation at 1 p.m. for lessons.

The rest of the time, Ezra learned about the State of Alabama, either by reading books and articles, meeting with selected people, or visiting

BUFFALO HUNTING IN ALABAMA

communities. He had thought he knew a lot about Alabama, but quickly realized he didn't.

"So how's it going?" asked Jack one afternoon as they were having beers.

"I can't decide what's being worked more," said Ezra, "my mind or body."

"That's good," said Jack. "We need you ready as soon as possible."

"I have a question," said Ezra, "I've visited much of the state in the last couple of months. I know there's some very poor areas—I've visited some of them—but I don't see Alabama being near the bottom in quality of life compared to other states."

"We're not," said Jack.

"But that's what the numbers say."

"Which numbers?" Jack asked.

"Median household income and per capita income," replied Ezra.

"You have to understand what those numbers really mean," said Jack. "First, they're before-tax numbers. Federal income taxes are progressive, so people with less income don't just pay lower taxes. They pay a smaller percentage of their income as taxes. And then Alabama's state and local taxes are lower than most states—property tax is the lowest. If you look at median income after taxes, Alabama ranks about forty-first—still not great, but better than forty-sixth or forty-seventh.

"Also, the cost-of-living is lower in Alabama—about fifteen percent less than the national average. You can buy a nice house here that would cost a fortune elsewhere, and you can fill up your car with gas for less, too. When median income is adjusted for cost-of-living, we rank about thirty-fifth or so compared to the other states. Still not great, but much better than forty-sixth or forty-seventh.

"And then there's a final factor to consider: When median or per capita income is calculated, the total income generated by everyone in the state is divided by the total population. The Labor Force Participation Rate is the percent of the population who are working or actively looking for work. In Alabama and much of the South, it's often ten or fifteen percent lower than other parts of the country like Iowa, Minnesota, and Massachusetts. This means that for those who work, their real income is typically higher than Alabama's mean or average income."

"Why the lower percentage of people working or looking for work?" asked Ezra.

"For some, it's a lifestyle choice. They choose to stay home and care for children or elderly parents, or they're willing to trade less income for more free time."

"On the downside, the loss of manufacturing from offshoring in the early 2000s wiped out a tremendous number of jobs, and it's easy for people to become discouraged when they can't find work—or work that pays a decent wage. That's a big part of our job—to help these people and help the state improve."

"For someone who supposedly doesn't know much about data, you're pretty well-informed."

42

DRINKS AT THE COLLINS BAR

Ezra met Amanda at The Collins Bar downtown for drinks after work. Massive paper airplanes hung from the ceiling, and the wall behind the bar featured a huge Periodic Table of Elements chart like Ezra remembered from high school chemistry. Instead of the two-letter symbols for oxygen and iron and other elements, the chart listed abbreviations and names of notable Birmingham places and people.

Amanda claimed to like the place for its cocktails, and they were superb, but Ezra knew she liked having her name on the Periodic Table. In big letters was "DR," with "Amanda Kling" printed in small letters below. While the attraction had been mutual and instant, Ezra still didn't know that much about Amanda.

They had ordered drinks, and Ezra was just about to ask her how she ended up on the chart with people like Taylor Hicks, Frank Stitt, and Condoleezza Rice when Scott walked in.

"Fancy seeing you here," said Ezra.

"Just coming to visit my little sister. And you," replied Scott.

"I got tired of Scott asking me questions about your new job, so I told him to ask you directly," said Amanda.

"Suits me," said Ezra, "but you may be disappointed. I'm not sure what the hell I'm doing."

"I'm disappointed you chose to go with those guys," said Scott. "Atmani's foundation may be around in a year or two, but their economic development effort probably won't be."

"Well, I've screwed up before," said Ezra. "And I understand why you're pissed off at me. If I were in your shoes, I'd be pissed off, too."

Scott just stared at him. "We know what you guys are doing. You're trying to make the Big Data thing work to generate prospects. We've looked at it, and we think it's too risky."

Scott pulled a piece of paper from his wallet. "Here's something that Dan Ariely, a professor at Duke University, wrote. He said 'Big data is like teenage sex: everyone talks about it, nobody really knows how to do it, everyone thinks everyone else is doing it, so everyone claims they are doing it...' "

"There's a lot of truth to that statement," said Ezra. "Whenever new technology emerges, there's always a sorting out of what will work and what won't. Failures happen, but every time you use Google Maps, you're using Big Data. We think what we're doing will work—it already has."

"There's a lot of front-end costs, and there's no guarantee it will generate significant numbers of prospects," said Scott. "We think it's more cost-effective to visit with site consultants."

"If Mr. Atmani wants to spend his money trying to make Big Data work for economic development instead of owning a sports team or sending a rocket to Mars, why not? Rich people do all sorts of crazy and innovative things with their money. And there are worse things than trying and failing," said Ezra. "Half of all startup companies don't last five years. Only a third make it to ten years. Business is risky. Most businesses, anyway."

"In our company's culture, failures get much more attention than successes. You can have a hundred successes, but a failure can kill your chances for advancement. I've been there too many years to risk a failure," said Scott.

And that's one reason I'm not working for you guys, thought Ezra.

43

TRIP TO JAPAN

It had still been dark when Scott Kling left home for the drive to the Birmingham Airport, then the forty-minute flight to Atlanta, then twenty minutes navigating through the airport to the International Concourse. The 11 a.m. departure had been on-time.

Scott settled into the Delta business-class seat for the fourteen-hour flight to Tokyo. He felt a twinge in his back from a long drive off the seventh hole at Shoal Creek the previous day.

He shouldn't have played golf with the Japan trip upcoming, but a friend had called with a tee time, and the temptation had been too much. It was such a beautiful course. Scott's goal was to own a house there, retire at sixty, and play golf for the rest of his life.

Scott was thankful that Ogg wasn't sitting nearby. He was six or seven rows up, out of sight, and mostly out of mind. They had met at the Atlanta airport, and Scott had found him sober and in the suck-up mode Ogg often used with elected officials.

Scott sipped a gin and tonic and hoped it would help his back. *Everything in moderation. It would be good for Ogg to learn that.*

He reclined the seat and closed his eyes. The rush of the outside air was comforting white noise. It was 10:30 a.m. Birmingham time, so he wasn't the least bit tired—just relaxed.

He couldn't remember the last time he'd had fourteen hours where he didn't have to go somewhere or meet someone, and where he could listen to music, eat, and drink what he wanted—and just think. And so that's what he did. He had never been to Japan and reflected now on why he was going.

Even as a teenager, Scott realized he didn't possess the sheer brilliance of his younger sister, but he was smart, loyal, persistent, and a hard worker.

He spent high school playing football instead of studying but still got accepted into Alabama and graduated with a degree in mechanical engineering. He had also made it into Sigma Nu, one of the best fraternities on campus.

In college, he had secured an internship with DG&L, and after graduating, they offered him a full-time job. At DG&L, one advanced by working in as many departments as possible, to gain the necessary experience for leadership. He had accepted every opportunity offered.

Another way to get ahead was to belong to one of the ruling families, either through blood or marriage. Scott had once heard DG&L described as an *aristocratic meritocracy*. Being a member of one of the ruling families didn't guarantee success, but if you were smart and loyal and kept your nose clean, doors were opened.

Esther had been a cute, blonde-haired Alpha Chi at Alabama, and they were married in July after graduating in May, but neither she nor Scott had any family connections at DG&L.

They had worked hard, and Esther had been the wife that any corporate climber needed to succeed. He could never have become Vice President without her. In recent years, reaching middle-age and with all the kids' activities, their passion had lessened, but it had been good for a long while.

He had devoted himself to DG&L, and DG&L had been good to him. Scott had started at the Letson Steam Plant and steadily advanced. He had hated the stint in Human Resources but loved his years in Gas Distribution Engineering. His last job was District Manager in the Birmingham Division, punching his ticket in local marketing and customer service.

Five months ago, the Vice President of Economic Development had suffered a massive heart attack and died during a prospecting trip to Chicago. The powers-that-be suggested Scott interview for the position, and when the offer came, he accepted it immediately. DG&L had resisted title inflation—being a Vice President meant something. Even the newer VP positions—in areas like ethics and diversity—carried real power.

DG&L had two types of management positions: One called for specialized knowledge, which limited the applicants. Promoting an engineer with no accounting experience to CFO, or taking a non-lawyer and putting him in a legal position just wouldn't work. Other positions, however, were those where up-and-coming executives could "punch their ticket" to gain experience. For these jobs, good managerial skills were considered more important than formal qualifications or experience.

The VP of Economic Development was one of those positions. DG&L viewed economic development as a variation of marketing or public relations—or even governmental affairs.

Scott had tinkered with cars as a teenager and viewed organizations as engines to be tuned. Sometimes, the carburetors needed to be adjusted. Other times, a component had to be rebuilt or replaced. Occasionally, the entire engine needed rebuilding.

Scott's new department was in good shape; only a minor tune-up was in order.

Economic development was a new experience. Almost immediately, he began meeting with the mayors and economic developers of numerous Alabama cities and towns to understand their needs. The message was clear: They wanted good-paying jobs for their communities.

From those interviews, Scott had formed an opinion about ADIT. His meeting with the ADIT Director confirmed his suspicion that the ADIT Director knew less about economic development than he did.

Scott had to tread carefully because he wanted ADIT's projects—as many as possible—to locate in DG&L's service area.

ADIT had multiple problems. First, it had good people and mediocre people, but improvements were difficult because people couldn't be fired, reassigned, or properly rewarded because of the state's Competence Plan.

Second, the Competence Plan didn't foster teamwork; a manager couldn't enforce consequences for not working together.

Third, many of the recruiters had little business experience and no in-depth knowledge of industry segments. ADIT had one recruiter with agribusiness experience, but many of the project managers and marketing people were lifelong government bureaucrats, kids just out of college, or people with friends or relatives in government.

Fourth, their marketing plan was outdated. It consisted of advertising in economic development trade publications, catering to a select few site consultants, inviting prospects and site consultants to turkey shoots and football games, maintaining offices in multiple foreign countries, and constant travel to wherever crossed their mind.

ADIT was an eight-cylinder engine operating on three or four cylinders; it needed an engine rebuild. Kling learned that Ogg had successfully resisted change for many years.

The current ADIT Director, Todd Nelson, seemed more interested in the New York and Washington restaurant scene than making tough management decisions. Scott had already talked to Governmental Affairs about pushing the Governor to make some needed changes.

ADIT had some good people. Mark Thornton, who headed Project Management, had been an executive with Hyatt in Australia and had returned to Montgomery several years ago to help care for his elderly mother. *Not many people would do that*, Scott thought. Scott and Mark were becoming friends.

Scott tried to schedule a meeting with Sam Atmani, but he was never available. *Generals meet with Generals*, Scott thought. A meeting with Jack Brannon was offered. Scott learned that Brannon was highly regarded among economic developers, so they met at the Atmani Foundation headquarters.

During Scott's meetings with local officials, many had complimented the Atmani Foundation's efforts to assist communities. *If that's all they did*, thought Scott, he wouldn't have an issue with them. He just didn't want them recruiting.

Scott had quickly realized that economic developers were fiercely protective of their turf, and the most coveted jobs were those that involved a lot of travel. Many people liked to travel, especially when someone else was paying for it.

"What advice would you give me, being new to economic development?" Scott asked.

"I'm in no position to give you advice," said Jack. "You guys are the oldest and most powerful economic development entity in the state, and you've got great people. If I suggested anything, it would be to listen to your people."

"I do, but I want *your* opinion," Scott pushed.

Jack paused for a moment then looked Scott in the eye. "OK, I would say that there is nothing particularly hard about any aspect of economic development; there's just so much to learn, and no matter how smart a person is, it takes time to learn the job—and a lot of what you need to know is the *politics* of various issues."

"What do you mean? Give me an example."

"OK, economic developers regard what they do as a specialized profession. When they see someone like you with no experience come in and want to change things, they're naturally skeptical and resistant."

"I've experienced a bit of that. How do you recommend I handle it?"

"Just do what you're doing now, and listen to people."

"I've listened to my people, and they're interested in knowing what the Atmani Foundation is doing in economic development. Can you give me an overview?"

Jack replied, "We view economic development as a 'big tent,' which includes many kinds of economic development efforts. Nothing we're doing in economic development competes with your initiatives. We're committed to being a partner with you and ADIT and the other economic development players." Jack then went on to detail some of the things that he and Mrs. Avery were doing in the way of local community development.

"That's impressive," said Scott, "but what about the other people on-board—people like Ezra Drake or that Simon guy."

"Nothing those people do interferes with what you and ADIT are doing."

"We keep hearing whispers...," pressed Scott.

"Most of our activities involve gathering information about companies and the economy. We're trying to understand better what makes the economy tick."

"Why do I feel you're not being straight with me?" Scott continued to press.

Jack stared at Scott and pushed back. "Mr. Atmani has had a good relationship with the last half-dozen CEOs at DG&L. Both entities have respected each other. It's our intention and hope to continue that relationship. We respect you and know you do much good for Alabama."

Jack then continued: "Have you seen us try to muscle in on projects? Have you ever heard of our meeting with a site consultant?"

"So, what *are* you doing?" challenged Scott.

"It's like this: If it's D-Day during World War II, you guys and ADIT are the troops landing on the Normandy beaches, and we're the guys who parachuted in a couple of days before to weaken the Nazis behind the lines.

"We're not interested in companies with projects; we're not interested in talking with brokers or site selection people; we're not interested in working projects. We want to talk to companies before they have projects. Our goal is to find the growing companies that are going to have projects and positively affect their perception of Alabama, so when they *do* have projects, they're more likely to include Alabama as a possibility. That's it. Nobody in Alabama is doing what we're doing; it's an unserved area."

"You're targeting companies that don't even have projects?" Scott sounded a bit incredulous.

"Yes, but they *will* have projects based on their growth rate."

"How do you find these companies?"

"That's proprietary information, but if we do our job right, you and your people will find more companies considering Alabama for projects. That doesn't mean Alabama *wins* more projects; that's up to you and ADIT and the communities, but our job is to help get Alabama into consideration."

Scott shifted gears. "What do you think of ADIT?" he asked.

"Probably about what you do," answered Jack. "They are what they are, and we don't see major change happening there anytime soon. The bureaucracy is just too entrenched.

"In some regards, the state doesn't treat economic development seriously. If the state has a big legal case, they often use high-powered, big-dollar lawyers to maximize their chances of winning, but if they've got an economic development project that can bring a thousand jobs and tens of millions of tax revenue to the state, they often have a $75,000/year project manager running it who may be a kid a few years out of college or a government bureaucrat who's never worked in the business world."

"But for big projects, I understand the Governor and the state's business and political leaders get directly involved."

"That's true, but many projects are lost in the early stages before the power players even know about the project. Site selection is a process of elimination, and early in a project, poor information, missing a deadline, or a wrong word from a project manager can get us cut. Then one day, out of the blue, Alabama's leaders read that North Carolina's landed a major project to do this or that.

"Also, while Alabama handles the big projects with their 'A-Team,' those folks aren't typically available for the 50- and 100-employee projects, and those can add up to a lot of jobs over time.

"ADIT project managers, over their careers, can win or lose the state tens of thousands—maybe hundreds of thousands of jobs, and given their job responsibilities, they're not paid much. What sense does that make?"

"As a start, I think ADIT's marketing efforts need revamping," said Scott. How do you feel about that?"

BUFFALO HUNTING IN ALABAMA

"It does," said Jack, "but it's been tried before and failed."

"I understand," said Scott, "but DG&L hasn't pushed it to be done."

"Watch out for Atlas Ogg," said Jack. "He's a drunk but a very smart and cunning drunk. Don't underestimate him."

Word had spread quickly in the economic development community that Scott wanted changes made to ADIT. Ogg had heard about it and came to talk. Scott learned that Ogg felt it his duty to periodically "educate" new ADIT directors and people at DG&L about how economic development worked.

"Scott," he said, "if you want to understand what we do, you need to experience it first-hand. Come with me to Asia, and I'll show you how we market to international prospects. It's not just about the language. It's understanding the culture and being able to navigate efficiently in foreign countries. The only way for you to understand is for me to show you. Also, we need to talk about the Atmani Foundation and how to get rid of it."

From his first day as VP, people had urged Scott to "go traveling." To date, he had resisted, except to visit a few site consultants. He preferred to spend time understanding the needs of his department and the communities in Alabama.

Also, he spent about a quarter of his time on chairing the United Way fund drive, serving on non-profit boards, and other such activities. After all, DG&L's core competence was relationships with public officials, and managing this core competence took time.

"I'll give you one week," said Scott, "including the time needed to get there and back." They talked dates and checked schedules, and they set a departure date.

Scott's recruiter who worked Asia offered to make the trip with him, but Scott turned him down. *Generals talk with generals*, Scott thought. His guy continued to insist there were things about Asia where he could be valuable, but Scott said, "I'll handle it."

Ogg wasn't exactly a general, but the principle applied. Scott wanted to talk directly with Ogg and make the evaluation himself, to be sure he was taking the correct course.

A month before the trip, Scott had received a call from Jack Brannon. "Scott? I understand you're going on a prospecting trip with ADIT to Japan."

"That's right."

"We have a couple of companies we think you should meet. Remember when the Tōhoku earthquake happened in Japan a couple of years ago? It created the tsunami that led to the Fukushima nuclear disaster. That created huge problems for Japanese companies with single-source suppliers in the affected areas. Honda had ten parts suppliers located in the evacuation zone around the Fukushima power plant. In all, about a hundred automotive suppliers faced problems from the disaster.

"There was already worry about single-source suppliers. Back in 2007, Riken controlled fifty percent of the Japanese piston-ring market, and their plant in Kashiwazaki suffered earthquake damage. Four automakers had to suspend vehicle production.

"About the same time as Fukushima, monsoon flooding in Thailand took out many electronics suppliers. These natural disasters have caused companies to take a hard look at the vulnerability of their supply chains.

"Companies continually pressure suppliers to lower prices, and the easiest way to do that is to optimize production at one plant, but if something bad happens to that plant, it can shut down the supply chain. So now they're pressuring their suppliers to have more than one production plant and to be geographically diversified.

"We researched Japanese auto suppliers who supplied Honda's, Nissan's, and Toyota's U.S. assembly plants from a single-plant location in Japan. That's produced a couple of prospects. I'll send you their contact information and backgrounds."

An email had followed with detailed profiles of the two companies and how to contact them. One company produced a special type of paint additive used in certain colors of Honda cars. The other manufactured an impeller used in water pumps used by Honda and Nissan. The water pump manufacturer was already manufacturing in the U.S.

Scott called Jack to thank him. "How did you get this information?"

"Our Analytics Group put most of it together, with help from one of our people who's a logistics expert," replied Jack. "Simon, our Japanese speaker, made the initial contacts and validated the prospects."

***

Scott woke to the steady roar of the jet engines. He had shifted in the seat, and his aching back had woken him. *Damned back.* He glanced at the flight map and saw they were almost to Anchorage, Alaska. *A long, long way still to go,* he thought.

44

TOKYO

The plane arrived mid-afternoon, Tokyo time, and Mr. Hayato Ito, ADIT's business development person in Japan, met them.

Tokyo astounded Scott. It looked like a larger and denser version of New York, with neon and video screens covering large areas of the city, like Times Square in New York. Vehicles drove on the wrong side of the road, and the traffic signs were almost all in Japanese. Driving would be a nightmare.

And the people! Tremendous numbers of young, beautiful, slim, fresh-faced Japanese girls on the streets enchanted Scott. There weren't many Japanese in Alabama, and the ones Scott had met tended to be middle-aged businessmen and their housewives. These young, beautiful girls in stylish business suits and fashion outfits captivated him and caused him to view Asians in a whole new light.

Ogg had provided Scott with a trip itinerary, and Scott had put his foot down about staying at the Park Hyatt Hotel. There was no way he was paying that much for a hotel room, and he wondered how Ogg, as a state employee, could get away with it. They ended up staying at the Imperial Hotel, a grand old place near the Imperial Palace, for less cost.

"It's a good hotel," Ogg admitted, "I've stayed here before. The Imperial Palace is just over there," he pointed, "and it's only a few minutes' walk to the Ginza District."

The lobby was massive, and the service and courtesy were impeccable. Scott appreciated the Japanese way of quiet understatement.

Scott's hotel room was modern and tastefully furnished. At first glance, one could mistake it for an upscale American hotel room. Details differed, however. Scott was most amused by the bathroom toilet seat with its panel of controls on the side containing more buttons than a TV remote. He felt like Captain Kirk commanding the Starship Commode. One button fired a stream of warm water directly at his anus. He had to admit it felt pretty good. Another button heated the toilet seat. The toilet even played music when he flushed.

Scott decided there was something about this that ran counter to his basic Christian values as if too much pleasure was being derived from the process of elimination.

Ogg had suggested Scott take advantage of the hotel's in-room massage service to help his back, but Scott just wanted to catch a few hours' sleep before dinner. He took a couple of Aleve and found a central control panel next to the bed that controlled the lights, drapes, shades, and air conditioning. *Very nice*, he thought. The sheets were clean and crisp, and he was soon fast asleep.

Scott met Ogg and Ito in the lobby at 9 p.m. for dinner.

"How is your room?" asked Ito.

"Very nice, Ito-san," said Scott, "though a few things are *different* than America."

"Such as the toilets?" asked Ito.

"Yes," said Scott.

"That is one of our fetishes," said Ito. "Perhaps because our houses are so small, we feel we deserve a bit of pampering when we take our rest. You know the toilets require electricity for all the extra features? After the Fukushima tragedy in 2011, we were very short of electricity because the government shut down all the nuclear reactors. A study showed that Japanese toilets account for four percent of household energy use. It also showed there were four thousand *pachinko* parlors in the Tokyo area—you know *pachinko?*—and they used two times as much power as Tokyo's main subway system, yet no one suggested we unplug our toilets and shut down our pachinko games. We must have our little pleasures," he smiled.

"I'm hungry," said Ogg. "The Ginza District is just a five-minute walk, so let's eat there."

As they walked, Scott was surprised to see several groups of well-dressed businessmen visibly intoxicated.

"It's part of our culture," said Ito, "But our people are not aggressive drunks. They mostly just fall asleep at the train stations." Scott wondered if Ito was subtly drawing a contrast with Ogg.

"Drinking is viewed differently in Japan," said Ogg. "Almost all cultures have lunch or dinner together to build trust, but in Japan, sharing large amounts of alcohol is just as important.

"The Japs," continued Ogg, "use drinking not just to communicate with clients and *Gaijin* like us but also among their own team. *Nomunication* is the word they have for it. *Nomu* means to drink. You know what *communication* is, so *nomunication* describes a way to build relationships through drinking."

As they dined at a fish restaurant in Ginza, Ito said, "Japanese culture is all about *wa*, or harmony within a group. It's about cooperation, understanding social roles, and avoiding open conflict."

"I don't see how they do it," said Ogg. "I'm not happy unless I yell at my people at least once a day. Isn't that right, Ito?"

Scott saw how a Japanese person showed embarrassment. Ito continued, "Drinking is a way for business people to express their real thoughts, their *hone* feelings. Things discussed during a night of drinking are never discussed the next day."

"So, you're supposed to get drunk and make a fool of yourself in front of people you don't even know?" asked Scott. "How will they take us seriously?"

"That's exactly the point," said Ogg. "Getting drunk tells them you are willing to remove social barriers. You won't look stupid." Ogg emptied his beer glass. "*Kampai*. That's the Japanese word for 'bottoms up.' You'll hear it a lot."

"Don't worry about looking stupid," Hayato Ito reassured Scott. "The more you drink, the more they will see you as trustworthy."

"There's also the karaoke," said Ogg. "You'll be expected to sing. You might start thinking about three or four good songs. You're going to have to do it. I always go with *New York, New York* and *Don't Cry for me Argentina*, so I've got dibs on those," Ogg said. He continued, "Japanese business relationships are built by eating, drinking, talking, laughing, and singing songs in karaoke rooms. Just relax; you'll get used to it!"

Scott wondered if Ogg really liked Japanese business culture or if he just liked getting drunk.

***

The next morning, they had breakfast in the seventeenth-floor breakfast room overlooking the Imperial Gardens. Honda was the first appointment of the day.

"Honda has invested more than $9 billion in North America," said Ogg. "They employ more than thirty-three thousand people and purchase more than $16 billion in parts and materials from suppliers in North America.

"Honda is a good example of how Japan is culturally different," said Ogg. "Compare Mercedes and Honda in Alabama: They each have huge plants, and each makes hundreds of thousands of vehicles a year, but otherwise they're very different.

"The Mercedes plant on I-20 west of Birmingham sits like a gigantic white city visible to everyone. You don't even see the Honda plant on I-20 east of Birmingham. It's very near the interstate, but they didn't want to be *visible* from the interstate. Most people drive that portion of I-20 without knowing the plant's there. Old Japanese saying," said Ogg in a sing-song voice, "The nail that sticks up from the others gets hammered." Ito said nothing.

Ogg continued, "There are other differences: The Mercedes plant mostly assembles parts, not makes them. The engines and transmissions and body panels come from suppliers, and the emphasis is on Just-in-Time and Just-in-Sequence.

"In contrast, the Alabama Honda plant is highly integrated. It casts and builds its engines, it stamps its body panels, and it even plastic-injects its bumpers. Mercedes workers wear different-colored polo shirts; Honda workers all wear white coveralls. The styles and operations are very different, yet they are both very successful."

As they took a short taxi ride to meet Honda, Scott knew that Ogg had some rough edges, but he was impressed that Ogg appeared to know his business.

Honda's headquarters was in Minami, only ten minutes from the Imperial Hotel. After a short conversation with the Honda executive in charge of North American production, an assistant gave Scott and Ogg a tour of the marketing center. It included previews of the new cars, Honda's business jet, which was almost ready for production (and manufactured in North Carolina), and a demo of Asimo, the four-foot-tall Honda robot that seemed to do everything.

Scott knew he was getting the *Gaijin* visitor's treatment. Nothing they were doing here would affect what Honda did in Alabama. It was an orientation for Scott and activity for Ogg and Ito.

BUFFALO HUNTING IN ALABAMA

After Honda, they had a light lunch and took a taxi to the American Embassy, where they met with the U.S. Foreign and Commercial Service. About halfway through the meeting, Scott realized the Commercial Service people weren't interested in Japanese companies investing in the U.S. Their mission was to help U.S. companies develop export markets in Japan. Again, more activity to fill an itinerary.

Scott was still jet-lagged, and his back was bothering him, and Ogg was either jet-lagged or hungover, so they had an early dinner in the hotel and adjourned to their rooms.

***

Ogg had organized the trip around an *Invest in the United States* seminar hosted by the Council of American States in Japan (CASJ). More than a hundred people were in attendance.

Twenty-one U.S. states had offices in Japan—mostly in Tokyo. At the seminar, each state gave a five-minute presentation, followed by a couple of minutes of questions from the audience. Most of the state representatives were native Japanese, like Mr. Ito, but two were Americans who had "gone native."

Scott found it interesting to watch the two Americans give their presentations. They not only spoke Japanese, but their body posture and the way they used their hands were characteristically Japanese. Scott could see that communication was much more than just speaking the language.

All the presentations were in Japanese, and Scott didn't understand a word, but the best presentations told their stories through good photos and illustrations. Scott had some suggestions for PowerPoint slides Mr. Ito might want to use.

A reception followed, and as Scott mingled with the attendees, he slowly realized that most of them either worked in Japan for an American state, had come over from the U.S. for the seminar, or represented some Japanese or American government agency. Someone who saw a seminar photo might mistakenly assume the audience was full of investment prospects.

Scott had given Ogg the Atmani Foundation leads, and Ogg had instructed Mr. Ito to arrange the appointments. When Mr. Ito had contacted Ata Chemical, he had invited them to attend the seminar, and they had accepted, so an *ichijikai*, or dinner party, was arranged following the symposium.

***

"Even companies located far away from the Fukushima tragedy and the coast where the tsunami hit are under pressure to have a manufacturing location outside Japan," explained the CFO of Ata Chemical, "because in Japan an earthquake can strike anywhere."

They were having dinner at a restaurant in Shinjuku, not far from the Park Hyatt. The CFO had already explained that Ata Chemical made a special additive used in the paint sprayed on cars manufactured by Honda and Nissan. Honda had plants in Ohio, Ontario, and Alabama, and Nissan had plants in Tennessee and Mississippi, so Ata focused on those states, plus others in the general area, such as Kentucky.

So far, they had talked with Tennessee. During dinner with the three Ata representatives, they discussed the company's criteria for a U.S. location, and Scott and Ogg talked about Alabama and its advantages, with Ito translating when necessary.

They all drank throughout dinner, and afterward, they went bar-hopping with the Ata representatives.

"We call this the *nijikai*, or afterparty," said Ito. After a few more drinks, they ended up at a karaoke place for more drinks. "This is the *sanjikai*, or after-afterparty," said Ito. By this time, Scott was wasted and did a karaoke rendition of *Louie Louie*. He was determined to win this prospect. The Ata CFO had ordered *sake* for everyone, and Ito whispered to Scott that it would be an insult to reject the offer, so Scott sipped the rice liquor warmed in a porcelain bottle and served in small porcelain cups. That went several more rounds.

As they said their goodbyes to the Ata people and stumbled back to the hotel, Scott said, "I couldn't have taken much more of that."

"You should be glad they didn't want to do the *yojikai*, which is the after-after-afterparty," said Ito.

The next morning, Scott blamed the liquor, in general, for his hangover, but he blamed the *sake* for his erotic dreams of beautiful Japanese girls in business suits and fashionable outfits.

45

GOTEMBA

Ogg knew that Scott loved golf, so he had arranged an outing. They left Tokyo Shinjuku Station at 7:15 a.m., and the train trip took about an hour. They were playing at a place called Gotemba at the base of Mt. Fujiyama, one of Japan's most famous landmarks.

Scott knew he was an idiot for playing golf with an injured back, *but how many opportunities do I have to play golf at the base of Mt. Fuji?* he thought.

The land in Gotemba was flat and lush, and the volcano cone of Mt. Fuji, topped with snow, towered overhead. According to Ogg, one could play golf here year-round. A friend of Ito's made the fourth, and they played the first nine holes then took an hour for lunch. Scott was careful, and his back seemed OK.

They were teeing off on the thirteenth hole when Ogg put the question to him, "So whatcha think, Scott? Hasn't this trip been worthwhile? Don't you see that understanding the culture is important to getting anything done?"

Scott didn't want to be rude. "Atlas, I appreciate what you've done, putting this trip together and trying to make it interesting, but I'm interested in results; we've got to produce. Otherwise, this is just sightseeing on the taxpayers' and shareholders' dime."

"Oh, we'll produce results," said Ogg, "but you've got to understand that economic development projects take time to develop; companies can't be hurried." *And how many years have you been doing this?* thought Scott.

Teeing off on the fifteenth hole, it all went wrong, and Scott ended up writhing on the ground. Ito and Ogg helped him to the golf cart and asked if he needed a doctor. Scott insisted the other three finish playing the back nine. He sat in the golf cart and gritted his teeth and tried to appear stoic as his back spasmed.

After golf, tradition called for relaxing in the natural hot springs bath at the clubhouse. Everything was provided, including towels, soap, and shampoo. The baths were separated by gender, and no swimsuits were worn. Hayato Ito had inducted many Alabamians into the Japanese bathing ritual, and he quietly advised Scott.

They removed their clothes in the changing room, put them in baskets, and locked them in coin lockers. They each had a small towel they carried for modesty into the bathing area. They first rinsed their bodies with tap water, then entered the large indoor bath filled with mineral water.

Scott slowly lowered his body into the water. It was very hot, but he didn't mind since the hot water helped mask the pain. They left the small towels at the side of the bath.

They soaked for a long while, and Scott could feel his back muscles beginning to relax and his pain diminish.

They grabbed their towels, emerged from the water, sat on stools, and washed their bodies with soap at the water taps. Ito helped Scott sit on the low stool. Scott noticed that Ogg tended to strut around—what his grandfather would call a "bank-walker."

"Don't get soap in the water," Ito advised in a low voice. Scott noticed everyone was very tidy, cleaning up their bath space. They re-entered the bath and soaked again. The setting was a bit strange, but Scott could think of nothing better for his back.

When they finally reemerged, they didn't rinse off, so the hot spring minerals could have full effect on their bodies.

Dinner was a huge buffet with Japanese sushi, American-style steak and ribs, and dishes from different countries. A sign in English said, "Seven different kitchens!" Scott found this ideal, being able to pick out the food he wanted because Japanese menus were confusing, and he was tired of Ito ordering for him.

The Gotemba Kogan Brewery featured five different types of beer brewed on-site using Mt. Fuji spring water, and each person drew their beer from "ever-flowing taps."

They stayed overnight on-site at the Gotemba Resort Hotel.

BUFFALO HUNTING IN ALABAMA

After helping Scott to his room, Ogg grabbed Hayato Ito by the upper arm. "Ito-san," Ogg said, "I want you to listen carefully…"

***

The next morning, it was three hours by train from Gotemba to Nagoya, to meet with the second prospect provided by the Atmani Foundation. Totyo Precision was situated in an industrial park on Nagoya's edge. They did a full-plant tour to see the various engine components produced by the company.

Walking on the concrete plant floor was agony to Scott's back. It had been a long process getting up that morning, but he had struggled through with Aleve and a long, hot shower.

The company hosted lunch at a local restaurant with traditional *zashiki* seating—low tables and pillows on the floor. Ito helped Scott sit down. At the end of the lunch and discussion, standing up caused beads of sweat to pop on Scott's forehead.

The train from Nagoya to Kyoto took only an hour; they were meeting that evening with a company that Ogg and Ito had been talking with for a long while and hoped would soon have a project.

Scott had looked forward to seeing Kyoto. For more than a thousand years, it had been the capital of Imperial Japan. While Tokyo looked like a *Blade Runner* version of New York, Kyoto was the home of the old Imperial Palace and hundreds of Buddhist temples and Shinto shrines.

Scott was a World War II buff, and he knew that Kyoto was the original target for the first atom bomb. Henry Stimson, the Secretary of War, had intervened to save the city because he had visited there on his honeymoon and diplomatic visits. Scott hoped that somewhere in the city, Kyoto had an appropriate statue honoring Stimson.

They stayed in a different hotel from the itinerary. "A last-minute deal opened up," Ogg said. Scott was glad to see that Ogg had become more interested in being thrifty.

Ogg and Ito helped Scott out of the train and to the hotel. Waiting for them at check-in was an older Japanese man in a long white coat and an attractive young woman, similarly dressed.

"We know you don't want a doctor, but as your hosts, it's our responsibility to take care of you," said Ogg. "We asked Dr. Takao to meet us at the hotel to check you out. Dr. Takao doesn't speak English, so Ito will translate. The young lady is his nurse."

Scott was in too much pain to resist. They assisted him to his hotel room and helped him take off his shirt and lay on his stomach, with a flat pillow underneath, to keep his back from arching. The doctor probed with his hands along Scott's spine and back muscles until Scott jumped and writhed in pain. Dr. Takao spoke to Ito.

"The doctor says you have a muscle injury, not a bone problem. That is very good! He say the muscle must be relaxed, so it doesn't tighten up and bring more pain. He will give you some medicine. Then you must sleep."

The doctor fumbled around in his medical bag and put several pills in a plastic bottle.

"He say you should take the blue pill now. It will help relax your muscles. In four hours, take another blue pill and also the white pill. It will help you sleep. I will call and wake you at 7 p.m. and remind you to take the pills. Dr. Takao's nurse is going to put hot packs on your back to help the muscles relax and heal."

"What about the meeting tonight?"

"We'll see how you feel."

***

Scott lay half-awake, his eyes closed, not interested in fully waking up because his back didn't hurt, and the bed was comfortable. Another dream; this one even more vivid. Dr. Takao's nurse had come to his room to put more hot packs on his back. She gently massaged his back muscles, to see if the medicine and hot packs were working, and then it had turned into something more. The nurse looked like one of the beautiful girls he had seen on the Tokyo streets, and in his dream, he had imagined her being even more beautiful naked and straddling him on the bed, her long black hair moving across her breasts and shoulders, and her perfume had an exotic smell. *How does one dream smells?*

Scott shifted slightly and pulled the covers up further. He froze. He could smell the same perfume now.

Was it maybe the cleaning lady's perfume? A rising panic. *Would a cleaning lady wear perfume?* Did his penis have that after-sex slight raw feel to it, or was that just his imagination? Had Ogg set him up? Scott didn't know what to think.

They caught the Shinkansen bullet train back to Tokyo. The trip took two-and-a-half hours. The long taxi ride to Narita was quiet. As they waited in the departure lounge for the 5:30 p.m. return flight to Atlanta, Ogg said, "I hope this trip has helped you understand how we do marketing."

BUFFALO HUNTING IN ALABAMA

Scott looked at him carefully, searching for a hidden meaning or threat in his eyes or body language, but Ogg gave no indication. "It was very educational," was all Scott would say. He reflected that the best appointments had come from leads supplied by the Atmani Foundation.

In a few moments, with a hard glint in his eye, Ogg said, "We have a saying in economic development that what happens on the road stays on the road."

Scott said nothing.

"So let's not talk about getting drunk or playing golf," said Ogg.

Scott wondered if Ogg was toying with him.

***

Esther had been remarkably welcoming after his return from Japan. They hadn't been that passionate in a long while.

Maybe I need to travel more, thought Scott, as he returned to his office after lunch. He was in a good mood because his back was better, and he was finally catching up on the work he had missed while traveling.

Scott spied a letter-sized manila envelope on his desk. It was addressed to him and marked "Personal and Confidential: To be opened only by Addressee." There was no return address. With a sinking feeling, Scott unsealed the envelope and pulled out several full-page color photos. He realized his marriage and career with DG&L might be over.

***

Ogg remembered the old days when all this had been much more work. The film cameras had been big and bulky, and shooting in low-light conditions had been difficult. They'd even had to put the camera in a small separate room with mirrored glass to shoot through.

Today, the same electronics used in smartphones meant half a dozen tiny cameras captured every action in high definition at the best possible angle.

Ogg watched as Kimi straddled Kling in the bed, Kling's mouth open in passion. She slowed her humping and slipped Kling's cock from between her legs and pumped him with her hand, as semen ejaculated in long spurts into the air.

Ito had even slo-moed the final few seconds, so the semen hung in the air like a porno version of an old Sam Peckinpah movie.

46

FAMILY PICNIC

Ezra was in Alabama for a week between Europe trips. On Saturday morning, he accompanied Amanda to the annual Kling family picnic at her parent's house at Lake Martin. In addition to Scott, Amanda had an older brother and sister, and they had children, so a half-dozen kids were playing in the back yard of the big old white house on the point of the lake. Ezra and Scott ended up talking.

"So, how was Japan?" Ezra asked.

"A lot of time and money spent for marginal results," said Scott glumly.

"Weren't our leads any good?" Ezra asked.

"Yours were the only good ones," Scott admitted.

Ezra said, "Credit Simon, our Japanese speaker; we really need an additional one."

"When you look for a Japanese speaker, also look for an alcoholic because working prospects in Japan almost demands it," replied Scott with a small smile.

The day was food and games and pontoon boat rides and all the things that made lake life so attractive. As the afternoon passed, Ezra and Amanda rode bikes to the small general store a few miles down the road.

Later, they sat in yard chairs and watched the sun drop behind the trees on the far side of the lake. As darkness set in, the crickets started their tunes, and tree frogs added their croaks. Lightning bugs made second-long streaks of light as they rose out of the dark green lawn. To Ezra, their cold yellow flashes were as magical as when he was a kid.

"Scott seems unhappy," said Ezra.

"He's certainly down in the dumps, but I don't think you're the cause," said Amanda. "Esther said he was OK when he first returned from Japan, but then he went into a deep depression. You know he hurt his back while playing golf?"

"In Japan?"

"Before, but then he re-hurt it in Japan."

"Maybe that's it."

"No," replied Amanda, "something else is going on. Something happened on that trip that's changed him."

"Let's go find some Mason jars," said Ezra, changing the subject, "and catch lightning bugs with the nieces and nephews."

Scott sat in a rocking chair on the front porch of the big old house, a black cloud of depression. *What if I caught something from that whore? And what if I've given it to Esther? What do I do? I'm doomed.*

***

During the drive back to Birmingham, Ezra and Amanda discussed his travel schedule. Ezra worried that being in Birmingham only a week a month would strain their budding relationship. He would have to do this for many months into the future until he generated some prospects, and even afterward, he would probably be traveling at least two weeks a month.

"So how do you feel about all this?" he asked her.

"I understand the beginning of a new job is always hard—I'm still establishing my practice, so I identify, and I know your job is particularly challenging, so let's not stress out too much about this, OK?"

"So, given how much I'm traveling, how would you describe our relationship?" he prodded gently.

"I would say," she said slowly, "that we're at least friends with benefits," and playfully elbowed him in the ribs.

Amanda had a way with words that always made him feel better.

***

The GO Team met every Monday morning, regardless of who was in town. Minutes were emailed to all team members. It was important to coordinate work and share rumors.

When it was Jack's turn to speak, he had several items, and then he said, "I understand that Scott Kling has given up on his campaign to change how ADIT does marketing."

"Heard why?" asked Simon.

"He's not saying."

"That's not like him," said Simon.

"No, it isn't," said Ezra.

After the meeting, Ezra found Simon. "I think something happened on the Japan trip between Scott and Ogg."

"What have you heard?"

"Nothing, it's just that Amanda and I have both noticed he's depressed. She says Esther told her it all started when he returned from Japan. I hate to say it, but I think Ogg's got something on him. I can't imagine what it would be. Scott seems a pretty straight arrow."

"Ogg's had a certain reputation over the years. Let me do some checking," said Simon. "By the way, he's complaining about you again. Says you shouldn't be meeting with IHK officials and auto suppliers in Europe. That's something the state should be doing."

"Nothing's stopping them," said Ezra. *Except it's hard to recruit companies sitting on your ass,* he thought. "Should I do anything differently?"

"No," said Simon. "Just make sure you identify yourself as being with the Atmani Foundation, rather than representing the State of Alabama."

"Understood."

Simon went to look for Jack, who'd seen a lot in his thirty-five years of economic development work. Maybe he'd know what was going on with Scott Kling.

47

SITE TROUBLE

"You have a big problem," the professor said to Jake on the telephone. "You need to come out here."

It's been like this virtually every week, Jake thought, as he got in his car. Last week, the endangered species people thought they had found a rare mussel in the small stream they had to mitigate in the middle of the site. Everyone had held their collective breaths as they took the tiny grey mussel in a chest of water to Montgomery for analysis. Luckily, it was a false alarm.

The college professor and some of his students were conducting the cultural resources study. Their job was to make sure no Indian villages, burial grounds, or old cemeteries existed on the tech park property and mega-site. If any existed, they were to mark them for protection. Such a find in the wrong location—like the middle of the property—could make the site unusable.

Jake arrived to find the professor and his team had set up a large folding table and chairs near the site entrance, covered by an open canopy popup. A second table held coffee and a chest for soft drinks. They had set up a base camp as if they were in the bush, instead of just driving to McDonald's ten minutes away and having a coffee.

Jake's project engineer pulled up behind him. He was a crusty old guy with Sagan Engineering who had worked hundreds of development projects. Jake had called him on the way to the site.

Arrayed on the front table were a dozen or so arrowheads along with a location map. Growing up in a small Alabama town, Jake knew that almost anywhere in the state where two creeks came together, one could dig down four to six inches and find arrowheads.

For thousands of years, Native Americans had built small temporary encampments where creeks came together. When they fished- and hunted-out an area, they moved to a new location. Only the remains of a permanent, substantial village would be a showstopper.

"Arrowheads by themselves don't indicate an Indian village," said Jake. "There's arrowheads everywhere."

"Yes," said the professor, "but look at this pottery fragment we found. Very fine work."

Uh oh, Jake thought.

The professor held up a dark brown fragment, perhaps two-by-three inches. The top edge was smooth and curved and appeared to have a lip. "Pottery is indicative of a permanent settlement. This is very troubling for your site," he said ominously.

"Let me see that," growled the Sagan engineer, and he grabbed the fragment from the professor and looked at it up-close, on each side, almost putting it under his nose and squinting his eyes, as if he were extremely nearsighted. Then he started laughing—not just laughing but guffawing.

"Professor, what would you say this pottery is made of?"

"Made of?" the professor said, puzzled. "It's fired clay."

"This is Bakelite," said the crusty engineer. "This is a piece of an old distributor cap, probably from a Ford F100 truck, if I had to guess. Probably leftover from when they were coal mining in the area."

Jake didn't mean to snicker. It was just a tension release.

48

INTERVIEW WITH CLARA OGG

"Yes?" She answered her phone.

"Ms. Ogg? My name is Jonathan Archer, and I have information about your ex-husband that will interest you. If we can meet for ten minutes, you'll find it worthwhile."

"What's your name again?"

"Jonathan. Jonathan Archer. I represent *another* woman who's been wronged by your ex-husband."

"I don't doubt that!" He had her curiosity now.

"We have some information we think you'll find interesting." He chummed the water again. "Can we meet?"

There was a pause on the phone. "When?" she asked.

"At your convenience, ma'am."

The appointment was set.

The two political operatives found the street where the townhouse was located, off the main road in the English Village area.

Atlas Ogg and his wife had divorced two years ago, and Clara had moved from Montgomery to the toney Birmingham suburb of Mountain Brook. According to rumor, Ogg's long-suffering wife had finally had enough of his philandering ways.

Reportedly, the divorce had been acrimonious. The operatives had used that information to decide how best to approach her for an appointment. The first rule of opposition research was to talk with any ex-spouses.

Mountain Brook was a bedroom community in the hills and hollows on the south side of Red Mountain. It was the wealthiest zip code in Alabama and one of the wealthiest in the South.

The "Tiny Kingdom," as some called it, consisted of estates set back into the hills, residential areas with fine homes, and a surprisingly large number of townhomes and condos. Several retail villages were interspersed among the residential areas.

For almost two decades, the two operatives had asked questions daily in their jobs as newspaper reporters, and they were good at it. Most of the time, the answers resulted in bread-and-butter stories that generated a paycheck, but occasionally, questions led to answers that resulted in a bombshell.

After they became political operatives, they used the same techniques to find dirt on their clients' political opposition. Most of their clients were elected officials who wanted to remain in office and who had the campaign resources to fund opposition research.

The primary interview technique was to get the subjects talking and keep them talking, always to keep asking questions, to display sincere interest, and to ask more questions about the answers given, continuing on-and-on until the process turned up something. It was important to stay on offense, always being the questioner and not the answerer. The ex-newspaper people knew countless ways to ask the same questions to elicit the answers they needed.

Doing campaign opposition research, most of the time, they never really knew what they'd find until they found it. In this case, they had an idea of what they wanted; they just didn't know if she knew anything.

She met them at the front door, all dressed-up as if she were going to a luncheon or bridge game. She was late middle age; early- to mid-fifties.

As they sat in her living room, the operative who had given his name as Jonathan watched Ms. Ogg as she crossed and uncrossed her legs, and he noticed her right hand twitch slightly. He could smell cigarette smoke in the house.

"Ma'am, if you want to smoke, that's not a problem."

She retrieved her cigarettes, lighter, and ashtray from a rolltop desk. After lighting up and taking a couple of draws, she seemed more at ease. She appeared to compose herself mentally, holding the long white cigarette to the side between her fingers.

He wondered if she would have any useful information. As the conversation progressed, it turned out she was a talker, and she hated her ex-husband.

"Who's the woman?" she asked.

"I'm not allowed to say," he replied.

Clara Ogg hissed, "Wives know things their husbands wouldn't dream they know. I knew for *years* that bastard was messing around, but what pissed me off is that he was *careless* and gave me a *social disease*."

"Our client's upset about that, too," the operative improvised.

"He's a bastard—a son of a bitch! He screwed me over for years and years. You know he liked those *Asian* girls. You know what they say about how they're different." She gave him a sideways look.

"Ma'am, please understand that we're just trying to get something for our client who's been treated horribly by your ex-husband. We understand your divorce case was settled with prejudice, so it can't be reopened, which means anything we can get for our client from your ex-husband won't allow you to reopen your divorce settlement.

"When you were divorcing Atlas, did he try to hide assets? Money? Jewelry?"

"I can't ever get rid of what he gave me," she sniffed, "and I'll never forgive him. So, what do you want?"

"Do you think your ex was hiding assets? Cash? Gold? Jewelry?"

"I'm sure he found a way to stash away money overseas, but we couldn't track it down. Somehow, he came up with more money than I thought possible because he wanted to keep the Ono House, and we split things equally. And he has a large safe in the Ono House!" she blurted out.

Carefully now, with no hint of unusual interest. "He has a house on Ono Island?"

"Yes."

"And you say he has a safe in the house?"

"Yes."

"Do you know what he keeps in it?"

"I checked one time when he was gone. All he had in there was his guns and his porn and some legal papers. He hid the money somewhere else."

"Long guns? Pistols?"

"Both. There was one of those assault guns."

"And porn, like magazines?"

"Naw, porn, like videos. I even played one of the DVDs, and it was disgusting!"

Bingo! "How did you get in the safe?"

"Oh, he tried to be smart and wouldn't ever give me the combination, but I figured it out. His sister's birthday! She died young."

The operative knew he would need to tread through the next part carefully. "You think there might be any money in the safe now?"

"There wasn't when I checked it before, but there might be now."

"Could you give me the combination?"

She scratched the side of her neck like she was trying to decide something. "I'll give you the combination if you promise me half of whatever cash you find."

"Ma'am, you have a deal. You have my solemn word."

She gave him the combination. "12-18-51. December 18, 1951."

49

MEETING IN AUGSBURG

Polite persistence had paid off. The Meyer Papierfabrik meeting was set for Monday morning. It was the first appointment of the trip. Ezra had left Atlanta late Friday afternoon and arrived at Stuttgart-Echterdingen Airport Saturday morning. He checked into the Graf Zeppelin, one of his favorite hotels, just across the street from the Stuttgart *Hauptbahnhof,* the central train station.

After nine hours sitting in a plane, Ezra visited the hotel's fitness center and spent a solid hour working the weight machines. He had turned into a gym rat since joining the GO Team and had put on fifteen pounds of solid muscle. After three weeks of jiu-jitsu training, there were no more takedowns by Ella. Once Ezra fully grasped the mental and physical commitment the GO Team demanded, he performed to expectations and regarded each second of spare time as a gift.

After a shower and short nap, Ezra took a stroll through the *Schloßgarten* and met an old banking friend at the *Weinstube Kachelofen* near the *Rathaus.* The next morning, he awoke early and worked on his Meyer presentation before adjourning to the breakfast room.

Ezra loved breakfast buffets in upscale German hotels. The tables of food were a feast for the eyes and stomach, with every kind of breakfast food and drink, all beautifully arranged.

Ezra then took the S-Bahn to Zuffenhausen to tour the Porsche Museum and visited Untertürkheim to see the Mercedes-Benz Museum. In the last half-decade, both Porsche and Mercedes had built new museums, and the Stuttgart area had experienced a severe case of auto museum escalation. Ezra continued working on the Meyer presentation throughout the evening, except for a solid two hours in the fitness room.

Early Monday morning, he picked up a rental car at the *Hauptbahnhof* and departed for Augsburg about 6:30 a.m. His appointment was at 10 a.m. with the *Finanzchef* of the Augsburg paper company.

It was typically a two-hour drive on the A8, but a nasty *Stau* in the hilly area around Mühlhausen im Täle brought autobahn traffic to a halt. Ezra regretted not taking the train. He finally reached Augsburg by 9 a.m.

Meyer Papierfabrik was one of the oldest companies in Augsburg, and its headquarters was located on Georg-Meyer-Strasse, a downtown thoroughfare named for the founder.

Ezra parked in a nearby *Tiefgarage,* had a coffee in a bakery shop, and caught up on email. Being late to a German meeting was poor form. Ezra always tried to arrive at a meeting location well ahead of time and then chill in a café until near the meeting time.

The Meyer Papierfabrik headquarters was a beautiful old, five-story building with ornate white trim and a particular shade of yellow that German buildings were sometimes painted. It was clearly pre-World War II, and Ezra was glad it had survived. A black iron fence surrounded the building, with a small reception office at the main gate.

"*Ich habe einen Termin bei Herrn Koehler um zehn Uhr,*" said Ezra. "*Mein Name ist Ezra Drake.*"

"*Bitte warten Sie einen Moment,*" said the receptionist.

In a couple of minutes, he was given a name tag. "*Geradeaus durch die Tür. Die erste rechts zum Aufzug. Dritte Etage.*"

When the elevator opened on the third floor, a young man in a black Hugo Boss suit met Ezra. "Please follow me," he said in English.

The décor was "grand old manor house" instead of "modern corporate offices." Ezra was shown into a large, spacious office. Sitting behind an ornate desk at the opposite end of the room was, presumably, Herr Koehler, who quickly came around the desk and shook Ezra's hand. They sat at a meeting table at one side of the room, where light from a large window highlighted the beautiful inlaid wood table.

BUFFALO HUNTING IN ALABAMA

The young assistant brought coffee to complement the plate of cookies and bottles of water and juice sitting on the table.

"I apologize for not seeing you before, but I have been traveling on business and then on holiday. You did a good job explaining your situation to my assistant. She told me you spoke beautiful German, which made me even more curious," said Herr Koehler.

"I'm grateful you could meet with me," said Ezra. "As I told your assistant, I work for the Atmani Foundation, a *Stiftung* that helps facilitate economic development in Alabama. I would like to talk to you about the property your company owns in Alabama. Have you ever visited it?"

"Mr. Drake, until you contacted us, I wasn't even aware we owned this property. I couldn't find anyone in the company who knew about it. We checked our records and found we were paying a small *Grundsteuer*—property tax—each year to this Forrest County. We contacted one of our retired managers who told us the story of how we purchased the land to build a paper plant."

"Do you see any possibility of ever constructing a paper plant there in the future?" Ezra asked.

"No. We still manufacture much paper, but the world paper market is very different now than twenty-five years ago. Still, real estate is very precious in Germany. Two hundred hectares—five hundred acres—is a large amount of land. Why should we sell it?"

"Because it's never going to be worth much," said Ezra. "Large parts of Alabama are prosperous, but this property sits in an area of Alabama where there's almost nothing and probably never will be."

Ezra opened his iPad to a map of Alabama. "Your property is located in the Alabama Black Belt. Forrest County has less than nine thousand people, and the population is decreasing each year. There are less than 5.5 people per square kilometer. The median household income is only $24,000 a year. Thirty-four percent of the population is below the poverty line. Eighty-two percent of the population is black. Thirty-one percent of the population is functionally illiterate. Forty-four percent of the population is obese. More than seventeen percent of the adult population has diabetes. There are only three restaurants and four gas stations in the entire county. The only industry is a catfish processing plant. Things are getting worse there each year."

"What is this Black Belt?" asked Koehler.

"It's a large area of land—like a belt—that stretches across Alabama. It accounts for about one-quarter of the land in Alabama, but only about twelve percent of the population. Before the American Civil War, cotton plantations dotted the county and slaves worked the fields. Now, there's nothing; it's like a sparsely populated Third World—*die Dritte Welt*."

Koehler pointed to Tuscaloosa on the map. "Our property, it's not so far from the Mercedes-Benz plant in Tuscaloosa. Maybe it will be valuable one day."

Ezra replied, "The Mercedes plant sits about halfway between Tuscaloosa and Birmingham," Ezra pointed it out. "It's about an hour's drive from your property, but culturally it's a world away. Once you travel south and west of Tuscaloosa, you enter a different world. There's almost nothing there. None of the Mercedes suppliers are located anywhere near your property." Ezra swiped to the next slide showing a map of Mercedes' suppliers in Alabama.

Koehler asked the obvious question: "If this place is so bad, then why are you trying to buy the land back from us?"

Ezra was silent for a moment. "Because the local people need some hope. I think the best use for Forrest County is hunting plantations and tourism, but the local leaders still want to try to attract industry. They know they have no chance to do that as long as you own the property, but if they can regain control of the property, they feel they have some chance, no matter how small."

Mr. Koehler thought for a moment. "I think we might be willing to sell the land, but we don't want a loss on our books."

"I understand that."

As Ezra walked back to his car, he had mixed feelings about his accomplishment. On the one hand, he was pleased that Forrest County would be getting their land back. On the other hand, he wished he'd had a better strategy than persuading the German company that Alabama was a shithole.

50

THE PROJECT

Ezra looked out at the audience. The *Stuttgart Industrie- und Handelskammer* was hosting an export seminar, and Ezra estimated the audience to be about two hundred people. He was the next speaker, but that would probably be a while.

Ezra was always amazed at the German tolerance for long-winded and boring speakers. By now, in America, half the audience would have slipped out to use their cell phones or grab a drink, but the German businesspeople all sat there patiently.

Sitting behind the long table on the raised dais, Ezra surreptitiously checked his iPhone for new texts and email messages. He saw an email titled *Request for Proposal*, which surprised him since he didn't work projects.

> *Mr. Drake:*
> *We are searching for a site for a major manufacturing project. If Alabama wishes to submit possible sites, please fill out the attached Request for Proposal and email it back to us within two weeks. Please do not submit sites that do not meet our site criteria.*

The sender was a generic-looking Gmail address.

Ezra slipped his iPad from his messenger bag and scanned the email's attached PDF—a long and detailed Request for Proposal with more than forty pages of questions about available sites, workforce, taxes, and such issues. The project required a site of at least five hundred acres and claimed it would initially create six hundred high-paying jobs, with a high indirect job multiplier. Ezra guessed it to be a chemical plant of some sort.

Someone probably mass-emailed this to economic developers across the state, Ezra thought, and they had somehow gotten his email address. He forwarded the email to Simon with a *'What do you think about this?'* added and returned his attention to the export program.

This was Ezra's sixth export seminar. His efforts to build relationships with the German IHKs were paying off.

Ezra was careful in his speeches not to give the impression he was trying to steal jobs from Germany. He emphasized the Southern U.S. as a market for German goods, not as a manufacturing location for German companies, though Mercedes-Benz and Airbus always slipped into his presentations.

Most U.S. state representatives who spoke at these seminars were German nationals working for U.S. states under contract. One year they might be working for Georgia and the next year Kansas.

Ezra was a curiosity—an American who spoke good German and who had worked for a world-famous company. In his speeches, Ezra always explained that he was born in Alabama, grew up in Alabama, and that Alabama was the only U.S. state he had ever represented. This distinguished him from the other speakers. His goal was to establish credibility as someone who could speak authoritatively.

Ezra always began by talking about the American South. "If they're not interested in the South, they're not going to be interested in Alabama," Simon had said.

Ezra described the South as the most populous U.S. region with the largest number of Fortune 500 headquarters. Only in the second half of his speech did he mention Alabama and its economy—not making a pitch, but just providing interesting facts, which Germans liked.

"Never exaggerate," Simon had said, "or you'll lose credibility. Economic developers often tell Europeans that their community is the best place in the U.S. to locate. By doing so, they destroy their credibility because the odds of their community *actually* being the best place is very remote.

"It's all about planting seeds," said Simon. "Unless you get lucky, you'll mostly be planting seeds at the beginning, and those seeds will take time to germinate.

BUFFALO HUNTING IN ALABAMA

"Most of your prospects will be middle-sized companies—*deutsche mittelständische Unternehmen*. These companies know a wrong location decision can cripple them, so they'll be very cautious. Often, they're pushed by their large customers to manufacture in the U.S. to shorten supply lines or be within NAFTA. It will take many meetings for them to develop confidence in you."

Ezra had always found the German *mittelständische* companies fascinating. Typically family-owned and located in small towns, they were often world leaders in their particular technologies.

One reason Germans found the U.S. so appealing, Ezra knew, was the relative lack of rules. "There was an engineer on the original Mercedes team," Jack had related. " 'I want to chop a tree down,' he said. We all laughed. 'We've got twenty-one million acres of trees in Alabama. Wear yourself out!' we told him as we presented him with a brand-new ax. The freedom to shoot a gun or go fishing without a lot of rules was exhilarating to them."

Everyone Ezra met went into the Atmani databases, and the Quants and their algorithms researched them.

***

An email from Simon:

> *No one else at the Atmani Foundation received this email. Jack checked with Scott Kling, and none of his people got one. Kling checked with ADIT and same story.*

Ezra emailed the generic email address:

> *Did you send this Request for Proposal to anyone else in Alabama?*

He received a prompt reply:

> *No. We will only accept Alabama RFPs from you.*

Maybe this is it, Ezra thought. A big project. *This is why I returned to Alabama.* He forwarded the reply to Simon.

***

Sixteen U.S. states had development offices in Europe. "I don't think much of them," said Simon. "Sure, they may occasionally save a few hours of travel time to meet a prospect, but they tend to have high overhead. Europe's a big place, and wherever you locate an office, it can still be many hours' travel to meet a prospect. That money's better spent on business intelligence and targeted travel.

"Overseas development offices are not retail offices. Prospects are not going to walk up like going to a grocery store. Offices *are* a place to work, but you can work anywhere with a phone, a laptop, and the internet. Overseas development offices isolate the people operating them from the area they're representing. I think you can accomplish more without one.

"A U.S. state office abroad is like having a house at the beach; it invites unwanted guests," Simon continued. "Once I was part of a group making prospecting visits in Japan, and in meetings, one of the Alabama guys would sit there with his legs crossed and dangle his loafer off the end of his foot. He might as well have stood up, turned around, and let out a huge fart.

"You see it all the time at dinner parties in Europe. The drinks come, and Americans start drinking without waiting for the host to make a toast. The food arrives, and the Americans start eating without waiting for the host to say *Guten Appetit* and take the first bite. It's a basic lack of European manners, and it interferes with relationship building.

"A U.S. state office in a foreign country is an invitation for that state's economic developers and politicians to come and visit. And of course, they want to be set up with appointments to justify their junkets.

"If you've spent months—maybe years—delicately building relationships with prospects, the last thing you want is to take a group of economic developers and politicians to visit them because it represents an uncontrolled situation with few advantages.

"Don't get me wrong: There are many economic developers, and some politicians, who know the proper etiquette, but a foreign state office rarely has the opportunity—or power—to vet these people in advance."

"But if a company's interested in Alabama, eventually the prospect's going to meet Alabamians, right? And then don't all these cultural *faux pas* happen?" asked Ezra.

"It's all about *where* the contact occurs. When you're in the *prospect's* culture, you behave according to the norms of that culture. When the prospect is in *your* culture, it's the prospect's responsibility to behave according to the norms of *your* culture. So when the prospect visits Alabama, they're trying to understand

BUFFALO HUNTING IN ALABAMA

Alabama and its culture and obey our norms. It's all about respect for culture," Simon said.

"I realize that local economic developers and politicians need to travel to gain experience, but wasting good prospects on them is not the way to do it. Send them to tradeshows and seminars, where the chances of them burning prospects are minimal, and accept that the trip is for the educational and cultural benefit of the travelers, not a serious attempt to generate leads.

"The truth is, if an economic developer doesn't speak a particular country's language, he's at a great handicap. Economic developers who deny this truth are generally the ones who don't speak another language.

"When I attended the Hannover Industry Fair in Germany for several consecutive years, I saw these two economic development representatives of a southern regional utility. They were both heavyset, good old boys. Each year they had the same corner position in the same trade show hall, which meant they'd been doing this show a while.

"Their trade show booth was an eight-foot-square banner which rolled up on the pole from which it hung. Two uprights, a cross pole, and a banner with a map of their service area—that was their exhibit.

"They'd sit there having a great time, watching people, occasionally talking to someone, and at noon they'd display an 'out-to-lunch' sign and eat *Haxen* at a trade show café. Same routine in the afternoon. At night, I imagine they put away a few beers. When the trade show ended, they'd call it a good week's work."

***

After the seminar and the question-and-answer session, the IHK held an attendee reception in an adjacent glass-walled room that opened to a hillside vineyard. The Stuttgart Region was a major wine producer, and vineyards covered the hills around Stuttgart. The Stuttgart IHK building in the city center backed up to such a hill.

Ezra found the real payoff for his speeches occurred during the *Kaffeepausen* and receptions. A German executive contemplating U.S. manufacturing wasn't interested in broadcasting that to his competitors. The receptions allowed prospects to talk casually one-on-one with the speakers. Much of Ezra's GO Team training had been devoted to what he was doing just now—sipping a nice 2006 Trollinger *trocken* while slowly luring in a possible prospect.

***

Ezra's recipe for success was to outwork everyone, and in that respect, Europe ideally suited him. After working all day, Ezra could still talk with Alabama people in the evening, since most of Europe was seven hours ahead of Alabama. Ezra had a 10 p.m. conference call scheduled with Simon, Jack Brannon, and Scott Kling.

"We've run the email through all the databases, but nothing turned up," said Simon.

Jack spoke up: "Scott, you know we don't work projects, but they sent the RFP to Ezra and have specified him as the channel of communication. We don't want to ruffle feathers. Can you work with ADIT to put together the RFP response, and then Ezra can forward it to the prospect?"

Kling agreed to manage the process with ADIT. "Ogg won't be happy, but even he understands the easiest way to be cut from a project is not to follow the prospect's or site selector's instructions."

***

Four days later, Ezra was in Munich and participating in another late-night conference call with Simon, Jack, and Scott. "We're submitting four sites," said Scott. "Huntsville has a site adjacent to Interstate 65. Baldwin County has a mega-site they've been developing, also next to Interstate 65, and Mobile is submitting a 500-acre site near Evonik and the other chemical plants."

"What's the fourth site?" asked Ezra.

"Birmingham," said Scott. "They haven't had a good mega-site in a long time—if ever—and they still don't have one, but they're working on one with Milltown. Everyone knows about it because that young economic developer, Jake Hatfield, is an excellent networker.

"Even though it's not one hundred percent ready, we've decided to submit it—as much of a reward to Birmingham and Milltown for working together as anything else."

"I think the Milltown-Birmingham site has a real chance," said Jack. "It's got interstate and airport connections, the labor supply, and the quality-of-life required for the management team."

For each site, they had to submit a plethora of data. They were careful to make sure the data was correct and footnoted because the site consultant probably already had much of it and was testing their honesty.

They wrapped the proposal into a 140-page document that answered the prospect's questions with maps, tables, and detailed data. Ezra sent the PDF to the Gmail address with several hours to spare.

"We'll probably never hear from them," said Scott. "We fill these out all the time. Some of them aren't even real projects—just site selectors or other states fishing for information."

***

Compared to working U.S. companies, Ezra had fewer data tools to generate European prospects. But with the IHK strategy, the speeches themselves were the hooks, and for meetings with German companies, his German fluency acted as a hook. He knew long-term, however, that he needed better research tools.

Ezra found business travel like chocolate cake. The first piece was delicious. The second piece was good. By the eighth piece, he wanted to throw up.

Weekends were nice; he could sleep late and enjoy a leisurely breakfast. He would typically stay in small *Gasthäuser* during the week and then splurge on a business or resort hotel on the weekend. He would sightsee and ride bikes and read and visit art museums. Some weekends, he traveled to France to practice the language. It was a sweet life, at least for a while.

"Working a project and generating a project are two completely different activities," said Simon. "Working an active project is a teamwork effort, with sometimes dozens of people on-board helping win the project, but generating prospects is generally a solitary art. Many economic developers go on prospecting trips together like a bunch of girls going to the bathroom together. That's done for the benefit of the developers, not for efficiency and effectiveness in recruiting.

"Every extra person in a meeting reduces the chance a prospect will take you into his confidence. Prospects want confidentiality, and groups make them nervous. If you're not comfortable being alone for long periods, you're not going to like this job. That's one thing the shrinks tested you for, whether you realized it or not."

Ezra averaged three weeks a month in Europe, with a week in Birmingham. He would do this until he had planted lots of seeds he hoped would sprout and bear fruit for many years.

51

EXISTENTIAL THREAT

It was one of those overcast European days where the sky hung like a blanket of grey cotton balls.

From his warm and dry hotel room—through the mist and drizzle—Ezra could see the European Parliament building on the far riverbank. It was as if a giant *Independence Day* spaceship had landed at the intersection of the Ill River and Marne-Rhine Canal.

Strasbourg was less than a two-hour drive from Stuttgart, and Ezra had driven over after a Friday lunch meeting. Though it was just over the border from Germany, speaking French in Strasbourg was *de rigueur*, and Ezra needed the practice. He sat on the bed and video-conferenced on his iPad with Simon and Jack.

"Ezra, my boy, I have to tell you that Atlas Ogg is on the warpath," said Jack. "He's furious we're working this project."

"What choice did we have? The prospect wants us involved."

"That doesn't matter. Ogg's determined to put a stop to it."

"What can he do?"

"We hear he's huddled with some of his legislator buddies, and they're gonna introduce a bill in the legislature in January to clamp down on us."

"How would they do that?" Ezra asked.

"We hear a couple of things: First, the bill would require anyone talkin' with a company about locating in Alabama to get the company to sign a form sayin' they understand they're not talkin' with an official representative of the State of Alabama."

"Wow, that'll send the prospect a message about economic development teamwork in Alabama," said Ezra sarcastically.

"There's more," said Jack. "Another provision would require us, if we're talkin' with a company that might request incentives, to fill out a form about the project and send it to ADIT for 'incentive budgeting purposes.'"

"So ADIT can butt in and take over the relationship," said Ezra.

"That'll be a mess," said Simon on the conference call. "It takes a year or two to build a relationship with most of our prospects before they have an actual project. ADIT will disrupt that whole process."

"How can he do this?" asked Ezra.

"Ogg has developed a tremendous amount of power over the years. He seems to have the ability to persuade—or twist—an awful lot of arms."

"What about DG&L? Would they help us?"

"Kling is starting to appreciate the value we bring to economic development, but I'm not sure DG&L would spend political capital on a fight like this."

"Can Ogg get the votes to pass the bill?"

"Maybe. But simply introducing the bill creates major damage because it means public committee hearings that expose us and our methods and techniques. If it passed, we could take it to court, but it would probably take years to overturn."

"This would essentially put us out of business, wouldn't it?"

"Yes," said Simon.

After disconnecting, Ezra sat on the side of the bed, his head hanging. He thought about having to return to New York with his tail between his legs looking for a job because he had failed in Alabama.

And then he realized it wasn't just about him. Mr. Atmani and Simon and Jack and his fellow employees—his friends—were trying to help Alabama. They were trying to do something noble and good, and they didn't deserve this kind of bullshit.

New York had been his home at one time, but it wasn't any longer. His home was in Alabama with the people he worked with and loved. He'd be damned if he would let Ogg destroy it all! These people had accepted him and helped him and loved him, and he was going to do his damnedest to defeat Ogg's plans.

But what to do?

52

ONO ISLAND

The Boston Whaler skimmed across the pitch-black water of Perdido Bay, its twin Mercury outboards making a steady roar. It looked like any number of boats out for a summer evening—perhaps headed to Pirate's Cove for dinner and drinks or beers at the Flora-Bama. The boat appeared to contain a single occupant.

Hundreds of lights twinkled in the black night. Perdido Bay was immense but bounded on all sides by land. To the South, a long east-west barrier island, Perdido Key, separated Perdido Bay from the Gulf of Mexico. Perdido Pass, a narrow cut in the Key, opened to the Gulf of Mexico. A breeze ruffled the dark water of the clear, moonless night.

The boat had left from a house on the north side of Perdido Bay. Ono Island was a fifteen-minute journey.

Ezra lay in the bottom of the boat, completely clothed in black, his apprehension a large bug with ice-cold feet crawling up his spine. Simon lay in the boat next to him, only his eyes visible. Ezra had seen some sketchy things on Wall Street, but even after the 2008 crash, not a single banker had gone to jail. *But this? If we're caught…*

Tonight's events began weeks ago when Ezra told Simon about Scott Kling's depression. "Do you want me to help?" Simon had asked.

"If you can," said Ezra. "Scott's responsible for me being in Alabama, and while he isn't happy I joined the Atmani Foundation, he's been warming up to us lately. And there's Amanda…"

BUFFALO HUNTING IN ALABAMA

Simon was silent for a moment. "OK, let me see what I can do."

When Ezra returned from his latest Europe trip, Simon said, "Ogg's intentions toward us have created a new urgency. Can you swim?"

"I'm a good swimmer," said Ezra.

"OK, I want you to be in Orange Beach for the AEDA Summer Conference."

"I thought the GO Team didn't attend those kinds of events."

"You won't be attending the conference," Simon said.

***

The Alabama Economic Developers Association met twice a year. Birmingham or Montgomery was the venue for the winter business conference. In the summer, they met at Alabama's Gulf Coast for business and pleasure. The business agenda was relaxed, and many economic developers brought their families.

Both meetings were popular and regularly attended by more than four hundred local and state economic developers, mayors, state officials, and service providers.

AEDA held the Summer Conference at the Grand Hotel or the Island Beach Resort. Neither venue was perfect. The Grand Hotel was superb, but it sat on Mobile Bay's Eastern Shore, an hour from the sugar-white Gulf beaches.

The Island Beach Resort sat in Orange Beach next to miles of beautiful beaches, but it was an older hotel.

It was an issue that the Alabama Gulf Coast had no world-class convention hotel. Many Alabama trade and professional associations had difficulty finding suitable venues at the Alabama Gulf Coast for their annual meetings, and holding such meetings across the border in Florida was politically difficult.

Jack Brannon and Mrs. Avery attended both yearly AEDA meetings. They provided an efficient way to meet with local economic developers, small-town mayors, and the community leaders with whom they worked.

It was challenging to keep the agenda fresh from meeting to meeting. Certain parts of the program were traditions, such as the ADIT Director's address, but there was a constant search to find new and interesting speakers and evening entertainment.

They had done Casino Nights and Luaus, and fish fries and shrimp fests. This year, they had booked Chevy 6, a popular oldies band, but it wouldn't start playing till 8:30 p.m., so they needed entertainment during the seafood buffet dinner.

Someone on the conference organizing committee suggested a professional hypnotist who they heard was hilarious.

"Why not?" they said.

***

The Atmani Foundation owned a guest house on the north side of Perdido Bay, on a point where the bay narrowed into one of the many bayous that fed it. The house had four bedrooms, a large dock, and a boathouse filled with marine craft. The property was eighteen acres and secluded.

In the late afternoon, Simon and Ezra and Augustus sat around a table on the deck. A map of Perdido Bay covered the table. A red cross marked the north side of a long island sitting entirely within the Bay, parallel to and north of Perdido Key. The map said, "Ono Island." The western end of Ono lay near the Perdido Pass, and a short bridge connected Ono Island to Perdido Key. A guardhouse at the bridge kept the public off the island, *at least by land*, Ezra thought.

The Alabama-Florida border took a convoluted turn east around Ono, and then back west so that Ono was a peninsula of Alabama jutting into Florida.

Whoever made that happen was smart, Ezra thought, because Alabama's property taxes were much lower than Florida's. Ezra had rarely visited Alabama's Gulf Coast because he had grown up in southeast Alabama, and everyone there frequented the Florida panhandle beaches.

Earlier in the afternoon, Ezra had searched for *Ono Island* on Google and found it to be five-and-a-half miles long and entirely private. The island had a water tower, fire station, private harbor, two recreation centers, a guardhouse at the entrance, and an administrative center known as Ono House.

The Spanish had discovered the island in the fifteenth century and named it "Orinoco," hence O̱rino̱co̱. Development began in the 1970s, and more than seven hundred houses now dotted the island. The houses on Ono weren't on the beach, but exclusivity trumped beachfront. Besides, when a hurricane hit, it was better to have a barrier island between you and the open water.

Photos of a house lay on the map. An airplane or helicopter appeared to have taken some of them. Others looked to be from a boat offshore. The Ono house was large, two-storied, and finished in a fanciful stucco design. A pier and small boathouse jutted into the water of the bay.

BUFFALO HUNTING IN ALABAMA

It must be worth a couple mill, thought Ezra. *How does a state employee afford a vacation house like that?*

"I flew the drone for the past couple of hours, and there's no activity at Ogg's house. No cars; nothing," said Augustus. The "drone" was a small $1,200 quadcopter that a Chinese company called DJI had recently introduced. Launched from a boat, the 2.5-pound aircraft had an effective range of 1,800 feet or so and could stay airborne for more than twenty minutes.

Augustus had five batteries that he swapped out to increase airtime. Hovering at seven hundred feet, the four tiny electric motors powering the propellers were inaudible from the ground. The drone had LED lights on each arm which helped make it more visible. Augustus had taped over them. At roughly eighteen inches square, the white plastic drone was difficult to see from the ground.

A radio transmitter controlled the drone, and it used an iPhone connection to "see" through the drone's camera. The Atmani Foundation had purchased it to photograph property and industrial parks, but Augustus had repurposed it.

"Jack says that Ogg is still holding court at the Flora-Bama," said Ezra. "He'll surely be sloshed soon if he isn't already."

"Where's Blunt?" asked Simon.

"No one's seen him," said Augustus.

***

It was mid-Summer, so sunset wasn't until almost 8 p.m. About 8:30, Simon told Ezra, "This is something that Marco and I would do, but his death has left us critically short-handed, so I'm asking you to step up. You don't have the background, but you're a quick learner. I'm asking a lot of you.

"We don't want fingerprints or DNA all over the place, and we don't want video cameras to identify us. These days, they're everywhere. Put this on. Carry nothing else. No ID, no phone."

"We're not going in armed?" Ezra asked.

"Just with your wits," said Simon.

Great. Ezra changed into a black suit, which completely enveloped his body, including hands, feet, and a balaclava for the face. *Ezra the Ninja*. He felt a little stupid. He had never even seen such a suit, except in martial arts movies.

"If something bad happens, get to the water," Simon said. "The belt on your suit has a homing device that Augustus will use to find you."

***

Augustus slowed the boat to a crawl as they neared the north side of Ono. In the darkness, Simon and Ezra slipped over the side of the boat away from Ono. The water was pleasantly cool.

Lights sparkled on the black water. A honky-tonk band played at the Flora-Bama down the highway, and the wind occasionally carried scraps of laughter and conversation. The air smelled of the sea.

Ezra thought, *I'm certainly jumping the shark on this.* He was acutely aware of the risk, but this had become a matter of self-preservation.

"Follow me," whispered Simon. The swim was only seventy-five yards or so. They avoided the boat dock and slid onto the sandy shore, staying low to avoid presenting an outline to adjacent houses. They crept slowly to the rear of the house.

Simon pulled something from his black waterproof backpack and worked on the rear door. In less than twenty seconds, the doorknob turned. *This isn't Simon's first rodeo*, Ezra realized.

Simon opened the door gently. No alarm beeped.

Careless of Ogg, Ezra thought. *Or someone's here.* The bug with cold feet was crawling up his back again.

They slipped inside, and Simon gently closed the door. They were in a mudroom. Creeping into the kitchen, Simon whispered, "No lights. You go that way," he pointed, "and I'll go this way. We're looking for a large safe."

Someone had plugged nightlights into the walls at intervals. Ezra rounded a corner and faced a staircase. He slowly climbed it on his hands and knees. The house was new, and the treads were solid and carpeted, so there were no squeaks.

As he climbed, Ezra began to hear something—TV or radio noise. The stairs opened to a hallway. The sound came from the first doorway to the right. Light from the room and a television reflected on the opposite wall of the hallway.

On his hands and knees, Ezra peeked around the corner of the doorway, and there was Ernest Blunt, eyes closed, sitting in a chair, a barbarian king on his throne, facing the television on the other side of the wall from Ezra.

The safe was probably in a bedroom further down the hallway. Blunt looked fast asleep.

Can we do this without waking him up? Ezra started carefully crawling past the doorway. Blunt's eyes opened wide, and he jumped up and charged, his massive hands outstretched like twin steam shovels.

BUFFALO HUNTING IN ALABAMA

Ezra scrambled to his feet, backed against the opposite hallway wall, and at the last instant, popped out a front stop kick. Blunt's gut slammed into Ezra's outstretched leg, but Ezra's braced back leg took the shock.

Like being hit by a bus, Ezra thought. Momentum forced Blunt's face forward, and his hands dropped, and Ezra slammed a straight left punch to Blunt's face, then followed up with a right and then a left again. Blunt backed up a step, blood streaming from his nose. *I've got to put him away quickly, or he's going to kill me*, Ezra thought.

He tried a straight back kick, but Blunt recovered quickly and blocked it with his forearm, knocking Ezra off-balance. He stumbled into the TV room to give himself more maneuvering room. *Advantage lost. All I've done is piss him off.* Blunt moved into a classic fighting stance, blood dripping on his shirt and murder in his eye.

Kicks do more damage but take longer to execute. Amateurs get knocked out by kicks but less often a pro. And this guy was a pro. Blunt didn't waste time with jabs, methodically throwing hooks and roundhouse punches and depending upon his greater bulk and strength to overwhelm.

Ezra backed and moved side-to-side, stepping in to punch and then backing out quickly. *One solid hit from those fists, and it's all over*, Ezra thought.

Blunt tried to back Ezra against a wall. Ezra closed quickly, tied up Blunt's arms, and slammed a knee into Blunt's gut and chest.

Blunt easily broke the armhold and pounded roundhouses into both sides of Ezra's ribs. Ezra headbutted him, pushed him backward hard with both hands, and caught him in the nuts with a front snap kick. Blunt took it with a grunt.

Blunt's right leg came around fast and caught Ezra's left thigh with a low roundhouse that almost knocked him off his feet. Ezra staggered backward. *I can't go down*, Ezra thought. *I can't win a grappling match with this guy.*

Ezra and Blunt both circled, Ezra throwing an occasional jab and Blunt just looking and waiting. Ezra focused on Blunt, the rest of the room a blur. Ezra had reach and more speed but lacked Blunt's brute strength. Ezra jabbed and punched and tried to block Blunt's punches, but Ezra's best defense was to keep moving.

Blunt threw a haymaker with his right just as Ezra was moving leftward, and for an instant, Ezra was behind him and slipped his right arm around Blunt's neck, grabbed his left bicep with his right hand, and his left arm wedged behind Blunt's neck.

And then Ezra squeezed *hard* and sagged downward so Blunt couldn't flip him. Blunt tried to shake him off and slammed him back into the wall. Ezra felt like a bull rider, but he held tight.

It wasn't a chokehold; Blunt's windpipe was in the crook of Ezra's elbow so Blunt could breathe, but Ezra's forearm and bicep were compressing the carotid arteries on each side of Blunt's neck, cutting the flow of blood to his brain.

As they went to the floor, Ezra's legs wrapped around Blunt's waist, and his heels locked into Blunt's crotch. In five seconds, Blunt was out, and Ezra rolled him onto his stomach.

"Nicely done," said Simon, standing in the doorway of the TV room, his black balaclava off and a leather shoehorn-like object in his hand. "The rear-naked choke or sleeper hold. Perhaps the most important submission in jiu-jitsu."

Ezra was on his hands and knees, panting hard. He looked at Blunt's face on the carpet, the blood from his smashed nose splattered on the white carpet. He wondered if this son of a bitch had killed Marco.

"I've checked," said Simon. "No video or audio, but keep your gloves on."

"What's that?" asked Ezra, gasping for breath and pointing at the black object in Simon's hand.

"It's a sap," Simon said as he zip-tied Blunt's hands behind him and his feet together. "Don't you watch old detective movies?" Simon pushed earplugs into Blunt's ears and slipped a black cloth bag over his head.

That sap might've been nice to have, thought Ezra.

The gun safe sat in the master bedroom closet on the second floor. Simon tried the combination they'd been given. The handle turned, and the door swung open. "His sister's birthday."

Inside, the safe held long guns and much more.

Two cardboard boxes contained old 16-millimeter film cans, DVDs, Blu-Rays, and USB drives, each with a name written on them. On one film can, someone had written the name of a famous politician—long dead. Ezra spied a USB drive labeled "Scott Kling—Kyoto."

"Oh my God," said Ezra.

The safe also held deeds and legal papers, an assortment of handguns, stacks of cash in dollars and Euros, a Thompson submachine gun, several long guns—probably automatics—and several bricks of a white substance wrapped in plastic.

Oh shit! Ogg, it's just not your night, thought Ezra.

Simon opened his waterproof backpack and methodically packed in the films and videos. He then started counting the stacks of bills and dividing them into two piles. A stack of dollars and Euros went back into the safe, and a stack of dollars went into Ezra's backpack.

They checked on Blunt, who was still out, but breathing, and then they slipped out the back door, leaving it ajar. Ezra slid into the water and turned to see Simon using the side of his foot to obliterate their footprints in the sand. Once in the water, Simon pushed a button on the device at his belt.

***

As they skimmed across the water, Ezra and Simon changed into street clothes and packed their gear. By the time Augustus had anonymously called the sheriff to report suspicious activity, the King Air had already lifted from Jack Edwards Airport, and Simon and Ezra were on their way back to Birmingham.

53

THE HYPNOTIST

About the time that Simon and Ezra were beginning their swim, and Ogg was drinking at the Flora-Bama, AEDA conference participants at the Island Beach Resort were enjoying a seafood buffet and open bar, and the hypnotist was beginning his show.

He looked like an old-time magician, with a pencil-thin mustache and classic black top hat. He explained that hypnotized people couldn't and wouldn't do anything against their beliefs. Hypnotism wasn't magic, but merely the power of suggestion, and hypnotists used it to help people stop smoking and lose weight.

He asked for audience volunteers and assured them they would have a great time. Mrs. Avery was in the audience, and she could tell the hypnotist was an excellent speaker and comedian and was good at making the audience comfortable and relaxed. After some urging, the hypnotist had about twenty-five volunteers sitting in chairs on stage.

He then told the audience to continue with their dinner, that he needed ten minutes or so to get the volunteers into a relaxed state and see which ones he could hypnotize. As he quietly talked with each volunteer, he eventually tapped about ten of them to return to the audience. He removed the extra chairs, and fifteen volunteers sat on-stage.

Art Bronson basked in a victory glow as he ate seafood and downed multiple Cuba Libres. Economic developers from three of the five losing Alabama communities had already congratulated him on the big win.

BUFFALO HUNTING IN ALABAMA

Last month he had beat them all to land a 400-employee call center for his small community. *What a trip!* They'd all had the right-size vacant Big Box, and some of the other communities had a better labor supply, but he had won.

The fools! He knew something they didn't; that incentives weren't just for the prospect, but also for those who could influence the prospect. And for this project, the "special incentive" hadn't cost him or his community a penny. In fact, he had thoroughly enjoyed the awarding of the incentive; it played to his natural proclivities, and he expected to win more projects in the future using the same strategy.

When the hypnotist asked for volunteers, Bronson decided it would be fun, so he volunteered. He was one of the fifteen who remained on stage.

"From this moment on, everything I say to you—every single thing I say, no matter how silly or stupid it seems, will instantly become reality. Everything I say will instantly become your reality."

The hypnotist told them that when he shook their hand, they would instantly fall into a deep sleep, and when he shook their hand again, they would be wide awake. It was amusing and a little startling to see the volunteers instantly go limp in their chairs when the hypnotist shook their hands. Mrs. Avery wondered: *Were they faking it?*

The hypnotist suggested they all had tacks in their chairs, and about two-thirds of the participants jumped out of their seats, grabbing their bottoms and searching for tacks. The other one-third continued sitting, as if half-asleep.

The hypnotist then told them he was naked from the waist down and "living large." The volunteers' expressions were hilarious as they looked at the hypnotist goggle-eyed, some staring, some giggling, and some putting their hands in front of their eyes. Mrs. Avery found it hard to believe these people were all faking.

The hypnotist then told them they were hot, and the volunteers' facial expressions and squirming signaled they were in deep distress. Bronson fanned himself as people did in church before the days of air conditioning.

The hypnotist asked him: "Sir, what's your name?"

Bronson stood up and said, "Art Bronson." And he continued to fan himself. The hypnotist was too close to Bronson to notice, but to some in the audience, it was apparent that Bronson's linen trousers sported an erection, and there were scattered giggles from the audience.

"Art, what's wrong?"

"I'm so hot!"

"Yes?"

"I'm so *hot* like when I met Atlas Ogg at the Seven Days Motel and gave him his special incentive." An immediate and massive *"Oohhhh"* came from the open-mouthed audience.

The hypnotist didn't miss a beat. He ignored the incident and told the volunteers they were all cold—freezing cold. He then had them do silly things, including two Elvis impersonations, and the audience started laughing again. But the lightheartedness of the event had been lost, and there was an undercurrent of murmuring. Eggs couldn't be un-cracked.

The hypnotist ended the session by thanking the participants and telling them they would remember nothing about what had happened.

Mrs. Avery sat in the audience. She didn't know if stage hypnotism was real or not, but it was entertaining.

***

About 10:30 p.m., Ogg stumbled into the Island Beach Resort restaurant. He saw Art Bronson sitting at the bar. Other conference attendees were present, but there was "distance" between Bronson and the rest as if he had a contagious disease. Bronson was confused about why everyone was snubbing him. They should be congratulating him on winning the big project!

"Art, how y'all doing?" said Ogg as he collapsed on a barstool next to Bronson and ordered a drink. There was a subtle shifting at the bar as if the contagion had just spread.

Jack had followed Ogg from the Flora-Bama, and he sat with the Milltown Mayor and some others. He had missed the dinner and hypnotist act but had heard about it. He now watched the disaster unfolding.

Ogg, he thought, *I don't believe this is going to be your night.*

***

The sheriff's department had responded to the call about suspicious activity on Ono Island. They found Blunt tied up and an open safe containing bricks of cocaine and illegal firearms, as well as a large amount of cash. Blunt was conscious but would say nothing without an attorney.

About that time, Ogg arrived at his house by taxi. He was in a particularly foul mood because Blunt had failed to answer his call to pick him up.

Seeing the flashing blue lights and the open front door, Ogg staggered in, cussing and demanding to know what was going on. They immediately cuffed him and charged him with possessing cocaine and illegal firearms, and for public intoxication.

Ogg's lawyers later claimed that someone had planted the cocaine and firearms to frame him. If so, it was an expensive frame, leaving the cocaine and not taking the cash. If it *was* a break-in, what did the robbers take? And why?

***

"You did good," said Simon, yelling above the noise of the King Air. He didn't say anything more.

Ezra sat still, exhausted. Finally, he asked, "So what are we? Ninja economic developers?"

Simon laughed, "Think of us as economic developers with a broad and unusual skill set," he replied.

By the time they reached Birmingham, the adrenalin had worn off, and Ezra's every breath produced pain. He hoped he'd only cracked some ribs.

"You OK?" asked Simon.

"Yeah," said Ezra as he stepped down from the plane, gritting his teeth and breathing as shallowly as he could.

"Why don't you take tomorrow off," Simon said, in a tone that wasn't a question.

Ezra drove the ten minutes downtown to Amanda's condo, used his phone to disarm her security system, and slipped into her flat. As quietly as possible, he took a shower, soaking under the hot water spray for a long while.

He gulped several Motrin, brushed his teeth, and then quietly entered her bedroom and painfully slipped under the sheets, lying on his back. He felt her hands slide over and gently start probing his ribs.

"Ow," he said. "How'd you know?"

"The way you're breathing," she said in the dark, continuing her inspection. "They don't seem to be broken. Anything else I should check?"

"Just the ribs," he said.

She slipped out of bed and returned with some ice packs, which she placed on his lower torso, and then she slipped back under the covers. "Let me know if anything else starts to hurt," she said and rolled on her side, her back to him. In the dark, Ezra heard, "I bet the other guy looks worse."

Ezra lay in bed, eyes half-closed. The ice packs were startlingly cold, but strangely enough, he felt warm and secure.

***

The next week, working through his In Box, Scott Kling spied a small package addressed to him, with TO BE OPENED ONLY BY ADDRESSEE printed in block letters.

Oh no. What now? thought Kling.

Inside was a USB drive and the simple message: *We have no reason to believe any other copies exist.*

That evening, in his study, Scott inserted the USB into his laptop and watched a few seconds of a video file before stopping it. He sat there in his chair, closed his eyes, and said a silent prayer of thanks.

He looked over at his paper shredder and saw it could shred paper, credit cards, and DVDs. He ejected the USB, stood up, and headed to his workshop to find a hammer.

***

Governor Smith sat at his desk, smoking a cigar. A VHS tape sat on his desk. He thought for a long while, then picked up the phone and ordered his ADIT Director to reorganize the department. "And find a small closet for Ogg's new office," he said.

The next day, an ADIT press release announced that Mark Thornton had been appointed the new General Manager of ADIT.

A separate press release said that Atlas Ogg had decided to retire from the state after twenty-one years of "loyal and dedicated" service.

54

SITE VISIT

It happened while Ezra was meeting with a company in Newcastle, in the northeast of England. The email was from SSAP, a site selection company. They wanted to visit the Huntsville and Birmingham sites, and they required everyone meeting with them to sign a non-disclosure agreement. The NDA was a masterpiece in requiring confidentiality while disclosing little about the proposed project.

"Good news," said Simon over the phone. "Let's just take it one step at a time." Ezra had set up a conference call to announce the new development.

"I'm surprised they replied so quickly," Ezra said. It had only been a couple of weeks since he had emailed the RFP response.

"Don't be," replied Simon. "Remember, most of the time, when a community gets an RFP, they've already made the semi-finals. They've survived the demographic data cut that eliminates most communities, and they likely have a decent site. I wouldn't be surprised if the site consultant—and maybe the prospects—have already visited and looked around."

Ezra had never met a site consultant, so everything he knew about them was hearsay.

"They tend to specialize," said Scott Kling. "We did some digging and learned that SSAP specializes in siting chemical plants, food processing operations, and pharma operations. We've tried to meet with them before, and we've invited them to our events, but never had any luck. We even checked to see if they do community assessment studies, but they don't."

"As usual," said Simon, "the site consultant has the upper hand. They know much about us, but we know little about the prospect."

***

The site selection process moved quickly. "There's no need to string it out," the site consultant told them later. "Patents expire, and the clinical trial process has already taken long enough. We want to start generating revenue as soon as possible."

The Sikorsky S-76 helicopter lifted off promptly at 8 a.m. from Atlanta's Peachtree-DeKalb Airport. It was full, with two pilots, Ezra, Scott Kling, and the three visitors.

PDK lay in northeast Atlanta. Birmingham was 140 miles due west, but Scott had instructed the pilots to fly southwest over metro Atlanta to maximize the views of Atlanta's congested rush-hour interstates. If they were considering Atlanta, the Alabama team wanted the prospects to see the glory of an Atlanta morning commute.

"We'll spend the morning examining the Birmingham site and then the afternoon at the Huntsville site," the SSAP man said. He was a tall, thin American in a dark suit. "We want to see the site by air and then on the ground, and then Messrs. Smith and Jones want to see all the documents related to the geology and planned infrastructure for the site." He looked at his two companions, who smiled sheepishly at the obvious pseudonyms but said nothing.

Ezra was sure both Smith and Jones were European and probably British. Their suits and shirts and shoes, the way they cut their hair, and even their stance, told him that.

Forty minutes after liftoff, they circled the Milltown-Birmingham site, east of downtown Birmingham. "The three-hundred-acre tech park is where you see site work happening. The 2,200 acres behind it—away from the interstate—is the mega-site," said Scott. Everyone looked at a large printed Google Earth photo enhanced with site boundaries and planned infrastructure.

"Do you have tenants yet for the three-hundred-acre park?" asked the SSAP man.

"Several companies are looking, but no one's committed yet," said Scott.

"We want to see the geo-tech and construction documents for both sites," said the SSAP man. Scott immediately texted the request to Jake Hatfield.

BUFFALO HUNTING IN ALABAMA

The ground reception at the Birmingham Airport FBO reminded Ezra of when he interviewed with DG&L, only there were now *two* Mercedes GLs waiting.

After a ten-minute drive to the site, they all sat around a conference table in the construction trailer. Jake Hatfield and the Milltown Mayor looked nervous.

The consultant drilled the construction superintendent with detailed questions regarding infrastructure capacity and the construction timeline. The questions addressed both the three-hundred-acre tech park site and the 2,200-acre mega-site.

At first, the SSAP man did the talking, but then the other two starting asking questions. Ezra was now sure both were Brits, and not just Europeans speaking English. The SSAP man, and Smith and Jones, then spent a half-hour walking the site, talking among themselves. They returned to the construction trailer.

"We're under a tight timetable," said the SSAP man. "We want to be in operation as soon as possible. We may prefer your tech park site to the mega-site. If we decide to locate here, we may want to use the entire three-hundred-acre tech park site, plus two hundred acres of the mega-site. The tech park infrastructure capacity looks fine, it's already under construction, and the site has better visibility from the interstate."

He looked at Mayor Brooks. "This is a $1.2 billion project that will produce six hundred high-paying jobs, several thousand indirect jobs, and hundreds of construction jobs. You interested in what we're proposing?"

Mayor Brooks choked out, "Yes, sir." Ezra smiled.

The last item was a discussion about employee training. Rick Cardoza, the state's workforce development chief, gave a short presentation about the state's ability to recruit, qualify, and train potential employees.

"That all sounds good," said the SSAP man. "Your program has a good reputation. If we locate here, we'll probably use it, but we require additional specialized training. We'll need four hundred trained technicians ready for work as this plant nears opening eighteen months from now." He handed Cardoza a document.

"Here is a curriculum and details for a specialized one-year certification program. We need a proposal from Alabama on how you would propose to train people and have them certified and ready for work. The curriculum is not that different from chemical production or food processing technicians."

"Please have Mr. Drake email your proposal to us as soon as possible. Is that acceptable?"

"Certainly," Cardoza replied confidently.

Scott asked about incentives, but the SSAP guy cut him off. "If we continue to be interested in your site, there'll be time for that. Incentives are the icing on the cake. Let's bake the cake first."

They had about a half-hour before needing to return to the airport. "We'd like to give you a short windshield tour of the metro area if you have time," said Scott.

"That's not necessary," the SSAP man said. "We visited last week and looked around. Some good food here."

They were back at the airport at 1 p.m. for the Huntsville people to pick up the site selection team. Ezra rode to the airport with Cardoza, who showed him the document given him by the SSAP man—a curriculum for Pharmaceutical Production Technicians.

The group flying to Huntsville included the SSAP man, the two Brits, Mark Thornton, and an ADIT project manager.

Several days later, the SSAP consultant informed Ezra by email that they had cut the Huntsville site.

***

Simon, Ezra, and Scott Kling were having coffee at O'Henry's in Homewood.

"A pharma plant!" said Ezra. "We've got to win this. Pharma jobs are high paying. This project can help us create a major new industry segment for the state."

"What are you doing to help us win it?" challenged Simon.

Ezra looked a bit frustrated. "I've searched our contact databases over and over," he said. "I haven't met with any British pharma company since I started this job, and I don't remember meeting one when I worked at Silverman. Yet the prospect singled me out as their conduit for this project. What am I missing?"

"Did you check to see if others in our group have had contact with British pharma companies?" asked Simon.

"I did, and nothing turned up," said Ezra.

"Maybe the Brits are working for a company of a different nationality. It could even be an American company."

"Maybe, but maybe I'm missing something here."

"Is it so important to know who they are?" asked Kling. "Let's just work it."
"It's always useful to have more information," said Simon.

55

SOLVING A PUZZLE

Ezra had spent all morning pouring over every scrap of information—no matter how tiny—related to the project. And then the "Aha!" moment had come. He walked into Jack's office, a big smile on his face.

"See there," Ezra pointed to a series of footnotes at the end of the forty-page RFP originally sent them. The footnotes—technically endnotes—were in tiny 8-point type and almost required a magnifying glass to read.

"What?" said Jack.

"See the typo."

"Where?"

"Here," Ezra pointed to one of the endnotes.

"So?"

"The letter should be 'y,' not 'z.' The word's 'laboratory,' not 'laboratorz.'"

Jack looked at Ezra as if he was crazy. "So? It's just a typo. We know what they meant."

"How do you make a typo like that?" asked Ezra.

"Just hit the wrong key," said Jack.

"It's not that easy," said Ezra. "Look at your keyboard. Where's the 'Z' key?"

Jack looked down at his keyboard. "Bottom row at the far left."

"And where's the 'Y' key?"

Jack looked. He said slowly, "Top row, middle of the keyboard."

"So how can someone accidentally hit the 'Z' instead of the 'Y' key?"

Jack said nothing for a moment, then said: "I don't know. You tell me."

"Keyboards are different for different languages. Sometimes there are only slight differences—sometimes big differences. Something you can do with an iPad"—Ezra pulled out his iPad and opened it to a Notes file—"is use different keyboards when writing in different languages, since the keyboard is virtual. Since I write in German a good bit, I can hit this 'globe' button, and it switches me to a German keyboard. Only a few keys are different between English and German keyboards. Pick them out as I switch back and forth between the two keyboards," said Ezra.

Jack watched as the two keyboards switched back and forth. "I see," he said, as he saw the 'Y' and 'Z' keys switch places. "So the typo was made by someone using a computer with an English keyboard when they were used to typing on a German keyboard. Or vice-versa."

"Yes, and now I think I know who our prospect is."

***

"Frau Kaufmann, I hope you are doing well," said Ezra.

"Very well, Mr. Drake. It's good to hear your voice. How are you doing?"

"Super. Especially now that I'm wondering if you are considering Alabama for a pharma manufacturing project."

There was a pause. "I wondered if you would figure it out. We sent our English partners to visit the site because their expertise is constructing and operating pharma plants. Congratulations on solving our little puzzle. This doesn't mean you win; you have some formidable competition, but it does give you some *Pluspunkte* for effort."

We got some Brownie Points, thought Ezra, smiling.

"By the way, please say 'hello' to my son when you see him. He is enjoying his internship in Birmingham."

56

SAILING OFF MALLORCA

*M*r. Drake,
We invite you to join the Project Victory Team for a Mediterranean sailing and team-building exercise. We will meet at the Munich Airport Center (Treffpunkt) at 12:00 on Saturday, 19 July, and will return approximately 12:00 on Saturday, 26 July.
Once you arrive at Munich Airport, we will provide for all trip expenses. The weather will be warm. Be prepared for a week on the open seas. Pack lightly using a soft-sided bag, since space is tight on the sailboats. We suggest you bring gloves for working the sails.
If you wish someone to take your place, please submit a name, since any substitute will require our approval. We look forward to your joining us on this adventure.
mit freundlichen Grüßen
Martin Kruger
Managing Director, OB-Bio

"Wonder if this means we've won?" Ezra asked.

"I don't think so," said Simon. "There's no draft development agreement, and we haven't even discussed incentives."

"At least it means they haven't cut us."

Simon, Jack, Scott, and Mark Thornton met and decided that Ezra would go. The prospect preferred him, and it was all about winning. ADIT ran the issue by Governor Smith since they knew he owned a marina, but the Governor was a powerboat man and had little use for sailboats. Ezra had no such prejudice since he had never been on one.

***

The Munich Airport lay north of the City. Twenty years ago, it had been cutting-edge, with enormous glass buildings and hangers. Since then, however, many incredible airports had been built in Asia.

At the *Treffpunkt*, Ezra greeted 'Mr. Smith,' who turned out to be Gordon Davis, the Managing Director of Rochdale Bio, located near Manchester, England. Ezra also met Martin Kruger, the Managing Director of OB-Bio.

About a dozen people had gathered when a tanned fellow in his mid-fifties strolled up. He looked familiar. Martin Kruger introduced him as Reuben Foster, the Governor of South Carolina. Foster shook hands with everyone, then looked at Ezra and said, "Nice to meet you."

In all, there were sixteen people, including the two Managing Directors, six Germans, six Brits, Governor Foster, and Ezra.

"So," said Martin, "we are off to beautiful Mallorca for a week. Paradise!"

Ezra made a bathroom stop and quickly emailed Simon and Sean the names of the fifteen people he had met. As Ezra climbed the steps into the plane, his phone vibrated:

> *Gov. Foster is an expert sailor and former Admiral of the Charleston Sailing Club. See attached PDF with summary of Mallorca. Bio of Gov. Foster and the others to follow.*

Just what I need, thought Ezra, but he was determined that Alabama would win this project.

The Condor flight to Palma, the capital of Mallorca, took two hours. Once they reached altitude, Ezra opened his iPad and started reading.

> *Mallorca sits in the Mediterranean Sea about 125 miles off the northeast coast of Spain. It is the largest of the Balearic Islands, roughly fifty by sixty miles. The capital, Palma de Mallorca, is surrounded by rocky inlets and harbors on the southern side, while most of the high-rise tourist resorts line the east coast. The northeast coast consists of two sweeping bays: the Badia de Pollença and the larger Badia d'Alcúdia.*

The PDF went on, giving more information than Ezra needed. It concluded:

The summer temperatures of around 27°C are perfect for swimming and other outdoor activities. Mallorca is a major tourist destination for much of Europe, with more than twenty-three million tourists per year.

***

As they circled to land, Ezra could see the coast was rocky bluffs interspersed with beautiful white beaches. Much of the interior was cultivated in patches of green and brown. Ezra could see sparsely planted orchards—poor soil and lack of rain, probably.

They landed about 3 p.m. The airport was large, with multitudes of tourists headed for the beaches, resorts, and bars. *A lot of them Germans with their multi-colored luggage,* Ezra noted.

A half-dozen taxis and a ten-minute drive to the port, and they were standing on the dock with several large piles of luggage next to two Bavaria 2000 sailboats, each fifty feet long, with white hulls and teak decks.

Martin Kruger addressed the group: "When Gordon and I met and started working on this project, we discovered that we both sailed. We decided a sailing trip might be a good team-building exercise for the Project Victory Team. Sailing requires teamwork and coordination—things this joint-venture must learn to be successful. So why not learn these things where it's pleasant and sunny—huh?" He looked up and waved his hand around in the bright sunshine.

"Some of you have sailed before, and some of you haven't. In each crew, we want experienced sailors and new sailors, but we also want a mix of OB-Bio and Rochdale people. About halfway through, we will shuffle the crews.

"The goal is to develop teamwork and camaraderie, but also to have fun racing the boats. Gordon and I will be the captains, and of course, we both want to win! So we will be looking for good team players.

"We have two guests with us this week," and Kruger introduced Ezra and Governor Foster. "They represent the states of Alabama and South Carolina—one of which will be our new home."

So, there it is. This week will be a competition in many ways, thought Ezra. *As Amanda would say, it's going to be "mano-a-mano."*

Martin outlined some ground rules for the trip: "When we're eating dinner or drinking together, no talking about Project Victory. We're here to focus on teamwork and camaraderie, and the subject this week is sailing. If two people want to discuss the project among themselves, that's fine, but it's not for group discussion."

Martin and Gordon went over some sailing basics: How to secure the boat to the dock using the cleats and the proper knots and using the fenders to protect it. It was stressed repeatedly to close the small cabin windows before sailing the boat on its side, or water would pour into the cabin.

Martin called out names, and Ezra was assigned to the *Luna de Cabrera*, captained by Martin. Luna had three Germans—Thilo, Frank, and Herb—and three Brits—Nelson, Clive, and Ian.

The other boat was the *Voodoo Lounge*—*where did they get these names?*

The sailboats looked huge, and from the outside they were, but inside they were a tight fit for eight people.

At the rear—the stern or *Heck*—was an open-air cockpit with a Bimini roof, a long narrow table in the center, and two rows of built-in bench seats facing each other. The stern side of the table displayed sailing instruments—depth gauge, heading, and speed.

The boat needed about six feet of water to float since it had a weighted keel—also *Kiel* in German. Twin steering wheels—*Steuerräder*—could steer the boat from either side. At the front of the table was a door and steps leading down into the cabin.

Below decks was a large room—the saloon—the width of the boat, which included a kitchen galley along the left, a captain's desk just inside the door on the right, and a large corner dining table with built-in seats and cushions wrapped around it.

The space was perfect for four or six people but very tight for eight. There were four small sleeping cabins, some with mere slots for the feet, and a head so tiny and claustrophobic as to make an airplane toilet seem spacious.

Behind the cabin and below the open-air seating area was the Volvo Penta engine, which propelled the boat when the sails weren't in use.

Ezra decided to sleep on top of the boat. He wasn't eager to put up with farts, snores, claustrophobia, and general lack of ventilation, so he bought a cheap air mattress from a ship store near the dock. He would spend his nights sleeping under the stars or canvas if it rained. The weather was warm and pleasant, even in the evening.

He found a niche below to stow his gear and heard they'd decided to take the boats out for a short shakedown cruise. It was only 16:30, and four or five hours of daylight remained.

As they motored out of the port of Palma, Ezra stood in the bow and looked to his left, where the *Voodoo Lounge* was cruising a hundred feet away. Behind the boat lay the old town of Palma, with its massive Santa María cathedral overlooking the harbor.

Ezra watched the South Carolina Governor hoisting flags up the mast. First was the British Union Jack and then—*shit!*—the crescent and palmetto tree and dark blue of the South Carolina flag. They might as well have raised the Jolly Roger.

Damn! He hadn't thought to bring an Alabama flag. Point One for South Carolina. In a short while, the *Luna de Cabrera* raised the black, red, and gold German flag, followed by the light blue and white checks of the Bavarian flag.

Once out of the harbor, they practiced hoisting the sails and performing simple tacking maneuvers. Ezra learned the boat couldn't sail directly into the wind, but it could cruise at an angle to it, and so they zig-zagged, each time momentarily emptying the mainsail of wind as it swung to the other side, then caught the wind and filled again.

The wind force on the sails was tremendous. The crew controlled the angle of a sail by tightening or loosening a rope that ran through pulleys to a winch that they could crank in either direction.

Martin's "ringer" was Thilo—they had obviously sailed together before. Martin barked orders from the ship's wheel, and Thilo tightened or loosened the sails as necessary.

The ships came into port under power about 21:00. After a few hours of sailing, they were already slightly sunburned and covered with sea salt, and they stank like men who did hard work.

Laughing and joking as they left the boats, walking as a group, they found a nearby restaurant where they were politely put on the roof at open-air tables under the stars and served large bowls of *paella* and bottles of good red Spanish wine.

When they returned to the boats, Ezra blew up his air mattress, pulled a lightweight sleeping bag from his duffle, snuggled in, and stayed awake long enough to compose several emails. He then drifted to sleep on the gently rocking boat.

BUFFALO HUNTING IN ALABAMA

***

Saturday had been a long day, so Sunday began with a leisurely breakfast. Some had rested well, but others hadn't, with vague joking references to farts and snoring.

Ezra helped clean up after breakfast while Thilo and the others readied the boat. They sailed south-southeast out of the Port of Palma on a nice wind.

People had sailed the Mediterranean for thousands of years, yet Ezra had never sailed even once. He watched how Martin barked orders, and the experienced crew members trimmed the sails and steered the boat.

It was easy to see how the wind pushed the boat downwind, but how could the boat sail against the wind?

"The key is the curved sail," said Martin. "As the wind flows around the sail, it must move faster on the curved side, and that creates lower pressure, which produces lift. The wind doesn't push the sail; the lower pressure pulls it. It's like an airplane wing.

"Sailors must adjust the angle of the sail to keep the curve tight. We call this trimming the sails. That's where the ratcheting comes into play. If the sail spills wind and the curve isn't perfect, the boat is wasting speed. The sailor's job is to keep the sail in an efficient relationship to the wind."

Ezra began to see that a good sailing team was a finely-honed machine, making sure the sails stayed trimmed, and when it was time to change directions, coordinating the turn of the rudder and the sails efficiently.

They sailed more than forty miles south-southeast to a beautiful bay called Platja des Trenc, filled with sailboats. They continued south along the coast for several more miles until they found a quieter place to anchor.

For dinner, they tied the boats together and cooked spaghetti, and they drank Spanish beer, Schnapps, a local drink called Palo, and whatever anyone had brought, including the Jack Daniels that Ezra had packed. They celebrated the semi-serious sailing they'd done that day.

Some of the Germans struggled with English, and only one of the Brits spoke German, but they all persevered because they knew they would be working together for years. Several were relieved to hear Ezra speaking German.

After a difficult time trying to explain something in English, one of the Germans declared, "I say the official language of this trip is the most common language in the world—bad English!" he roared.

"He's talkin' about you Yanks!" said Clive, pointing at Ezra and the Governor and laughing.

Governor Foster was an expert sailor, but he spoke not a word of German. Ezra knew nothing about sailing but spoke English and German interchangeably. Ezra wondered which skill would prove more useful during the week.

Martin gave sailing orders in German. He was determined to win the races and wanted no chance of miscommunication with Thilo. Ezra learned to sail using German sailing terminology.

After dinner and drinking and conversation, they separated the boats, so they had room to drift on their anchors.

Ezra checked his iPad before turning in and downloaded a PDF from the Quants, giving profiles of everyone on the trip. He spent a long while studying the report. It was interesting that both companies' pharma operations people were assigned to the *Luna de Cabrera*. He also received an email from Simon, which simply said:

Remember, to these people, you are Alabama.

***

Ezra woke to a breakfast of scrambled eggs and ham, fruit salad, coffee, and croissants. One savored and celebrated breakfast on a trip like this. It was not something to be gulped on the way to work.

According to the Quants' report, Ezra was the youngest person on the trip, and he knew nothing about sailing, so he was junior in every way. He decided to work harder than everyone else, do the crappy jobs (there weren't many), keep his head down and listen a lot.

He made breakfast whenever possible, washed dishes, put out the fenders when they docked or tied up beside the other boat, and learned how to trim the sails, which was a lot of work when they were racing because Martin was always making changes to the trim.

Today, they sailed eastward under a stiff wind, staying several miles off the southern coast of Mallorca until they turned southward toward the open sea. Martin announced they were sailing to an anchorage in Isla de Cabrera, the largest island of an archipelago that included ten uninhabited islands.

"The Spanish Government made Cabrera a National Maritime and Terrestrial Park in 1991 to preserve the rare plant and animal life. Access is limited," Martin said. "We have a reservation to anchor in the bay there."

Sailing at nine knots didn't sound fast, but it felt as if they were flying, the boat heeled over on its side, the sail tight and straining with the wind, and water spraying from the hull as it pounded into the waves. Cranking the winch to trim the mainsail, Ezra laughed out loud that he was paid to do this.

It was about thirty-five miles to Isla Cabrera, and in several hours, they could see a rocky landmass. As they sailed closer, they saw the outline of a fortress at the highest point. The nautical chart showed the island to be about six square miles with no permanent population.

High winds guarded the entrance to the bay, but they were finally able to tack into the channel. It was a matter of pride not to use the motor when wind was available.

The narrow channel opened into a protected bay called Puerto de Cabrera, overlooked by the fourteenth-century castle "built as a defense against pirates," Martin said. The surrounding rocky hills were dense with scrub vegetation.

To protect the Neptune grass, they attached to mooring buoys, instead of dropping anchors. The harbormaster was an older man with white hair pulled into a ponytail and skin burnt to dark mahogany. He motored close enough in his skiff to read the names on the boats to be sure they had reservations.

There were no tourist resorts or jet skis—only a few other sailboats and raw nature.

57

BIOPROSPECTING

The obvious thing was to hike to the castle, perhaps five hundred feet up and three-fourths of a mile by a winding path. They put the two dinghies in the water, attached the small outboards, and started shuttling the crews to shore.

Small green-and-black lizards slithered across the path as they hiked. Ezra found himself walking next to Gordon Davis, the Rochdale Bio head.

"Most of the vegetation you see here is wild olive, juniper, and pine. There are more than 460 plant species on the island, thirty of which are unique to Cabrera," Gordon said.

Ezra leaned down and smelled a bush on the side of the path. "This is rosemary, isn't it?" he asked. Ezra's mother used to grow it in their backyard as seasoning.

"Jolly good," said Gordon. "There are all kinds of rare and interesting plants here." He started pointing to different varieties. "Over there are mastic pistachio and oleaster, and that's éphèdres, and that's euphorbia. And among the rocks over there, you can see the Balearic wort. It's that small woody evergreen shrub. The leaves are leathery and glossy and sticky, and see the yellow flowers? It smells like lemons."

"How do you know all this?" Ezra asked.

"My first degree was in botany. Also, our company is heavily into bioprospecting, and we have a contract with the Spanish government to study possible pharma uses for rare plants and animals in the Balearics. That's why we chose to do the team-building here; I'm familiar with the area."

"Tell me about bioprospecting," said Ezra as they hiked the path to the fort.

"Since ancient times, people have used plant and animal products to treat illnesses. They didn't know *why* they worked; they just learned over time which ones worked for which diseases. We now know that plants are an essential source of pharmacologically active compounds, and we have created many important drugs from plants.

"Aspirin originally came from a substance in willow tree bark; penicillin came from a mold. Taxol, the cancer drug, came from the bark of Pacific yew trees. Despite the current preoccupation with synthetic chemistry and biologic drugs, plant-derived drugs still contribute enormously to disease treatment and prevention.

"Eleven percent of the 252 drugs considered as basic and essential by the World Health Organization are exclusively of flowering plant origin. At least 120 distinct chemical substances derived from plants are used as important drugs in one or more countries in the world.

"Up to fifty percent of the approved drugs during the last thirty years either directly or indirectly came from natural products, and from the 1940s to-date, of the 175 small molecules used for cancer treatment, eighty-five were natural products or directly derived from them.

"We've barely scratched the surface with bioprospecting; less than ten percent of the 250,000 flowering plant species in the world have been examined scientifically for their medicinal potential. There may be a cure for AIDS, lung cancer, or some other debilitating disease right here on this island in the chemistry of one of these plant species," said Gordon.

This conversation sounds familiar somehow, Ezra thought, *like a classroom lecture,* but he couldn't pin it down.

The castle had a tight spiral staircase up to the battlements where there were views north toward Mallorca and overlooking the bay where they had moored the boats. From the castle, Isla Cabrera was blue sky and bright sun and rocks topped with native scrub above crystal-clear blue waters.

"Just think," said Martin, "of all the great civilizations that have moored their boats in that small bay down there—the Phoenicians, the Carthaginians, the Romans, and the Byzantines—the Barbary and Moorish pirates."

Supper that night was peeled potatoes boiled with salt, then sliced and fried in vegetable oil; thin-sliced sweet peppers with vinegar and oil; mutton shish kabobs; and fruit salad. *Fantastic!*

Our provisions are a strange combination of healthy food and vast amounts of hard liquor, wine, and beer as if the healthy food offsets the unhealthy alcohol, Ezra thought.

They tied the boats together and ate and drank and joked and sung songs as the sun set on the water of the rocky, arid island. People getting to know each other.

At night, sitting on a boat on the dark water, the sky opens above you. Away from the lights of civilization, you understand why the ancients called it the Milky Way because it truly looks like milk spilled across the Heavens.

You sit and talk and drink in the mystical quiet and peace on the water, and see other boats floating silently in the distance, their portholes lit up, perhaps a faint tune barely audible. Lovers whispering and people sleeping in the peace of the primal night. It's no wonder some people choose to abandon the modern world and live this life.

Ezra checked, but he had no cell service. *Just as well*, he thought, as he slipped into his sleeping bag and watched the occasional meteor streak across the Heavens until he fell asleep.

***

In the stillness of early light, Ezra sat in the bow, legs hanging over the side, drinking coffee. He had woken up thinking about a course he had taken at Harvard his sophomore year. A famous biologist, originally from Alabama, had taught it. That's why he had taken the course. Ezra remembered the professor discussing the vast amount of biodiversity in Alabama.

About 9 a.m., they detached from the mooring buoys and sailed out of the harbor, leaving Isla Cabrera. They sailed northwest, racing each other to Cala Figuera, a small fishing port cut into the rocks on Mallorca's southern coast, where they took on drinking water and had a late lunch.

Text messages had started popping up as they sailed closer to Mallorca. One was from Simon:

How's the new job going?

Ezra replied: *I have an office with a window view you would not believe!*

They sailed northward along the coast to Cala Mondragó, where they had a late-afternoon swim and moored for the evening.

BUFFALO HUNTING IN ALABAMA

With the return of cell service, Ezra was back living in two worlds—a world of sun and sea, and a world of bits and bytes, thundering across the Mediterranean by day and sending messages halfway around the world in the evening or early morning.

***

"Un paquete para Luna de Cabrera." A skiff pulled up to their boat while they were eating breakfast. It was the first time Ezra had ever had a package delivered to a boat, and he'd paid extra for that. He opened the box and pulled out the Alabama flag—a crimson St. Andrews cross on a white background.

"Better late than never," he said, as he added the State of Alabama flag to the German and Bavarian flags flying from the mast.

Today was the day they switched crews, and Ezra transferred to the *Voodoo Lounge* and Captain Gordon Davis. Thilo stayed with Martin Kruger, but Frank—one of the Germans—transferred with Ezra. Governor Foster moved to the *Luna de Cabrera*.

Ezra applied what he had learned under Martin and spent most of the day trimming sails and cranking winches. The sailing was vigorous, with twenty-knot winds and white caps and the boats pounding through the waves. They anchored at the end of the day at Portocolom. Ezra felt tired but happy.

As the week progressed, some of the Germans and Brits opened up about the project. Ian Blake, Rochdale Bio's marketing manager, and Ezra sat in the bow of the boat at the end of the day, drinking beer, and Ian asked, "Have you ever been to South Africa?"

Ezra hadn't.

"We did most of our clinical trials there because it was cheaper and because South Africa is a heart disease hotbed. It's one of the world's fattest countries. Six out of ten South Africans are now clinically overweight or obese. So are twenty-five percent of the teenagers and one in six children under nine years of age.

"Three-quarters of South African women are overweight; forty-three percent are obese. Sixty-two percent of the men are overweight. One in eight suffers from diabetes. It's amazing because forty percent of South Africa's fifty million people live on less than two dollars a day.

"Rapid urbanization has caused it—easier work, too much TV, and eating out instead of home-cooking.

"The last time I was there, the newspapers had an article about a nine-year-old, 250-pound boy who had a heart attack and died in front of his classmates.

"It was gratifying to see the clinical trial results of our drug. We used MRI machines to do cross-sections of major blood vessels, and in just a few weeks of administering the drug, we could see a visible reduction in the plaque.

"South Africa was an ideal place to do the clinical trials, but we plan to manufacture and first begin sales in the U.S. because the U.S. has the wealth to buy the drug. Seventy-four percent of U.S. people over fifteen-years-old are overweight, compared with sixty-four percent in the U.K. and sixty percent in Germany.

"The U.S. is also the safest market. Recently, in India, the government forced us to grant a license to the local generics manufacturer for one of our cancer drugs. They said the drug was too expensive. Our price reflected how much it cost us to develop it.

"What are we supposed to do? Develop drugs for free? We thought India had more respect for intellectual property rights than China, but we were wrong. If pharma companies can't recover their costs for drug development and make a return for their investors, there won't be any new drugs."

***

Ezra woke as dawn was starting to break. He saw Gordon up in the bow, his mug steaming.

"Get some coffee, and come join me," Gordon said.

He found the coffee on the stove, and as he made his way to the bow, he looked over at the *Luna de Cabrera* and saw Martin and Governor Foster talking.

"How's it going so far?" asked Gordon.

"It's great. I'm learning a lot. Never sailed before."

In a few minutes, they started talking business. "At one time the pharma business was lucrative," said Gordon, "but in recent years the perfect storm's hit us: Insurance companies have become more tightfisted, generic drug makers steal revenue from some of our best drugs, and it's getting harder to discover new drugs. In a sense, we're victims of our success. There are good drugs now for a wide variety of diseases.

"At the same time, we've had to expand our presence in emerging markets or risk losing those markets to other drug companies.

"We're doing our best to cut costs. No more pretty ex-cheerleader pharma reps with company cars full of free samples. We've replaced them with lower-cost telemarketers and online marketing tools." He smiled, "Some of the doctors aren't so happy.

"We're also looking at new approaches to drug research. We've eliminated many of our large research labs and are creating alliances with universities and small biotech companies.

"If we're going to build this new pharma plant in the U.S., we're going to need some incentives to help make it work financially. We're not the old pharmaceutical industry. We eliminated over three thousand jobs just two months ago. That makes almost nine thousand jobs we've cut in the past five years. Most of those cuts have been in the U.S. and Europe."

Stein Stewart analysts had studied both OB-Bio's and Rochdale Bio's financials, and while Gordon was poor-mouthing a little, Ezra knew most of what he said was correct.

Ezra said, "It sounds as if you have a blockbuster drug. We want your pharma plant in Alabama. We believe it would be an important step forward for us, and we believe Alabama has bioresearch capabilities useful to you as well. We are going to be competitive regarding incentives."

"Do you have a sailing club in Birmingham?"

A question from left field, Ezra thought. "Not that I know of," he said truthfully.

"Good," Gordon said emphatically.

***

They put in a long day of sailing, first southwest, and then west. About noon, the air violently shook with enormous booms. "It's like World War II here!" yelled Gordon. Through binoculars, Ezra could see the grey outlines of large navy ships firing big guns. *Probably the Spanish navy on exercises.* The shells were (hopefully!) blanks.

Maybe they see the South Carolina flag and think we're an Islamic terrorist group, Ezra thought. He started to make that joke but knew it would be a cheap shot. While the rest of the world was not nearly so politically correct as Americans, Ezra's gut told him to hold off.

They finished the day by sailing west of Palma into Puerto de Andraitx, which had beautiful steep slopes with houses clinging to the hillsides.

That night, as they sat around talking and drinking, one of the Germans asked Governor Foster what the crescent moon and palm tree in the South Carolina flag meant.

"No one knows for sure," said Foster. "Both date to early in the state's history. The crescent is thought by some to represent the *gorget* that covered a knight's neck to protect him, and the palmetto tree supposedly comes from the palmetto logs of Fort Moultrie withstanding the British fleet's bombardment of Charleston in the War of 1812, though again no one knows for sure."

***

Palma was only about three hours sail away, so the next morning they took their time, sleeping late, drinking coffee, and having a long, leisurely breakfast. There was a bit of sadness in the air. It had been a great time, and the group had forged relationships.

The wind was still, so they used the motor for about half the way back. As they neared the Port of Palma, Gordon told Ezra to take the wheel and bring the boat in to dock. From the mouth of the harbor, it was probably a mile of navigating to get the ship into its slip. Ezra sweated bullets getting there, but about 16:30, they anchored in the Port of Palma.

That evening, they thought about eating in a restaurant but decided to tie the boats together one last time. They had a good dinner, drank a great deal of liquor, and told stories about the great week they all had.

***

They woke at 5 a.m. to catch taxis to the airport for the two-hour flight back to Munich. Simon texted: *How was it?*

Ezra replied: *I know all the terms for a sailboat now, in both English and German.*

58

THE WOODPECKER

Jake knew it would be a difficult meeting, and so far, it had met expectations. The Birmingham city councilors felt the Birmingham mayor had pulled a fast one on them, and they were determined to re-trade the tech park deal. Jack had warned Jake this would happen.

"But we have a deal to do this tech park together, and they agreed to it!" Jake protested.

"Yeah, but that means *nothin'* to them, and there's a thousand ways they can slow it down or kill it if they want to," replied Jack.

"Milltown's already put a lot of money in this. If Birmingham messes it up, we're going to sue."

"They don't care," said Jack. "That's what they want. A lawsuit will delay the project indefinitely, and fighting it lets them use city money to hire their lawyer friends as payback for campaign contributions. Goin' to court doesn't get the tech park built."

"What about the fact that we've already got a serious prospect looking at the park?" asked Jake.

"We can't tell them that yet. We've signed NDAs, and this project must stay secret for now. Everyone knows the Birmingham city council can't keep a secret. If we tell them about the project, in twenty-four hours, it'll be all over town."

The meeting was all about minority participation. *The idea was admirable in concept*, Jake thought, *but sometimes challenging to implement.*

Clarence Simmons, the Birmingham city council president, led the discussion, and next to him sat Linden Lloyd, the city councilor most often quoted in the news. Lloyd never missed an opportunity to complain about real and perceived social injustices.

The City of Birmingham pushed for substantial minority participation in development projects that received city support. Someone had joked that, if Lufthansa ever considered establishing a nonstop Stuttgart-Birmingham flight, Birmingham would demand that forty percent of the Lufthansa pilots and attendants be black.

"We want companies who locate in the tech park to employ minorities for at least forty percent of their workforce," said Simmons.

That wasn't an unreasonable goal, thought Jake, *if the definition of "minorities" included not just blacks, but women and Hispanics.*

"You know you can't make that kind of demand," said Milltown's city attorney, who sat next to Jake. "The courts have ruled against quotas."

Jake continued, "If we agreed to that requirement, site consultants would automatically disqualify us. Site selection is a process of elimination. Companies already operate under federal employment laws that prohibit discrimination, and the last thing they want is additional local bureaucracy.

"Besides, companies who have located in Alabama from elsewhere have been some of the most progressive in employing minorities." It was obvious to Jake that the Birmingham city councilors knew nothing about attracting economic development projects.

The two sides argued back and forth, but Jake knew the law was on Milltown's side.

"OK, then we want at least forty percent of the construction work on the tech park and forty percent of the construction by companies who locate there to be done by minority-owned companies," said Linden Lloyd.

"That's two different issues," said Jake. "Regarding the construction of the tech park, we're OK with that in concept, as long as minority-owned companies meet standard vendor qualifications and they're cost-competitive. We believe all companies should compete for work on a level playing field."

"If the minority companies' bids are no more than ten percent higher than the lowest bidder, we want you to select them for up to forty percent of the total work," said Simmons.

BUFFALO HUNTING IN ALABAMA

"Look," said Jake wearily, "We have twelve thousand people in Milltown. A few have some money, but most are simply hard-working people. We've sacrificed spending money on parks and schools to build this tech park. The idea that we should pay more to meet some minority quota would not be viewed well. Our citizens understand there have been past injustices, but they don't see why they should shoulder the burden of correcting them."

"But these minority companies are having to play catch-up from centuries of discrimination," said Simmons. They argued back and forth and were rapidly reaching an impasse when the project engineer entered the room and whispered into Jake's ear. As the engineer talked, Jake's face turned visibly whiter. "No sense in keeping secrets," he said. "Tell them what you just told me."

The project engineer paused and then spoke to the councilors: "To do a project like this, we are required to make sure we will not harm any endangered species. We surveyed the tech park property and didn't find any such species. We thought we were thorough. We were finishing our report and went back to take some final photos, and we found a problem—a red-cockaded woodpecker."

The councilors looked at each other. "So?" said Lloyd.

"They're endangered. We found it in a stand of mature pine trees in the middle of the site, hopping around on the ground. It had a broken wing."

"So?"

"So, it means we may not be able to build the tech park."

"You're shittin' me," said Simmons.

"I wish we were," said Jake.

"Let me show you," the engineer said, and one of his assistants brought in a birdcage and sat it down on the conference table. Inside was a bird about the size of a cardinal. The bird's head was black, and the sides of the face were white. One wing was wrapped in white tape. The little bird stood there in the cage, looking up at them.

"This one's a male. See the red streak on the side of his cheek? That's the cockade."

"And that bird can stop a multi-million-dollar tech park from being built?"

"It sure can. It's been on the endangered list since 1970. There are about twelve thousand of these birds left—about one percent of the original population. They like to nest in old-growth longleaf pine trees. They're the only type of woodpecker that excavates a cavity in living pine trees.

"The good news is we think there's something fishy about all this."

"What do you mean?" asked Simmons.

"We think that maybe this bird was planted there."

Everybody looked at each other. "Please explain!" demanded Jake.

"You would expect to see these woodpeckers where we found this one—in stands of mature pines, but red-cockaded woodpeckers are usually found in groups of three or four—even up to nine—and this one was by itself. We couldn't find any others, and we couldn't find any nests. Often you find sap running down the sides of the trees below their nests, but we found no sap and no nests.

"And then there's the broken wing. Frankly, it looks a little suspicious, like someone intentionally *snapped* it." Jake noticed that Simmons winced at hearing that.

"Who would want to do that?" Simmons almost whispered.

"People who don't want us to have the tech park," said Lloyd. "The same people that want to keep Birmingham down; the same people that make sure the state legislature has most of the power instead of the cities, and the same people who keep stealing companies that should have located in *Birmingham!*"

Jake thought for a moment that Lloyd was going to say *Those Honkies!*

***

"Did you break that poor bird's wing?"

"Of course not. You know Carter's first rule: Don't break the law. A friend at the Red Mountain Wildlife Refuge loaned it to me—for a nice donation." The two operatives were sitting at the Red Hat at Pepper Place, drinking coffee and comparing notes.

"You should have seen the look on Simmons' face when I brought the bird into the room!"

"How did you know he was a bird lover?"

"From his profile. Keeps a parakeet, for God's sake, in his apartment downtown. That's why we brought in the bird. We used a cage like one in a photo on his Facebook page."

"I wish we hadn't lied to the city councilors."

"We didn't lie. We said we thought the bird was planted. And it was."

A pause. "Well, it worked. Sounds like the tech park is back on schedule. Those city councilors didn't much like the Milltown people, so we had to find someone else they hated more. That wasn't too difficult."

59

SOUTH CAROLINA

"South Carolina is formidable competition."

Simon and Ezra were talking over drinks in the Delta Sky Club at the Atlanta Airport. Ezra had just arrived from Mallorca via Munich, and Simon was headed to Tokyo via New York. Through the windows, Ezra could see overlapping pairs of lights in the sky—planes stacked four-deep in approach formation.

"South Carolina landed BMW before we landed Mercedes," Simon continued. "They won Boeing before we won Airbus. They have 187 miles of coastline, compared to our fifty-three, and Charleston, Myrtle Beach, and Hilton Head are better-known than Mobile, Bayou La Batre, and the Alabama beaches.

"Both Alabama and South Carolina lost many manufacturing jobs in the last decade, and both states have seen their median household income—in real dollars—decline in the last fifteen years.

"South Carolina's often had an edge in leadership. They had Carroll Campbell when they won BMW and Nikki Haley when they won Boeing. Governor Foster's certainly competent, and he's looking for the signature economic development win to define his administration. Governors can be key in winning projects—they're a state's chief economic development recruiter.

"Our Governor Smith has a certain charm, and I don't think he'll win or lose this project for us as long as he plays ball on incentives.

"A greater challenge is the population issue. Companies want to go where the labor force is growing. In the year 2000, Alabama had 435,000 more people than South Carolina. Now we only have 66,000 more people. Last summer, South Carolina passed Alabama in total employment. Less than sixty percent of South Carolinians were born there, compared to more than seventy percent of Alabamians.

"We don't know where in South Carolina they're looking, but let's assume it's Charleston. The Charleston Metro is only slightly more than half the Birmingham Metro's size, but since 2000, Charleston's grown more than twenty-nine percent. Birmingham's grown only eight percent.

"We don't want or need the wild growth of an Atlanta or Texas, but we're not growing fast enough. Half of Alabama's sixty-seven counties lost population in the last ten years, and unless we grow faster, it's going to be harder for Alabama to compete with other states.

"The problem's not the birthrate; it's attracting people from elsewhere. Part of it is our 'police dogs and firehose' reputation from the 1960s. And every time we start to overcome one controversy, another one seems to erupt—generally self-inflicted. In 2011, the Alabama Legislature enacted HB56 to restrict illegal immigration, but it got horrible national publicity, and it made legal immigrants feel unwelcome—both real problems.

"Alabama shortchanges itself if it thinks immigrants aren't valuable to an economy. Do you know what ethnic group has the highest average family income in America?" Simon asked.

"Jewish people, perhaps?" said Ezra.

"Asians from India. Which two states have had ethnic-Indian governors?"

"Louisiana and South Carolina," said Ezra, who had learned that from his required GO Team study.

"There you go," said Simon. "When highly-educated legal immigrants bypass Alabama, we lose in many ways. Perhaps most importantly, immigrants start up new companies at a much higher rate than native-born Americans. There is certainly a problem with illegal immigration, and Alabama and the U.S. certainly have the right to have immigration policies that further their self-interest, but we must be careful not to exclude people who could help raise the standard of living for everyone."

"That's something I immediately noticed about Birmingham. There seem to be fewer Indians and Orientals than other cities I've spent time in."

"Let's talk about how we win," said Simon, shifting focus. "When it's down to the last two or three sites in a big site search—like now—each location meets the company's requirements. The site works; the labor force's there. They'll be looking at soft factors to make the difference. What's going to shift it our way?

"If South Carolina's site is near Charleston—which I think it is—would you prefer to live in Charleston or Birmingham?" Simon asked.

"Amanda loves Charleston," Ezra admitted. "She's talked about us getting away there for a long weekend."

"Unless we come up with something special, I think we're going to lose this project," said Simon. He stared at Ezra with that 'Simon' look: "So what are you doing about it?"

60

GIVING THE FARM AWAY

"Tell us about the Mallorca trip. What did you accomplish—besides getting a good tan?" Jack asked.

Ezra, Jack, Scott Kling, and Mark Thornton were meeting over coffee at O'Henry's in Homewood.

"The trip was a team-building exercise for the two companies," said Ezra. "Governor Foster and I were invited so they could ask us questions and size us up.

"I found out why we're a finalist: First, they liked the large sub-bachelor's degree STEM workforce in the Birmingham metro—more than ninety thousand workers. They see these people as candidates for their Pharma Technician positions.

"Second, they liked our site and its proximity to the interstate, the airport, and the rest of the metro area.

"Third, they like having UAB nearby.

"Finally, OB-Bio's parent company is OB-Chemie, and the son of OB-Chemie's Managing Director has been interning with a major construction company in Birmingham, so they've gotten good feedback there." *Many site decisions have a strong emotional component*, thought Ezra.

"How did the South Carolina governor do?" asked Jack.

"We were on different boats, except for evening dinners, but I heard he knew a little too much about sailing."

Jack grinned.

"So what else?" asked Mark Thornton.

"They started with three hundred sites in twenty-seven states, but it's now down to South Carolina and us. I couldn't find out *where* in South Carolina, but Simon thinks it's near Charleston."

"There's nothin' we can do about that, so let's focus on what we can control," said Jack.

Ezra described the project: "It's even bigger than we thought. It's not just a biologic pharma plant but a super-high-profile project that will produce a landmark drug. If we win this project, we'll be the only place in the world that manufactures a drug that reverses heart disease. They think the plant will expand to three or four times its initial size, and in addition to the direct and indirect jobs and the investment, the publicity should take our bio industry to the next level. It can do for us what Mercedes did for our auto industry and what NASA and Airbus did for our aerospace industry."

"Anything else?"

"It wasn't a primary site factor, but they did consider locations in terms of their rates of heart disease, and Alabama has the fourth-highest rate, behind Oklahoma, Mississippi, and Arkansas. They felt the project might have stronger public support in states with higher heart disease rates."

"Anything else?" asked Mark.

"Until recently, they were considering three sites, but they dropped the third one because the community was giving them problems with incentives."

"In what way?" asked Jack.

"In return for incentives, the community wanted the pharma project to construct low-income housing, make certain public infrastructure improvements, and commit to various types of social programs. So Project Victory dropped them.

"Here's what the OB-Bio head told me: They will be a good corporate citizen and contribute to the community and various charities, but their first and foremost job is to make drugs—specifically this new drug. They've got to get this plant built, get it certified, and then get the drug in production and start producing revenue for the company.

"They're not a housing construction or infrastructure company, and they wouldn't be very good at it; they need to stay focused on their core business, and while they're willing to commit to job and tax revenue targets—with clawbacks—they're not interested in government making them a role model for social engineering.

"He advised me to base our incentive package on what Project Victory will do for the community and state in terms of good jobs and tax revenue, and if the community wants these other programs, they should take the tax revenue the project generates and do them."

"That's pretty clear," said Scott.

"Damn!" said Jack. "I like this company."

Site selection is a process of elimination, Ezra thought.

Scott Kling interjected, "So let's start putting together our incentives package, and then we can discuss getting broad-based support for it."

"Before we do that, I want to say somethin'," said Jack. "We often talk about the Mercedes project because it transformed the state, and we were such underdogs when we won it. After the 1993 decision, the head of Fluor Daniel's site selection group wrote an article summarizing the site search; how it began with more than two hundred sites in twenty-one states, and how the final sites ended up being in North Carolina, South Carolina, and Alabama. He said that Alabama won because they showed the strongest partnership among the Governor, state legislature, state government agencies, city and county governments, and the business community.

"We have our differences, but we all love Alabama, and we all want to win, and our best chance to do that is to work together."

Scott Kling lifted his coffee cup, and they all did likewise, and everyone clinked them together. "Let's win," said Kling in a determined voice.

"And *now* let's talk incentives," Mark said.

"Whatever we offer, we're going to need an economic impact study to justify it," said Jack.

"We'll use that AUM economist who's done a lot of work for us," said Mark Thornton, who led the discussion, since ADIT was the gatekeeper for incentives.

"It should look good," said Ezra. "Pharma production jobs are high paying, and pharma production plants generate almost ten indirect jobs for every direct job, so we're talking roughly 6,600 jobs total, and that's just this first phase."

"We *know* we'll have to give them the land," said Thornton, "and it's got to have the necessary infrastructure in place—roads, sewer, electricity. Five hundred acres at, say $50,000 an acre. That's $25 million. That's not a lot of money for a $1.2 billion project. The challenge will be who pays for it. Realistically, it'll have to be some combination of Birmingham, Milltown, and the state. Let's assume for starters that the state picks up half the cost, and Birmingham and Milltown pick up the other half."

"Milltown may be close to being tapped out financially," said Jack. I'll talk with the state pension fund and see if they can help with a loan. They have a fiduciary responsibility to their pensioners, but they've helped us win many projects, and they may be able to help."

"We know the project will qualify for the state investment tax credit," said Kling. "It's the biggest paper tiger around, but at least it'll help."

"What's wrong with it?" Ezra asked.

"Because it sounds bigger than it is. It lets a qualifying company take five percent of the cost of their capital investment each year for twenty years and apply it against their state corporate income tax liability. So, if Project Victory invests $1.2 billion in plant and equipment, then five percent of that is $60 million. Alabama's state corporate income tax is effectively about five percent because federal taxes are deductible.

"Here's the catch: To fully use a $60 million yearly state tax credit, the Project Victory plant would have to generate a yearly taxable net income of $1.2 billion. Have you ever heard of a company that makes a hundred percent return on their investment *each year?*

"Assuming the pharma plant generates an eleven percent return from the $1.2 billion investment, that would generate a yearly taxable income of $132 million, creating an Alabama state income tax liability of about $6.6 million. So, the company has a $60 million yearly tax credit, but they can only use $6.6 million of it. The rest is lost; it can't be carried over.

"If the company earns eleven percent a year for all twenty years, its actual incentive is $6.6 million x 20, or $132 million, instead of $1.2 billion. But $6.6 million in tax credits per year in the future is not the same as $6.6 million received now, so at a four percent discount rate, the $132 million is worth about…" Mark fiddled with his calculator, "…$90 million in today's dollars.

"So, the company announces they're coming to Alabama, and the state announces an incentives package that includes $1.2 billion in state corporate income tax credits. The anti-incentives crowd goes apeshit, yelling that Alabama is giving the farm away, but we aren't. It's a decent incentive, but it's not giving away the farm."

"In one sense, it's not giving anything away because if they don't locate here, they won't be generating *any* corporate income tax," said Scott.

Jack spoke up, "Since this is a new blockbuster drug, I would think they'd make more like twenty percent return on investment, at least the first few years. Why don't we use that? It pumps up the total amount of incentives given."

Mark quickly did the math. "OK, let's assume a fifteen percent return over twenty years. That boosts their yearly taxable income to $180 million, giving them a $9 million yearly state corporate income tax liability, which over twenty years is $180 million, but discounted to present dollars is about $122 million. So, we've just upped our incentive package by $32 million. We'll surely be accused of giving away the farm *now*." They all laughed at the absurdity of incentives calculations.

"Next is property tax. We can abate the non-educational portion of the project's local, county, and state property taxes for up to ten years. After that, they pay full property tax.

"At this site, the total non-educational property tax is 29.2 mills, so a $1.2 billion investment assessed at twenty percent is $240 million. Apply the millage rate, and we can abate $6.96 million of property tax yearly. At a four percent discount rate, ten years of that abatement comes to $56.4 million in present dollars. Again, if they don't locate, they don't generate the property tax, so we still come out ahead.

"Incidentally, 30.1 mills of county and city property tax go to education, and that can't be abated, so Project Victory generates $7.44 million in new property tax revenue each year for education *if we land them*.

"State law allows localities to abate the sales or use tax normally paid on the construction materials and equipment purchased for qualifying plants. It's a $1.2 billion project: Let's say half of this project is materials and equipment. Local, county, and state sales tax totals ten percent, nine percent of which is abatable. Nine percent of $600 million is $54 million. That's a huge one-time savings, and it's a benefit received now, not years in the future. Yet again, we're not giving anything away because if the company doesn't come, the company never generates the sales tax we're abating.

"Finally, there's workforce training. I don't consider it an incentive but an investment. Instead of pouring more money into the black hole of higher education—often for useless degree programs—we spend money training people for real jobs awaiting them when they graduate.

BUFFALO HUNTING IN ALABAMA

"I've talked with Ricky Cardoza, and he's priced out the Pharmaceutical Production Technician curriculum that Project Victory gave us. Plus, he'll do the usual workforce recruitment and pre-employment screening and training for all their employees. The budget is $30 million. He can absorb $10 million of that in his normal budget, but he needs $20 million extra to make it work.

"Then there's the usual 'soft' incentives, like host family programs and the like. Current operating budgets can absorb that. So, the total is:

Land	$ 25.0 million
Investment tax credit	$122.0 million
Property tax abatement	$ 56.4 million
Const. materials sales tax abatement	$ 54.0 million
Worker Training	$ 30.0 million
Total (present dollars)	$287.4 million

"Call it $288 million."

"That'll *surely* bring out the corporate welfare protestors," said Scott.

"What's the actual 'ask' of the legislature?" Jack asked.

"Project Victory will statutorily qualify for the state investment tax credit, and the localities can abate the property tax and construction sales tax, so we're asking $12.5 million for the land and $20 million for the additional training. $32.5 million. Is that doable?"

"That's easily doable," said Jack. "The problem won't be the legislature, but the Governor. You know how he feels about incentives."

"Will we be competitive against South Carolina?" Ezra asked.

"I'm not sure. The site consultant will probably give us some feedback about that."

The site consultants always seem to have the upper hand, Ezra thought. He spoke up: "I have an idea for a different type of incentive that South Carolina can't easily copy, but it will take a few days to put together. Can you give me that?"

"Sure," said Mark. "We're waiting on Project Victory. They haven't asked for a final proposal yet."

As they continued talking, Ezra wrote an email to Sean Howard:

> *Working on a high-priority project. Who might know A.K. Jackson, the Harvard biologist?*

A few minutes later, Sean answered: *Mr. Atmani knows him.*

***

"People scream about 'corporate welfare,' but I see it's much more complicated than that," said Ezra, as he and Jack returned to the office.

"Most arguments deal in soundbites," said Jack. "Not in-depth analysis."

"Welfare—deserved or not—is giving somebody something they haven't earned. Incentives aren't welfare; they're just a negotiation," said Ezra. "People negotiate the price they pay for a house or car, their salary when they join a company—all of life's a negotiation. For a mega-project like this, in return for a corporation bringing thousands of jobs to an area and generating millions in direct and indirect tax revenue, they're just asking the state and community to help out a bit."

"What's that book the MSNBC morning person wrote a couple of years ago? *Knowing Your Value.* It's about helping women negotiate for what they're really worth. I'm all for that, but shouldn't a company bringing a billion-dollar mega-project to a state have the same privilege?" asked Ezra.

"Yeah, but by the time you've said all that, the other side has yelled 'corporate welfare' a dozen times. If you're explainin', you're losin'," said Jack.

"Maybe so, but the public doesn't seem to have a problem with a pro team giving a $20 million signing bonus to a hot prospect who plays in a stadium heavily subsidized by the taxpayer."

"Unfortunately, we live in a society where sports stars are heroes, and corporations are villains," said Jack.

Ezra sat deep in thought.

"I guess there *is* an issue of tax equity," said Ezra.

"How so?" asked Jack.

"Small businesses complain they don't get the same incentives as large corporations."

"Yeah, but small businesses typically only employ a few people each, and they're generally non-traded businesses. Mega-projects are like the anchor tenants in a mall—they attract customers for the small shops. This pharma project will employ thousands, but it will also generate tons of business for all kinds of other businesses—big and small.

"Kid, when you've been doing this a while, you'll realize that tax equity is rarely practiced in real life. It's all negotiation. Why do you think the U.S. tax code is more than seventy thousand pages long? Even at the local level, Birmingham's business license tax ordinance is over a hundred pages long. Why? Because every type of business has a different tax rate, and there's no logic to it. Poor people in Alabama pay sales tax on groceries. What's the logic in that? On the other hand, you can argue that corporations should pay no tax at all because they're owned by stockholders who already pay taxes on stock dividends.

"In the end, public officials and economic developers must make a value judgment: Do the benefits of attracting a particular project exceed the costs? Like any negotiation, you don't want to give away more than you must, so you make the best guess what it'll take to win. It's easy for the folks sittin' in the cheap seats to criticize those in the arena makin' things happen."

***

The Alabama State Capitol building sat like an antebellum crown on Goat Hill in downtown Montgomery. The domed white Greek Revival building featured a brass star on its front steps that marked where Jefferson Davis was sworn-in as President of the Confederacy in 1861.

The Governor's office was located on the first floor of the North Wing of the building. The office was remarkable for having a complete absence of modern technology, except for a telephone. The Governor's desk sat at one end of the office, and a long conference table filled much of the rest of the room.

"You know my feeling about incentives. I'm not going to call a goddamn special session for this," said Smith.

"Now Governor," said the Senate Majority Leader, "this is exactly why a pro football team pays big bucks to draft a star to build a team around. That's what we're doing here."

"Yeah, and half the time, the star turns out to be a dud."

"Please just call the special session and let the legislature debate the bill on its merits," pleaded the Senate Majority Leader.

"Not going to do it," said Smith.

***

That afternoon, Ezra received an email from the SSAP consultant:

> *The cake is almost baked. Within five days, please submit your best proposal for Project Victory. Please include detailed information regarding incentives you are offering.*

61

IN THE DITCH AGAIN

An economic development project is like a chain. Each part of the project is a link. One weak link, the chain breaks, and the project is lost.

Ezra visualized the Project Victory chain exploding as he read the editorial page of that morning's *Wall St. Journal*, where every business in the country read that Alabama was reverting to its tort hell ways.

The *Journal* blasted the Alabama Supreme Court for an 8–1 decision where they ruled that Helms Pharmaceutical could be liable for damages caused when a generic drug maker copied Helms' drug, and the plaintiff suffered harm from taking the generic company's medicine. The court based its reasoning on a trial lawyer theory called "innovator liability" that courts had rejected almost everywhere—except California and now Alabama.

Shit! Ezra could imagine the economic developers in South Carolina laughing their asses off.

He started Googling and pieced it together: When a pharma company's patent for a drug expired, a generic drug company often manufactured and sold the drug in competition with the original manufacturer. In such cases, the FDA required the generic manufacturer to use the same ingredients and labeling as the original manufacturer.

In 2011, the U.S. Supreme Court ruled that plaintiffs couldn't sue generic drug manufacturers for failing to warn consumers of a generic drug's risks since the FDA required them to use the original labeling.

BUFFALO HUNTING IN ALABAMA

In the Alabama Supreme Court case, the Plaintiff claimed to suffer side effects from the generic version of a stomach medication. Since he couldn't sue the generic manufacturer, he sued Helms Pharma, who originally created and manufactured the drug.

But Helms had quit making the drug *five years* before the Plaintiff took the generic version. The court ruled that Helms could be held liable for injuries because the generic manufacturer couldn't change the warnings on the Helms product it copied. The decision went against decades of Alabama tort law and product liability precedent.

When the U.S. Supreme Court in 2011 ruled that generics couldn't be sued, the trial lawyers started going after the original drug makers. Judges mostly laughed these "innovator liability" lawsuits out of court. Since June 2011, fifteen courts, including the federal courts of appeal for the Fifth, Sixth, and Eighth Circuits, had rejected the idea of targeting the innovators. But not Alabama.

The one dissenting Alabama justice—with good sense—said the decision "creates a precedent that poses a danger for the prescription-medicine industry and, by extension, for all industry."

The generic manufacturer wasn't free to change the labeling, Ezra thought, *but they freely made the decision to copy Helms' drug and manufacture it for profit, so they should bear the consequences of that decision.*

The message from the SSAP consultant came swiftly:

> *Are we making the wrong decision to consider Alabama for this pharma plant?*

Ezra replied:

> *No. Be back with you shortly.*

Ezra called an emergency meeting of the Project Victory team.

"We'll have a draft bill ready by this afternoon, and we'll run it through the legislature the same time we pass the incentives legislation. Be sure and tell them that!" said the Senate Majority Leader.

"I will, but the Governor hasn't committed yet to hold a special session."

Jack sat for a moment, thinking. "Maybe this unfortunate situation is an opportunity."

***

The Senate Majority Leader began the conversation: "Governor, how would you feel if a competitor copied the design of one of your fishing lures, and a child swallowed the copy, and the parents sued you instead of the company who copied your lure."

"That would be total bullshit."

"Well, that's essentially what the Alabama Supreme Court just ruled. If we let this stand, Alabama's going back to the 'tort hell' situation we were in for much of the last thirty years."

"I thought we'd gotten all those fuckin' liberals off the state supreme court."

"We did. The state Supreme Court justices are now all Republican, but there's a big difference between a Republican and a Republican lawyer."

"What should we do?"

"We need to pass a law overruling the Supreme Court as quickly as possible, so companies looking to locate in Alabama don't get the wrong message. We've already got it drafted."

"You want me to call a Special Session?"

"Yes, sir. And since you're calling the session, *please* consider adding the pharma incentive bill as well, so the legislature can debate its merits."

The Governor just sat there, visibly thinking and rapping his knuckles on his desk. He looked at Ezra. "You're the young fella at the dinner in Germany a few months ago, aren't you?"

"Yes, sir," Ezra replied.

"And I understand you've played a big part in this company considering Alabama?"

"I'm part of the team—yes, sir."

"Those quail salt-and-pepper shakers. Have them at my hunting lodge."

"I'm glad you liked them, sir," Ezra said.

Ol' Bo sat there, knuckles rapping on his desk, thinking. "Tell you what, I'll call a Special Session, and you get that bill ready to override the Supreme Court," he paused, "and I'll agree to put the pharma incentives bill on the Special Session Order—but I intend to veto it. You know I'm opposed to incentives!"

"Yes, sir. Thank you, sir," said the Senate Majority Leader.

***

Walking down the steps of the Capitol, Ezra was sad and confused. He looked at the others. "Why is everyone so happy? He said he'd veto the bill."

BUFFALO HUNTING IN ALABAMA

"Because," said the Senate Majority Leader, "in Alabama, the legislature can override a governor's veto with a simple majority. His veto isn't worth a gallon of warm spit. The legislature will adjourn *sine die*, and if the Governor vetoes the bill, we'll come back and override it with the same vote that passed it."

62

A UNIQUE INCENTIVE

"So we're taking the lead on working the legislature, and you're taking the lead on getting the local politicians and economic developers in line—right?" said Scott Kling to Jack Brannon.

"Yep, for the next week or so, I'll be doin' nothin' but talking with local folks, locking down their support for the project. The local economic developers won't be a problem, but you know politicians—they love publicity—and they'll go squirrelly on you in a heartbeat. We don't need any of 'em startin' a crusade against the project. The worst thing that could happen is to get the ball down to the five-yard line and not get the touchdown because the team wasn't blockin' and tacklin' together."

"What will you tell them?" Ezra asked.

"Certainly not the name of the company, and not even the type of company. We'll say we have a chance to bring a major-league company to Alabama that will do for our life sciences industry what Mercedes did for automotive and Airbus did for aerospace. And along with the carrot, we show 'em the stick," and Jack pointed his finger at an imaginary politician. "You don't want to be the one who fucks up this project."

***

Ezra and an older gentleman entered the lobby of the Boston Harbor Hotel. Gordon Davis spied them and came over.

"Gordon, I'd like you to meet A. K. Jackson," Ezra said.

BUFFALO HUNTING IN ALABAMA

"The Father of Biodiversity," said Gordon. I was in college when you published your book on spiders. It influenced me to study the biological sciences. I am honored to meet you."

They sat and ordered coffee, and Ezra looked at Gordon and began his pitch: "When we hiked to the castle on Isla Cabrera, you taught me about bioprospecting, and it reminded me of a biology course I took from Dr. Jackson at Harvard. I took the course because Dr. Jackson was from Alabama.

"From him, I learned that Alabama is one of the most biodiverse places in the world. Given your company's interest in bioprospecting—even if you didn't have this pharma project—you should have a presence in Alabama."

"OK," said Gordon. "Tell me more."

"Alabama has more than 4,500 plant and animal species; more diversity than any U.S. state per square mile. Alabama leads the U.S. in species of freshwater fishes, mussels, snails, turtles, and crawfish. The Mobile-Tensaw Delta has eighteen turtle species, more than the Amazon, Nile, Yangtze, or Mekong Rivers.

"Alabama has eighty-four different crawfish species, compared to thirty-two for Louisiana and nine for California. Alabama has 350 species of freshwater fish, about a third of all the species in the U.S.

"Alabama is home to more species of flesh-eating pitcher plants than anywhere on Earth. In one Alabama pitcher plant bog, an Auburn scientist counted sixty-three species of flowering plants in one square meter of ground. That's among the highest biodiversity ever recorded on the planet."

"I've visited Birmingham and Huntsville but nowhere else in Alabama. Where is all this biodiversity?"

"The biggest single concentration is in the Mobile-Tensaw Delta," said Ezra. "Alabama gets almost five feet of rain a year which drains into seventy-seven thousand miles of rivers and creeks that flow four hundred miles south to the Mobile-Tensaw Delta and the Gulf of Mexico.

"The Delta floodplain is roughly ten miles wide by forty miles long, and it's the second-largest delta in the U.S."

Dr. Jackson spoke up, "It's a jungle wilderness where dozens of river channels intertwine and create hundreds of islands. Alligators, bull sharks, bears, bobcats, feral hogs, and five types of venomous snakes live there. A few years ago, people spotted a bull shark near where hunters had recently killed a thousand-pound, fifteen-foot-long alligator. It's like *The Lost World*.

"The Delta floods in the Springtime and pushes fresh water out into the Gulf. In the summer, the Delta dries out, and salt water moves in, so there's fresh and saltwater species constantly intermingling. Huge cypress trees grow like islands in the black swamp waters. Trees on the hillsides are what you see much further north in West Virginia or New Jersey—maples, American chestnuts, beech, and mountain laurel. The Delta has twenty-four species of oak trees. By comparison, the entire Smoky Mountains National Park has fourteen oak species.

"Strange and exotic plants are everywhere. At your feet, Indian pipe flowers—ghost plants which have no chlorophyll—poke up through the decaying leaves. In the trees above, you see some of the fifty-four species of rare orchids present in Alabama.

"If you visit, I can show you places in the Mobile Delta you'll see nowhere else. It's as if a time machine deposited flora from different times in Earth's history all in the same place."

"And it's not just in South Alabama," said Ezra. "Alabama has twenty-three million acres of forest—the third-largest in the U.S.—and scattered throughout the state are biological hotspots like the Bibb County Glades, where the Little Cahaba River flows over Ketona dolomite, which has levels of magnesium toxic for most plants. So far, we've identified eight plants there that grow nowhere else in the world.

"And in the northeastern part of the state, Alabama has more than 4,200 caves which contain the third most biodiverse cave fauna in the temperate world—and we've barely started exploring them, so we may eventually rank first for cave biodiversity. The National Speleological Society, the largest caving organization in the world, is headquartered in Huntsville, Alabama."

"How did Alabama end up with all this biodiversity?" asked Gordon.

"Geology and evolution," answered Jackson. "Over the past few hundred million years, most of Alabama has been submerged under seas multiple times. Combined with ancient volcanic activity, this created sedimentation layers of limestone and chalk and other elements, with different types of soils and topography, and that created different environments for plants and animals.

"Alabama has more than sixty distinct habitat types, including sawgrass meadows like the Florida Everglades, grasslands and prairies, floodplain jungle, mountains, ancient rock formations, hundreds of miles of brackish shoreline and marshes, coastal dunes, and fifty miles of Gulf beaches.

"Then there's evolution. During the multiple ice ages of the past hundred thousand years, glaciers up to a mile thick covered large parts of the U.S., destroying much biodiversity. Most U.S. forests are no more than ten thousand years old.

"But Alabama was never covered by glaciers. Through the Ice Ages, life continued to multiply and diversify in Alabama. Evolution continued, and the result is a lot of speciation.

"All this biodiversity is a treasure for bioprospecting. Native Americans and early settlers knew about and used some of the medicinal plants found in Alabama, but we've barely scratched the surface in seriously exploring bioprospecting. I *know* there's a treasure of potential medicines waiting to be discovered in Alabama," Jackson said.

Time to close, thought Ezra. "Gordon, you're considering Alabama for your pharma production plant, but we also want you to explore Alabama's biodiversity for biopharmaceuticals. If you build your pharma plant in Alabama, in addition to the incentives already offered, we'll establish the Victory Biodiversity Institute to help preserve Alabama's biodiversity and to search for pharmaceuticals from Alabama's biodiversity. We'll base the Institute in the Mobile Delta, and the legislature will fund it with an annual appropriation. And Alabama will give your company a twenty-year license on pharma-related discoveries."

"I'd like to see some of this biodiversity," said Gordon, his eyes gleaming.

"We have a private jet ready at your convenience to bring you and Dr. Jackson down for a visit."

Gordon thought for a moment. "You're right. This would interest us, regardless of the pharma project."

"The Institute is something we should've already done, but your project provides the opportunity to do it," said Ezra. "If you locate in Alabama, you get the best location for your new pharma plant, *and* you get to expand your bioprospecting efforts and perhaps create new drugs. We get a pharma plant with good jobs, but we also educate Alabamians about the importance of preserving our biodiversity."

"Could we go tomorrow?" asked Gordon.

"Yes."

"Why don't you go ahead and start drafting an agreement, and I'll talk with Martin and the Board," said Gordon.

"We've already started it," said Ezra. "There's some bioprospecting deals we copied from, like the deal between Merck and the Costa Rican government. If you have model documents you'd like us to consider, we'd appreciate seeing them."

***

"People usually think of incentives as giving free land, tax credits, job training, or cash, but an incentive—in its truest sense—is anything of value that can help close a project," said Ezra. "Most Alabamians aren't aware our biodiversity has value, but it does.

"Who knows if Project Victory will ever produce a drug from the twenty-year license, but *they* view it as an incentive, and establishing the Institute is a good thing for Alabamians, the Delta, and our biodiversity.

"Locating the Institute in the Mobile-Tensaw Delta makes the most sense, but politically, it also spreads out the benefits of Project Victory, which will help it get through the legislature."

"How did you come up with this?" asked Simon.

"You told me to find a game-changer," said Ezra.

"Well, let's hope it works," said Simon.

63

MAKING SAUSAGE

Approaching Montgomery from the north, the interstate is elevated, and the surrounding land is a flat floodplain of cotton fields and woods, and downtown Montgomery can be seen in the distance across the river. The gleaming white capitol and state government buildings sit on a low hill, and one is tempted to recall Reagan's 'shining city on a hill' quote, but that would be a mistake.

The Alabama State Legislature meets thirty days each spring, generally meeting two or three days a week and stringing out the session for several months. Other times, if an issue is urgent, the Governor can call a Special Session. The reasons for doing so are listed on a Special Order, and those items can pass with a majority vote, but other bills brought up require a two-thirds vote for passage.

The Alabama State House sits behind and right of the State Capitol. The thirty-five Senators and 105 Representatives have offices on floors four through seven, where they also meet in session. The space would be snug, but adequate, if not for the 550 registered lobbyists representing more than eight hundred companies and organizations who often line the hallways during the legislative session.

The eight-hundred-pound gorilla of lobbyists was the Alabama Teachers Association, the ATA head sitting in the Senate gallery and giving a slight up-and-down or sideways nod to bills. The legislature consistently voted down anything that negatively affected the stream of taxpayer money going to teachers' salaries.

***

The Special Session met and passed the pharma liability law, which provided that "a manufacturer is not liable for damages resulting from a product it did not design, manufacture, sell, or lease." The business community was happy; the trial lawyers weren't.

The Alabama legislature had historically supported incentives for economic development projects. Jobs were a high priority.

ATA had issues with the Project Victory incentives bill, but they were outgunned. The bill had strong support from both the Birmingham and Mobile delegations since both areas stood to benefit, and for once, the environmentalists supported "corporate welfare."

And while ATA was known as the eight-hundred-pound gorilla, DG&L was known as the eight-hundred-pound ghost. DG&L's governmental affairs department employed a squadron of lobbyists, including their own people and the most powerful lobbying firms in Montgomery. When it wanted to, DG&L could blow a hole through the legislature.

The Project Victory incentives bill easily passed both houses, and Governor Smith was pleased enough he didn't veto it.

***

The Governor's office had chummed the press for several days about the upcoming economic development announcements. One announcement would be about "good jobs for Alabamians," and a landmark project to "benefit mankind." The other would be "a major announcement about preserving and making use of Alabama's precious natural resources."

Politicians who hadn't heard of the project until the last few days and who had voted for the incentives bill without knowing the details fought for seats on the announcement stage. Everyone wanted to be a part of bringing good jobs to Alabama.

64

THE ANNOUNCEMENT

It was a bright September morning with a crisp blue sky. The announcement was set for 10 a.m. They had built a raised platform at the entrance to the Milltown-Birmingham tech park site with a podium in the center and rows of chairs behind it for dignitaries. For insurance, they had also erected a canopy over the platform, though they wouldn't need it.

In the front row, Mayor Burton and Mayor Brooks sat next to each other—best buddies. Next to them sat the Governor and the pharma officials and the Presidents of UAB, Southern Research, and HudsonAlpha. Birmingham and Milltown city councilors occupied the second row of seats. Federal, state, and local legislators, as well as economic development officials and assorted hangers-on, filled the rest of the seats.

They had arranged several hundred chairs in rows facing the grandstand, and they were filled by the press, those hoping to provide business services for the project, those who planned to seek employment at the plant, team members who had helped land the project, and the curious.

Billy Jeff Jenkins sat in the second row. Jake had told him about the project at church and had already written him a letter of recommendation. Billy Jeff was determined to make a career with this new company.

Scott Kling had chosen to sit in the audience to get a better view of the announcement. As he waited for the program to begin, he sat and pondered the events of the past few months and said a silent prayer that everything had turned out for the best.

Dr. James Carter sat in the audience, surrounded by people, so there was no sightline on him. Purely by coincidence, he sat next to the previous mayor of Milltown.

Jake Hatfield stood at the side of the grandstand, checking his listing, talking on a phone, and coordinating everything. Todd Nelson, the head of ADIT, who had almost nothing to do with the project, served as Master of Ceremonies.

The Governor's security detail and their fleet of black Expeditions with smoked-glass windows, stood ready at the rear of the grandstands to protect the Governor against any imminent terror attacks—and also to ferry him to the airport.

After the 10 a.m. announcement, the Governor and the pharma officials would fly to Mobile for the 2 p.m. biodiversity institute announcement. DG&L was providing a corporate jet to help ferry the group.

"You getting this?" Jack streamed video to Ezra from his phone as the minutes counted down, and the crowd built for the announcement. It was almost 5 p.m. Ezra's time, and he was sitting in a large hotel room.

"*Dahling*, should we play tennis or go to the casino?" Amanda asked off-camera with an exaggerated sophistication.

"Don't mind her," said Ezra to Jack. "She thinks she's Grace Kelly in *To Catch a Thief*."

They were staying at the Hotel de Paris in Monte Carlo, just across the street from the Casino. It was an old-fashioned place for people their age, but Amanda had never been there, and everyone needed to stay in Monte Carlo at least once.

"Does that make you Cary Grant?" asked Jack. Ezra ignored him.

"Let me finish talking with Jack, and we can go to the casino," said Ezra to Amanda. He turned back to Jack. "I'm glad you're there, and I'm here. This is your type of event, not mine. It's set up for your politician friends to get all the credit. I'm just a working stiff. My job is to stay below the radar."

"This announcement will be great," said Jack, "but I'm waiting for the 2 p.m. announcement where all the business folks and the greenies will sit on the same stage together. Usually, they're at each other's throats."

Jack knew the devil was in the details, and there would be times during the rollout of the biodiversity project where businesspeople and environmentalists would be at odds. But for now, it was a big win for everyone.

"Glad you're getting a thrill out of it," said Ezra. He had known for a week that Alabama had won the pharma plant. Gordon and Martin had called him and told him the project team had voted to choose Alabama. South Carolina's incentive package had been slightly better monetarily, but Alabama's biodiversity initiative had made the difference.

"Have the pharma guys told you they talked with the Governor, and he agreed to name the biodiversity institute after A.K. Jackson?" asked Jack.

"That's perfect," was all Ezra could say.

"You did a good job on this project," said Jack. "Just don't let it go to your head. When are you back in Alabama?"

"We're going to drive down to Saint-Tropez for a few days, but we'll be back in Alabama by the weekend. This is football season."

"Alabama's not playing this coming weekend."

"I know that," said Ezra shortly.

"What game are you going to?" asked Jack innocently.

Ezra sighed. "Going to watch Auburn play."

"Auburn? I thought you were an Alabama fan."

"I am, but I support any team from the State of Alabama. I think it's time we got over these silly rivalries which divide us. Besides, watching an Auburn game is what got me into all this." He paused. "And Amanda went to Auburn. That's really why I'm going." And he could have added *So there!*

"That's a good reason," said Jack.

THE END

If you enjoyed this novel, please consider leaving a review on www.Amazon.com. You can also write me at www.donerwin.net.

AUTHOR'S NOTE

Buffalo Hunting in Alabama is a fictional work of entertainment and should be read as such. It is not reality. Names, characters, companies, organizations, places, and incidents are either the product of the author's imagination or are used fictitiously.

I worked as a professional economic developer for twelve years and loved doing it. While traveling, I would often read books, particularly thriller novels. They come in many varieties—spy, legal, medical, technothrillers.

I wondered whether anyone had written an economic development novel. Economic developers were perhaps not as exciting as spies, but we could hold our own with lawyers and doctors. I resolved one day to write such a novel.

Life intervened, but five or six years ago, I searched Amazon.com and found economic development textbooks but no novels. So, I started writing.

I was initially inspired by *The Phoenix Project: A Novel about IT, DevOps, and Helping Your Business Win*. It's sold a half-million copies and has more than four thousand reviews on Amazon. Surely if a novel about data processing could sell, so could an economic development novel, I thought. We'll see.

This story could be set in many places across the U.S. The economic development players are mostly the same everywhere—the local communities; the state economic development agency; the utilities; the site consultants; companies looking to relocate, expand, and start-up; the politicians; and people wanting good jobs. I set the story in Alabama because I know Alabama, and creating a fictional state of "Dixie" didn't seem appropriate.

AUTHOR'S NOTE

Conflict is the heart of any good novel, but my corporate background had taught me to avoid conflict when possible because it interferes with people working together and getting things done.

But no one would read a novel without conflict, so I "bit the bullet" and wrote about Ezra's struggle whether to return to Alabama, the struggle of Alabama's fictional economic development entities to work together, and Alabama's struggle to create more and better jobs for its citizens.

"You must entertain before you can instruct or inspire," I was told at *The New York Pitch* event I attended in December 2017. The book's primary purpose was to entertain, but I hoped it might also inform. No ten-year-old aspires to be an economic developer, and most adults have only a vague idea of what economic developers do. Perhaps, through fiction, I could help explain the profession a little.

At *The New York Pitch*, I also learned that "if you're going to write a thriller, somebody's gotta die." I had never heard of anyone being killed doing economic development, but I guessed it was possible…

I'll surely be criticized for sensationalizing economic development, and for that I'm mildly guilty. In defense, most spies aren't like James Bond.

This novel's characters, organizations, and situations are fictional, but I tried to accurately depict Alabama's economy in 2014. Since then, Alabama has made remarkable progress. Ernst & Young's most recent *US Investment Monitor* ranked Alabama first among the U.S. states in capital investment as a share of state GDP and fifth among U.S. states in announced jobs as a share of state employment.

Likewise, more people continue to move to downtown Birmingham, more great restaurants and breweries have opened, and Birmingham's home-grown tech startup scene has caught fire. In recent years, Birmingham has been more successful in retaining its startup companies. A milestone was reached in 2018 when Shipt, a four-year-old Birmingham startup, was sold to Target for $550 million, and the company decided to stay headquartered in Birmingham. Two home-grown, Birmingham-based companies, Vulcan Materials and Encompass Health, are steadily approaching Fortune 500 status.

Many people deserve credit for this progress, but it begins with leadership.

Greg Canfield, Alabama's Secretary of Commerce, and Governor Kay Ivey have done a magnificent job attracting companies to Alabama, and Neal Wade and Governor Bob Riley did a great job before them.

AUTHOR'S NOTE

Likewise, Birmingham is fortunate to have a fine young mayor in Randall Woodfin, who gives the city a youthful face and who has a rare talent for bringing people together.

Alabama has been gaining momentum, and I expect that to continue. I am proud to be an Alabamian, and I am proud of the economic and social progress that Alabama has accomplished in recent decades.

Some comments regarding selected scenes in the story: Montgomery has no Möbius Mansion, though it has many fine old homes. Möbius LLC is a fictitious political consulting firm, but such firms are often used these days by political campaigns.

In 1860, Montgomery was indeed a major center for the slave trade. Montgomery's Legacy Museum is a must-see for learning about this shameful time in Alabama's history.

The author fully intended to watch Alabama play in the 2013 SEC Championship at the Ainsworth in New York, but like Ezra, ended up watching Auburn play at Tavern on Third and Van Diemen's.

After many years as a finalist, Highlands Bar & Grill won the James Beard Foundation Award in 2018 as the most outstanding restaurant in America. Well deserved! The Chris Hastings–Bobby Flay competition happened as described, and I look forward to dining at Hot and Hot's new location at Pepper Place in Birmingham.

The Barber Motorsports Park is as described; a wonderful world-class gift to the city and state created by George Barber and his team.

The discussion about Peter Thiel's *Wall St. Journal* article titled "Competition Is for Losers" occurs about nine months before it was published on September 12, 2014. Fiction-writing makes such things possible.

Regarding the discussion about site searches and the use of site selection consultants, Development Counsellors International regularly publishes research on this and other topics in a publication titled *Winning Strategies in Economic Development Marketing*. Every economic developer should thoroughly study and understand the latest version of this publication. It's gold and can be found at DCI's website.

I decided not to translate the German passages in the story into English, to help make the point that if one is doing international work without knowing the relevant language, one is at a disadvantage.

AUTHOR'S NOTE

Like Ezra, I spent a cold dark January at the Goethe-Institut in Frankfurt with only one other person in the class.

The fictitious "miracle drug" in the story drew heavily from a 1970s discovery of people in an Italian alpine village who had a mutation that helped them resist heart disease. For many years there was hope this might result in a drug to help others.

I've had several good conversations with Don Walls regarding his magnificent achievement—the National Establishment Time Series.

Various software products have been developed since 2014 to help economic developers identify companies with investment projects. This is progress, but only the first step. Finding the hooks that secure appointments, and persuading these decision-makers to consider a state or community is much more challenging.

The sailing chapter drew inspiration from a Mallorca sailing trip taken with friends from Auburn and Hoerbiger, a European company.

The use of incentives to help attract industry is a highly-charged issue. I doubt this book will change anyone's mind who has already formed an opinion, but perhaps it gives some insights.

The fictitious generic pharma case described in the story borrowed heavily from *Weeks v. Wyeth*, a case decided by the Alabama Supreme Court in 2013, reaffirmed by the Alabama Supreme Court in 2014, and effectively overturned by the Alabama Legislature in 2015.

Alabama's biodiversity is as described. A.K. Jackson is a fictional character. The true "Father of Biodiversity" is E.O. Wilson, a Harvard professor and Alabama native. Alabama owes many thanks to Dr. Wilson, Ben Raines, and many others who have helped educate the public about Alabama's incredible biological diversity. There is still much work to be done.

If you've reached this point, I hope you enjoyed reading the book, unless you've cheated and read this first! Your thoughts and feedback are appreciated.

A review on www.Amazon.com would be great. Write me at www.donerwin.net.

Don Erwin
Birmingham, Alabama
September 2020

ACKNOWLEDGMENTS

Many people helped make this novel possible. My sincere thanks to those who read drafts of the book and provided comments and suggestions. Their assistance doesn't imply they agreed with all or anything I wrote. Opinions and errors in the book are mine.

Special thanks to those who endured the early drafts!

Professional economic developers who reviewed the book and provided comments include Dean Barber, Phillip Dunlap, Ed Gardner Jr., Ron Kitchens, Doug Neil, Arndt Siepmann, and Rick Weddle. Neal Wade, a superb economic developer, gave me much encouragement over many breakfast meetings.

German-speaking friends who provided comments include Patricia Hübner, Arndt Siepmann, Friederike Suess, and most especially Rainer Bauer, a great friend and mentor regarding European business and culture.

While writing this story, I continually straddled a fine line between writing a novel primarily for economic developers and writing something that might be interesting to a general audience, or at least a general business audience. People who tried to help me maintain a balance include Earl Cooper, Alex Erwin, Dr. and Ms. Sydney Gibbs, Cindy Morton, and Rosalie Parkey.

I appreciate Art Tipton, bio-expert extraordinaire, for reading an early draft of the novel.

I leaned on fellow authors Kenneth Griffiths and Roger Reid for ideas on how best to publish and market the novel, and their thoughts were much appreciated.

ACKNOWLEDGMENTS

I attended an intensive four-day workshop in December 2017 called *The New York Pitch*. I'm not sure my book pitch improved, but I learned much about the book publishing industry, thanks to Paula Munier and Patrick LoBrutto. Our pitch class included writers from across the world. Many thanks to Neil Laird and David Riegel for reviewing my book draft. I enjoyed reading your manuscripts!

Two books by Larry Brooks, *Story Fix* and *Story Engineering*, opened my eyes to the structure of novels and thrillers. I learned they had to fit a time-tested formula—especially a first novel. So, I rewrote and rewrote.

I am most grateful to my wife, Julie Gibbs Erwin, for reading multiple drafts of the book, for her suggestions which improved the book, and for putting up with me when I came home from a full day of work and spent the entire evening writing. Or an entire weekend writing.

One must be a bit crazy to write a novel, but when finished, it's a great feeling of accomplishment.

www.ingramcontent.com/pod-product-compliance
Lightning Source LLC
Chambersburg PA
CBHW020628220526
45464CB00001B/61